Minnesota
Atlas & Gazetteer™

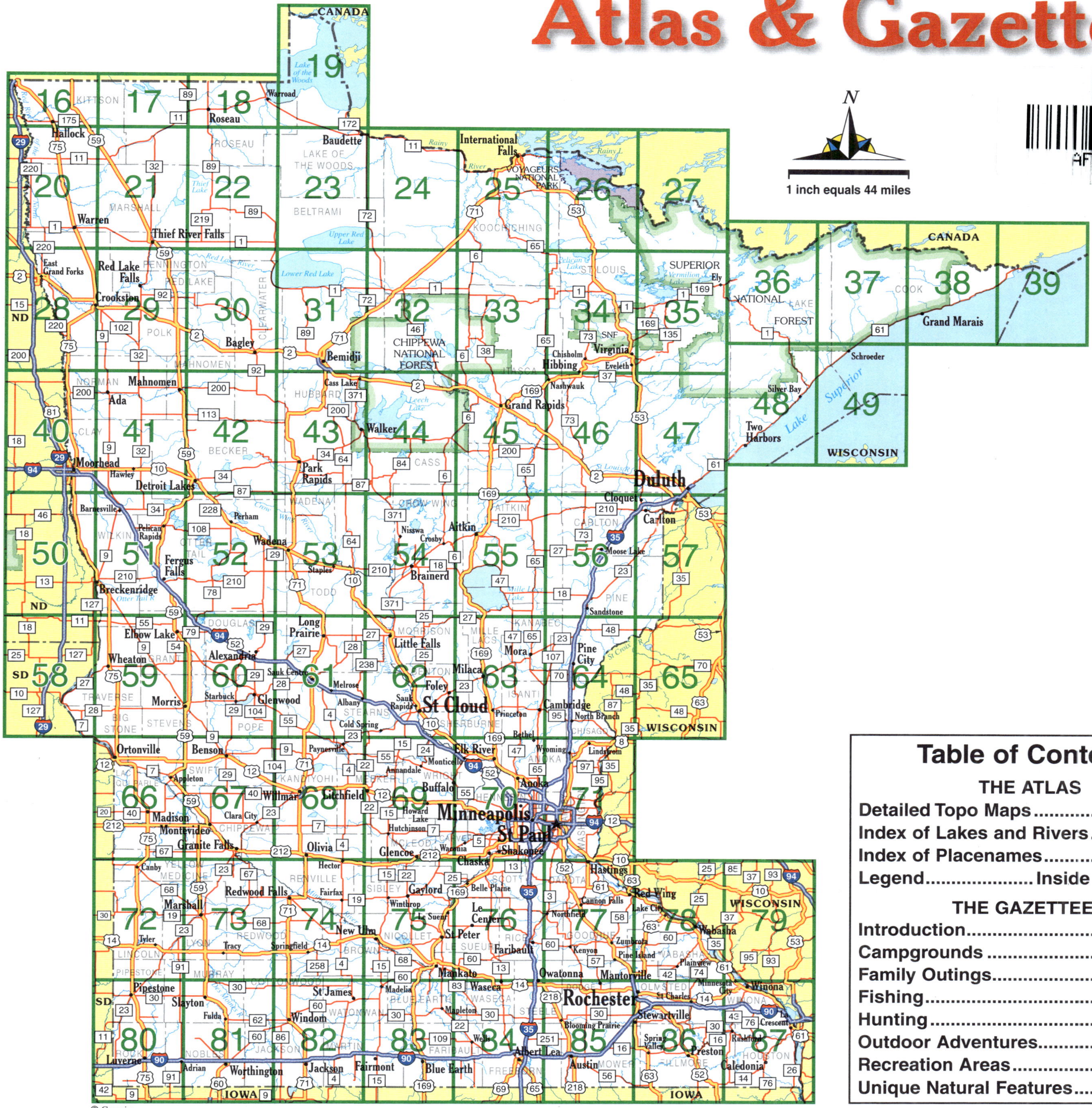

N

1 inch equals 44 miles

AF120106

Grid numbers refer to detailed map pages

© Garmin

No portion of this atlas may be photocopied, electronically stored or reproduced in any manner without written permission from the publisher.

Important Notices

Garmin has made reasonable efforts to provide you with accurate maps and related information, but we cannot exclude the possibility of errors or omissions in sources or of changes in actual conditions. GARMIN MAKES NO WARRANTIES OF ANY KIND, EITHER EXPRESS OR IMPLIED, INCLUDING THE WARRANTIES OF MERCHANTABILITY AND FITNESS FOR A PARTICULAR PURPOSE. GARMIN SHALL NOT BE LIABLE TO ANY PERSON UNDER ANY LEGAL OR EQUITABLE THEORY FOR DAMAGES ARISING OUT OF THE USE OF THIS PUBLICATION, INCLUDING, WITHOUT LIMITATION, FOR DIRECT, CONSEQUENTIAL OR INCIDENTAL DAMAGES.

Nothing in this publication implies the right to use private property. There may be private inholdings within the boundaries of public reservations. You should respect all landowner restrictions.

Some listings may be seasonal or may have admission fees Please be sure to confirm this information when making plans.

Safety Information

To avoid accidents, always pay attention to actual road, traffic and weather conditions and do not attempt to read these maps while you are operating a vehicle. Please consult local authorities for the most current information on road and other travel-related conditions.

Do not use this publication for marine or aeronautical navigation, as it does not depict navigation aids, depths, obstacles, landing approaches and other information necessary to performing these functions safely.

California Prop 65 Warning

⚠ WARNING: Cancer and Reproductive Harm - www.p65warnings.ca.gov

ELEVENTH EDITION
Copyright © 2023 Garmin Ltd. or its Affiliates. All rights reserved.
2 DeLorme Dr. Suite 200, Yarmouth, Maine 04096
www.garmin.com/DeLormeAtlas
Printed in Canada.

Index of Placenames

Index of Lakes and Rivers

Simon Lake 53 B7
Simonson Lake 30 D2
Sink Lake 48 A2
Sinneeg Lake 27 D8
Sioux Falls 27 D6
Sioux Lake 32 C2; 69 C5
Sioux River 27 D6
Sisabagamah Creek 55 B6
Sisabagamah Lake 55 B6
Siseebakwet Lake 45 B6
Sisseton Lake 83 C5
Sister Lake 37 D5
Sitas Lake 45 D6
Sitka Lake 37 B6
Siverson Lake 52 D3
Sivertson Lake 42 D3
Six Lake 52 A1
Sixmile Brook 44 A3
Sixmile Creek 37 D6
Sixmile Lake 34 D3; 44 A3
Sixteen Creek 46 C1
Sixth Crow Wing Lake 43 C7
Sixth Lake 30 B4
Skaein Lake 41 D8
Skataas Lake 68 B2
Skeeter Lake 33 D7
Skeleton Lake 35 B7
Skelly Lake 45 B5
Skimerhorn Lake 32 C1
Skimmerhorn Creek 32 C1
Skipper Lake 37 B8
Skogman Lake 64 D1
Skoota Lake 36 B4
Skull Lake 16 B4; 68 A1
Skunk Bk 45 B5
Skunk Creek 43 A6; 46 C3; 48 C2; 56 B4; 62 A3; 81 D8
Skunk Lake 43 C6; 45 B5; 55 D5; 59 A8; 62 A2; 71 A5; 81 D8
Skunk River 62 A3
Slade Lake 48 A4
Slate Lake 36 D2
Slauson Lake 33 C6
Slawson Lake 61 B6
Sleepy Eye Creek 73 C7, C8; 74 C1, C3
Sleepy Eye Lake 74 C3
Sletten Lake 35 A8
Slim Lake 27 C6; 35 A8
Sloan Lake 43 C5
Slotsye Lake 60 A1
Slough Lake 42 D1; 61 B5; 69 B7
Slow Creek 34 C3
Slowfoot Lake 36 B3
Slumber Lake 36 B2
Small Lake 42 C4
Smart Bay 35 B5
Smite Lake 36 B4
Smith Creek 45 B6; 74 A1
Smith Lake 30 A3; 31 B6, B8; 33 D6; 43 A5; 45 B6; 55 A5, C5; 60 B4; 69 C7, D8
Smithwicks Lake 59 D5
Smoke Lake 37 C6
Smoky Hollow Lake 44 D4
Smyth Lake 31 B7
Snail Lake 71 C5
Snake Creek 36 D2; 44 A4; 78 D3
Snake River 20 C2, D2, D4; 21 C5; 36 C2; 55 C8, D8; 63 A8, B8, D5; 64 B1
Snaptail Lake 33 D7
Snetsinger Lake 42 A2
Snider Lake 42 B2
Snipe Lake 37 B6
Snodgrass Lake 55 A5
Snow Bay 27 C6
Snow Lakes 52 D3
Snowball Creek 45 A8
Snowball Lake 45 A8
Snowbank Lake 36 B3
Snowshoe Brook 63 A8
Snowshoe Lake 63 A8
Soap Lake 48 A3
Sock Lake 42 D3
Sockeye Lake 42 C4
Soderman Lakes 55 B6
Solberg Lake 30 C4; 60 A1
Soldier Creek 82 D3
Solem Lake 51 A7; 60 B2
Solid Bottom Creek 42 B3
Solitude Lake 36 B4
Solvie Slough 60 D1
Solwald Lake 41 C6
Somdahl Lake 42 C1
Somers Lake 69 A7
Sommer Lake 52 D1
Sonju Lake 48 A4
Sorby Lake 30 C2
Sorensen Lake 54 B3
Sorenson Creek 86 D4
Soroll Lake 35 A6
Source Lake 48 A2
Sourdough Lake 36 B1
South Arm Knife Lake 36 A4
South Arm Lake Lida 51 B8
South Badger Lake 81 B6
South Barnes Lake 41 D8
South Bay 75 C6
South Bluff Creek 52 C4
South Bog Lake 26 D3
South Branch 32 A1
South Branch, Battle River 31 A8
South Branch, Buffalo River 40 D4; 50 A4; 51 B5, B6
South Branch, Little Elk River 61 A8
South Branch, Manitou River 48 A4
South Branch, Middle Fork, Zumbro River 85 A6
South Branch, Mud Creek 47 B8
South Branch, Partridge River 35 D8
South Branch, Rapid River 23 C5, C7
South Branch, Root River 86 C1
South Branch, Rush River 75 B6, B7
South Branch, Snake River 20 D4; 21 D5
South Branch, Sunrise River 71 A5
South Branch, Two Rivers 20 A3; 21 A5, A6, A7
South Branch, Water Hen Creek 47 A6
South Branch, Whiteface River 47 A7, B7
South Branch, Wild Rice River 41 B5, B7
South Branch, Yellow Medicine River 72 B3
South Branch, Zippel Creek 19 D6
South Brule River 37 B8; 38 B1
South Buckley Lake 69 B5
South Center Lake 71 A7
South Cormorant River 32 B1
South Creek 83 C6, C7
South Farm Lake 36 C1
South Fork Pine River 43 D8
South Fork, Black River 24 B3
South Fork, Bradbury Brook 63 A5
South Fork, Coon Creek 33 C6
South Fork, Crow River 68 C2, C3; 69 C5, D6; 70 C1
South Fork, Elm Creek 82 C3
South Fork, Groundhouse River 63 B7
South Fork, Kawishiwi River 36 C2
South Fork Lake 33 D8
South Fork, Nemadji River 57 B5
South Fork, Pine River 54 A1
South Fork, Rabbit River 59 A6
South Fork, Root River 86 C4; 87 C5
South Fork, Roseau River 22 A2, B2
South Fork, Watonwan River 82 B2, B4; 83 A5
South Fork, Whitewater River 86 A3
South Fork, Willow River 45 C5
South Fork, Zumbro River 85 A8
South Fowl Lake 38 B3
South Greenwood Creek 48 A1
South Hegman Lake 35 A8
South Heron Lake 81 C8
South Hope Lake 36 C4
South Lake 27 C6; 37 A8; 69 C7
South Lemmerhirt Lake 52 C4
South Long Lake 52 B1; 54 C3
South Maple Lake 52 D4
South McDougal Lake 36 D2
South Pool 21 C8
South Rice Lake 52 B1
South Rothwell Lake 59 D5
South Silver Lake 83 D5
South Stanchfield Lake 63 C7
South Sturgeon Lake 34 C1
South Temperance Lake 37 B6
South Turtle Lake 52 C1
South Twin Lake 31 D8; 42 B2, D3; 73 D6
South Two River 62 C1
South Wilder Lake 36 C3
Spark Lake 38 B2
Spaulding Lake 38 B2
Spawn Creek 36 B1
Spear Lake 41 D8
Spearhead Lake 43 A6
Speckled Trout Lake 38 B4
Spectacle Lake 55 C5; 63 D7
Spellman Lake 73 A5
Speltz Creek 78 D4
Spence Lake 63 B8
Spencer Brook 63 D7
Sperry Lake 68 B3
Sphagnum Creek 36 D2
Spicer Lake 84 B2
Spider Creek 46 C3
Spider Lake 33 D6; 43 B5, C7; 46 C3; 53 A8; 54 B3; 71 A7
Spike Lake 30 C4; 43 A8
Spinach Lake 42 B1
Spirit Lake 53 A5; 55 B5; 57 A6; 82 D1
Spitzer Lake 52 D2
Splash Lake 36 B3
Split Hand Creek 45 C7
Split Hand Lake 45 C7
Split Rock Bay 48 C3
Split Rock Creek 80 A2
Split Rock Lake 56 C1
Split Rock River 48 C3; 56 B1, B2
Spoon Lake 36 B4
Spooner Slough 59 D8
Spot Lake 53 A8
Sprague Creek 18 C2
Sprague Lake 76 D3
Spring Branch, 44 D4; 61 A7; 87 C8
Spring Brook 63 B8; 83 A5
Spring Creek 27 D8; 29 D6; 32 B1; 41 A5, A8, B8; 42 B1; 44 D3; 45 B8; 51 A5, A8; 64 A2; 66 D4; 67 A8, C6, D7; 72 A4; 73 A5, A6; 74 C2, C3
Spring Lake 26 C4; 27 C5; 30 D2; 31 C5; 32 C4; 33 B7, B8, D7; 34 D2; 42 C1; 43 B8, C8; 44 B4; 45 A6, B5; 47 C7; 51 C8; 55 B6, D5; 56 B4; 60 A3, B1; 64 D1; 66 B4; 69 B6, C7; 71 D6; 76 A3
Spring Mine Creek 35 C7
Spring Mine Lake 35 C7
Spring ValleyCreek 86 C1, C2
Sproul Lake 51 C8
Spruce Creek 53 D5; 61 A5
Spruce Lake 32 B4; 35 B7; 44 C1; 45 B5; 48 A3; 56 A3
Spunk Creek 62 B2, C1
Spur End Creek 48 A2
Spur Lake 33 C5; 36 D4; 43 B6
Spurzem Lake 70 C2
Square Lake 37 C5; 54 A4; 71 B7
Squaw Creek 31 B8
Squib Creek 57 D5
Squire Lake 37 C7
Squirrel Lake 29 C8; 42 B1
St Clair Lake 42 C1, D1
St Croix River 64 C3, D2; 65 A5; 71 A7, D7
St Francis River 63 C5, D5, D6
St Francis River 70 A1
St James Creek 82 A3
St Johns Lake 68 B1
St Louis River 35 D5; 46 B3, D3; 47 A5; 57 A5, A6
St Marys Lake 34 D4
Staege Bay 26 C4
Stag Brook 68 A4
Stahl Lake 69 C5
Stakke Lake 41 D7
Stalker Lake 52 D1
Stallcop Lake 61 B5
Stanchfield Creek 63 C7
Stanchfield Lake 54 C1
Stanjikoming Bay 25 A7
Stanley Creek 47 C8; 48 D1
Stanley Lake 54 B4
Star Lake 37 C7; 52 B1; 53 D8; 54 A3; 60 C3; 62 B1; 68 C4
Staring Lake 70 D3
Stark Lake 55 A5
Starlight Lake 36 B3
Starry Lake 45 D5
Starvation Lake 55 B8
Stassen Lake 42 B4
State Lake 29 C8; 37 B8; 44 D4; 60 C4
State Line Creek 57 B6
State Line Lake 84 D3
Stauffer Lake 64 C1
Steamboat Bay 43 B8; 54 C2
Steamboat Bay Lake 43 A8
Steamboat Lake 43 A8; 55 A7
Steamboat River 43 B8
Steel Lake 43 C8; 70 B1
Steele Lake 76 D1
Steenerson Lake 60 D3
Steep Bank Lake 72 B2
Steer Creek 58 C3
Stem Lake 37 C7
Stemmer Lake 52 D3
Stenlund Lake 30 C4
Stephens Creek 35 D6
Stephens Lake 54 C2
Sterling Creek 27 D8
Sterling Lake 27 D8; 30 C3
Stevens Creek 64 C2
Stevens Lake 38 C3; 44 D3; 45 A5; 56 C3; 61 B5; 68 C1; 69 C5
Stewart Lake 44 D2; 48 C1
Stewart River 48 C1, D1
Stickney Lake 62 D3
Stieger Lake 70 D2
Stiner Creek 41 C7
Stingy Lake 34 C1
Stinking Lake 41 C7
Stockade Creek 48 A2
Stockhaven Lake 60 A2
Stockholm Creek 87 C6
Stockhousen Lake 60 A2
Stocking Creek 43 D6
Stocking Lake 43 C6, D6
Stocking Lakes 44 C1
Stokes Bay 26 B4
Stokey Lake 45 B6
Stone Creek 35 D8; 46 B3
Stone Lake 31 B5, D6; 35 D8; 46 A4; 47 B8; 68 B4; 70 A2, D2
Stoner Lake 32 C1
Stones Lake 53 C7
Stoney Brook 46 D4; 56 A3
Stoney Creek 62 C4
Stony Brook 34 C1; 53 C7; 54 B1; 63 B5
Stony Brook Lake 51 D8
Stony Creek 19 B5; 40 D4; 44 D3; 48 C2; 51 A5; 51 A6; 61 D7; 62 C2
Stony Lake 30 C3; 36 D2; 43 C6; 44 C1; 46 D1; 51 D7; 52 C3: 61 B8; 63 D7
Stony River 36 D1, D2; 48 A2
Stony Run Creek 67 D6
Store Creek 48 B1
Store Lake 30 C1
Storer Creek 87 B6
Stormy Creek 61 A5
Story Brook 82 D2
Stowe Lake 33 D8
Stowe Lake 60 A2
Straight Lake 42 C4; 47 C8
Straight River 42 C4; 43 D5; 76 D4; 84 A4, B4
Strand Lake 30 C1; 47 B5
Strandness Lake 60 C3
Stratton Lake 63 D8
Strawberry Lake 42 C2; 44 A1; 54 A2
Stray Horse Lake 31 C6
Strike Lake 53 A7
String Lakes 82 B1
Stringer Lake 37 C5
Strom Lake 75 D6
Stroud Lake 47 C6
Struggle Lake 36 B4
Strunk Lake 41 D8
Strup Lake 36 B4
Stuart Lake 27 D7; 34 D1; 52 C2
Stuart River 27 D7
Stub Lake 36 B1
Stub Lakes 61 B7
Stud Lake 62 A2
Studhorse Lake 45 C6
Stumble Creek 49 A5
Stump Lake 31 D7; 42 B2; 54 C1; 62 D1
Stump River 38 B3
Stumpy Lake 53 D8
Stuntz Bay 35 B6
Sturgeon Channel 19 A7
Sturgeon Creek 24 A4
Sturgeon Lake 56 C3; 77 A8
Sturgeon River 24 D2, D4; 34 B1, B2, C2
Sucker Bay 44 B1
Sucker Brook 45 A7
Sucker Creek 18 D2; 26 B2; 31 A7, B8; 32 B1, D1; 42 A4, D1; 44 A1; 47 C8; 62 C3; 69 C5, C6
Sucker Lake 33 B7, D8; 36 B3; 42 A4, B2; 71 C5
Sucker Lakes 44 A1
Sugar Bay 45 B6
Sugar Bowl Lake 30 D2
Sugar Brook 45 B6
Sugar Bush Lake 42 B4
Sugar Lake 32 D2; 45 B5; 55 C7; 69 A7; 84 C3
Sugar Loaf Cove 49 A5
Sulem Lake 82 A3
Sullivan Bay 26 B3
Sullivan Creek 47 C5; 48 B1; 87 C7
Sullivan Lake 44 B4; 47 B7; 48 B1; 54 D4; 55 A5; 69 B8
Summit Lake 68 B3; 82 B1
Sumpet Lake 36 C4
Sunday Bay 27 D8
Sunday Lake 27 D8; 43 D6
Sundial Lake 27 D8
Sundling Creek 37 C8
Sunfish Lake 38 B2; 52 B1; 71 C6; 76 C2
Sunhigh Lake 37 C6
Sunlow Lake 37 C5
Sunrise Lake 33 D6; 64 D2
Sunrise River 64 D2; 71 A6
Sunset Bay 55 D7
Sunset Lake 34 A3; 47 D5; 52 C2; 55 B5; 71 B6
Suomi Lake 33 D5
Superior Bay 57 A7
Superstition Lake 36 C2
Susan Bay 26 D2
Susan Lake 34 A4; 82 D4
Sustacek Lake 69 C6
Sutton Lake 76 A2
Swag Lake 83 D5
Swamp Creek 27 D7
Swamp Lake 31 C7; 35 D8; 37 B8, C8; 38 B4; 43 B8; 55 B7; 62 C2; 71 A6, A7; 76 A2
Swamp River 38 B4, C3
Swamper Creek 38 B1
Swamper Lake 38 B1
Swan Creek 26 D2; 53 B7
Swan Lake 26 D2; 37 B8; 46 A1; 51 D8; 59 B8; 60 C1, D3; 61 C5; 68 A1, B2; 68 B1, C2; 69 B6, D6; 70 A4, D1; 74 B4; 75 C6; 76 D4
Swan River 45 A8, B7, C8; 46 B3; 61 A8, B7; 62 B1
Swanson Lake 42 A2; 66 D4
Swansons Bay 27 C5
Swartout Lake 69 B7
Swede Grove Lake 41 C7
Swede Lake 44 C2, D1, 70 C1
Swedes Bay 76 C1
Swedetown Bay 35 B6
Sweetwater Lake 59 D6
Sweitzer Lake 43 C6
Swenoda Lake 60 D4
Swenson Lake 31 D8; 68 A1
Swift Coulee 20 C3, C4
Swift Lake 44 B3
Swift River 44 C3
Sybil Lake 52 A1
Sylvan Lake 44 D1; 60 A1; 70 B2
Sylvania Lake 36 D4
Sylvia Lake 61 C7
Syverson Lake 30 C1

T

T Lake 37 C5
Taflin Lake 30 C3
Tail Lake 37 D6
Tait Lake 37 C7
Tait River 37 C7, D7
Taïts Lake 68 B3
Takucmich Lake 27 C6
Talcot Lake 81 B7
Talge Lake 30 B3
Talmadge River 47 D8
Tamarac Lake 42 C2, D1
Tamarac River 20 B2, C4; 21 B5; 24 D1, D2
Tamarack Bay 35 B7
Tamarack Creek 35 B7
Tamarack Lake 30 D3; 32 D3; 35 B7; 42 A2, A4, B4; 43 D7; 44 B4, C3, D2; 51 A7; 52 B1, C2, D1; 54 A1, A3, C1, C3; 56 A2; 61 B8, C8, D5; 64 A4; 69 B8; 71 A5
Tamarack Pool 21 C8
Tamarack River 46 D1; 56 A1
Tank Lake 45 D5
Tansem Lake 51 A7
Target Lake 87 B8
Tatley Lake 41 C6
Taylor Creek 61 B8; 62 B1
Taylor Lake 33 D5; 38 B4; 44 B4, D4; 45 C6; 53 A8; 69 B7
Tea Cracker Lake 42 C2
Teal Lake 39 B5; 82 B1
Teapail Lake 42 A3
Tee L Grassy Lake 35 A8
Tee Lake 29 D8; 52 A1, B2
Temperance Lake 82 C4
Temperance River 37 C6
Ten Lake 31 D8; 44 A2
Ten Mile Lake 43 C8
Tenmile Creek 66 D4; 67 C5
Tenmile Lake 31 B6; 51 D8
Tennyson Lake 63 D7
Tenth Crow Wing Lake 43 C7
Tepee Lake 31 C5; 37 A6
Tepee Lakes 43 B6
Terrapin Lake 71 B7
Terrebonne Creek 29 B7
Terry Lake 55 A5
Terway Lake 42 A3
Tess Lake 52 D3
Tetagouche Lake 48 B4
Tetonka Lake 76 D2
Thatcher Lake 43 A7
The Cascades 38 B4
The Inlet 73 D6; 82 D4
The Narrows 23 D6; 31 A6; 43 B8; 44 B1
Thelma Lake 37 B6
Thiebault Lake 45 C5
Thief Bay Pool 21 C8
Thief Lake 22 B1
Thief River 21 B8, C8, D7
Thielke Lake 66 A1
Thimble Lake 33 B7
Third Crow Wing Lake 43 D7
Third Guide Lake 45 D5
Third Lake 27 D7; 30 B4, D3; 47 C5
Third River 32 C2, D2
Third River Flowage 32 D2
Third Silver Lake 52 C1
Third Sucker Lake 45 A8
Thirteen Lake 55 C5; 56 D1
Thirty Lake 33 D8
Thirtysix Lake 46 D3
Thirtythree Lake 36 B1
Thisius Branch, 84 C1
Thistledew Lake 33 B8
Thoen Lake 68 B4
Thomas Lake 36 B4; 48 C1
Thompson Creek 23 B8; 37 C8; 44 D2; 87 C7
Thompson Lake 47 C7; 55 A5; 60 B1; 68 A1, B2, C3; 70 A1
Thompson Slough 21 B7
Thomson Reservoir 57 A5
Thornton Lake 55 B5
Thorson Lake 60 A2
Thorstad Lake 60 A1
Three Finger Lake 54 D1
Three Island Lake 33 D6; 44 C2
Three Mile Creek 69 A7; 72 C4; 73 B5; 74 B3
Threemile Lake 34 D3
Thumb Lake 27 C6
Thunder Creek 56 D4
Thunder Lake 27 D8; 31 B6; 44 C4; 53 D7
Thunderbird Lake 37 D5; 46 B1
Thursday Bay 36 A1
Tibbetts Brook 63 B5
Tibbits Brook 70 A2
Tidbit Lake 35 A7
Tidd Lake 44 B4
Tiesen Lake 45 D8
Tietz Lake 76 B2
Tiger Bay 27 D7
Tiger Lake 69 D8
Tikander Lake 47 A5
Tilde Lake 41 C7
Tilson Bay 25 A8
Timber Creek 37 C5
Timber Lake 37 C5; 68 A1; 82 B1
Timm Lake 73 B7
Timms Creek 74 A1
Tin Can Mike Lake 36 B1
Titlow Lake 75 B6
Toad Lake 42 D3
Toad River 42 D3; 52 A3
Toe Lake 27 C7
Tofte Lake 36 B2
Toimi Creek 47 A8
Toivola Swamp 46 B2, C2
Tom Cod Bay 26 B1
Tom Cod Creek 26 B1
Tom Lake 38 B3
Tomahawk Lake 36 C4
Tomash Lake 37 C7
Tomato Creek 19 D6
Tomato Lake 38 B2
Tomlinson Creek 36 D4
Tomlinson Lake 69 C6
Tommila Lake 48 B1
Toms Lake 52 D2; 53 C7
Toners Lake 76 D2
Tonic Lake 36 C2
Tonseth Lake 51 B8
Toohey Lake 37 D5
Tooth Lake 26 C4
Topaz Lake 37 A5
Torchlight Lake 56 A3
Torgerson Lake 41 D8; 52 D1
Torkelson Creek 86 B4
Torstenson Lake 60 B1
Tote Lake 37 B8
Tovson Lake 42 C1
Tower Creek 47 B6; 53 B8
Towers Lake 68 B4
Town Lake 52 A2
Town Line Lake 44 C2; 55 B5
Town Slough 68 B4
Townline Lake 33 B8; 55 A7
Trace Lake 61 B7
Traders Bay 44 B1
Trail Lake 27 B8
Trap Lake 38 B1
Trappers Creek 48 B1
Trappers Lake 36 D3
Travois Lake 37 B5
Trestle Lake 33 C5, D8; 34 C1
Triangle Lake 36 B2; 38 B2
Trident Lake 36 B3
Trieglaff Lake 42 D2
Trillium Lake 27 C6; 44 C1
Trimble Creek 35 C7
Tripp Lake 43 D7, D8
Trollin Lake 64 C1
Trott Brook 70 A2, 3
Trotterchaud Lake 41 C8
Trout Brook 77 C8
Trout Creek 45 A7; 61 B7; 78 D4; 86 B3
Trout Lake 27 C5; 33 D6; 35 A6; 38 C2; 45 A7; 54 A4
Trout Run 86 A3
Troy Creek 23 B8
Trulse Lake 52 D2
Trulson Lake 71 A7
Tub Lake 41 D7; 51 A7
Tucker Lake 37 B7; 53 C7
Tucker River 37 B7
Tuefer Lake 32 B2
Tulaby Lake 42 B2
Turner Lake 55 A7
Turpela Lake 35 D6
Turtle Creek 33 C5; 53 D7; 61 A7; 84 A4, B4; 85 A5
Turtle Lake 30 C2; 31 C7; 33 C5; 36 C2; 37 C7; 41 D7; 44 C1; 53 D7; 60 B1, B3; 71 B5, B6
Turtle River 31 C6, D8; 33 D5
Turtle River Lake 31 D7
Tuscarora Lake 37 B6
Tuttle Lake 32 D4
Twelve Lake 51 B8; 55 D5
Twelve Mile Creek 69 C8
Twelvemile Creek 59 B6, C7, C8
Twenty Lake 55 C6; 68 A2
Twentyone Lake 51 B8; 55 C8
Twentytwo Lake 55 D5
Twin Bays 55 D7
Twin Island Lake 42 B4; 54 C4; 61 B6
Twin Lake 33 D7; 43 A8; 46 B1; 61 B6; 64 C1; 69 A6, A8; 71 A6
Twin Lake Creek 42 A2
Twin Lakes 21 A5; 31 D6; 33 C5; 35 A8, B8; 44 C3; 45 A8, D8; 46 A4, D4; 47 B6, C8, D5; 48 C1; 52 C1, D3; 53 C8; 54 B3, D2; 55 A5, B7; 61 B7; 62 A1; 64 B1, D1; 66 A2; 68 B2; 69 A8; 70 A2, C3; 71 A5, B6
Twin Oaks Lake 42 A1
Twinkle Lake 37 B5
Twite Rapids 34 B3
Two Island Lake 33 C5; 37 C8
Two Island River 37 D5; 49 A5
Two River 62 B1
Two Rivers 16 A1
Two Rivers Lake 62 C1
Twomile Creek 34 A4; 35 A5
Twomile Lake 32 D4
Tyler Lake 76 C1
Tynjala Creek 47 A6
Typol Lake 64 D1
Tyson Lake 73 A7

U

Uhl Lake 70 B1
Uhlenkolts Lake 61 C8
Underberg Lake 30 C2
Union Creek 53 B5
Union Lake 29 C7; 60 B4; 76 B4
Upland Lake 48 A1
Upper Bass Lake 43 C8
Upper Bear Creek 86 B2
Upper Bottle Lake 43 C6
Upper Bug Lake 47 B6
Upper Camp Lake 42 B3
Upper Cormorant Lake 41 D7
Upper Cullen Lake 54 B2
Upper Dean Lake 54 A4
Upper Egg Lake 42 C2
Upper Fifth Lake 43 C8
Upper Hanson Lake 33 D7
Upper Hay Lake 54 A2
Upper Hunt Lake 60 A2
Upper Iowa River 85 D8
Upper Lightning Lake 51 D7
Upper Lindgren Lake 31 C7
Upper Loon Lake 54 A1
Upper Menton Lake 44 B4
Upper Mission Lake 54 B3
Upper Mud Lake 43 C5
Upper Panaca Lake 45 A8
Upper Pauness Lake 27 D6
Upper Pine Lake 56 D1
Upper Red Lake 23 D7; 24 D1; 31 A7
Upper Rice Lake 42 A4; 63 C8
Upper South Long Lake 54 C3
Upper Spunk Lake 62 C1
Upper Tamarack River 57 D6
Upper Trelipe Lake 44 C3
Upper Twin Lake 43 D6; 84 C3
Upper Twin Lakes 32 C2
Upper Whitefish Lake 54 A2
Upstead Lake 46 B2
Uram Bay 44 C1
Uran Lake 41 B8
Us-Kab-Wan-Ka River 47 B6, C5

V

Vaara Creek 46 C2
Vadnais 71 C5
Vails Lake 69 A5
Valley Creek 33 B8
Valley Lake 47 B8
Valley River 33 B8
Valley Rose Creek 87 B7
Van Patter Lake 45 B5
Van Sickle Branch, 44 D4
Vance Lake 37 B8
Vanduse Lake 45 C8
Vanose Lake 30 D1; 42 A1
Variety Lake 43 D8
Varner Lake 69 B8
Vat Lake 37 D7
Velvet Lake 54 A3
Venning Creek 33 C8
Venoah Lake 57 A5
Venstrom Lake 51 B8
Vera Lake 36 B3
Vermilion Lake 34 A4; 35 B5; 44 B5
Vermilion River 26 C4, D4; 27 D5; 35 A5; 45 B5; 77 A6
Vermont Lake 52 D3; 60 A4
Vern Lake 37 C7
Vern River 37 C7
Vernon Lake 37 B8
Vibo Lake 64 D2
Victor Lake 36 D3
Vigoren Lake 30 C2
Villard Lake 60 C4
Vinegar Lake 54 D3
Vineland Bay 55 D5
Vinge Lake 52 D1
Virgin Lake 32 C2
Vista Lake 37 B8
Vizenor Lake 42 C1
Volden Lake 30 C2
Volen Lake 52 D1
Vos Lake 61 C8
Voyageur Narrows 26 B3
Vyre Lake 37 C5

W

Waage Lake 30 B3
Wabana Creek 45 A7
Wabana Lake 33 D6
Wabang Lake 27 C7
Wabanica Creek 19 D7
Wabasha Creek 74 B2
Wabedo Lake 44 D2
Wabegon Lake 44 B1
Wabisish Lake 43 B5
Waboose Bay 44 A2
Waboose Lake 42 C2
Waboose Lake 43 C7
Wabuse Lake 47 A6
Wade Brook 33 B5
Wadena Lake 42 B2
Wadop Lake 36 D2
Waffle Lake 37 D6
Wagner Creek 32 C3
Wagner Lake 32 B2; 52 B1; 70 B1
Wagonga Lake 68 C2
Wagosh Lake 36 A1
Wahkon Bay 55 D6
Wahneshin Lake 44 B4
Wail Lake 35 A7
Wakefield Brook 55 B8
Wakefield Lake 42 A2; 45 D8
Wakeman Bay 45 A6
Wakemup Bay 34 B4
Walker Bay 43 B8
Walker Brook 30 D4
Walker Brook Lake 30 D4
Walker Lake 52 B2
Walkins Rapids 53 A7
Wall Lake 51 C8
Wallace Lake 64 A3
Waller Lakes 87 D8
Wallingford Creek 43 D7
Wallow Creek 47 A7
Wally Lake 60 B2
Walnut Lake 84 C1
Walter Creek 37 C5
Walter Lake 66 A2
Walters Lake 33 C7
Wambach Lake 42 A1
Wamp Lake 33 C8
Wampus Lake 36 D2
Wanihigan Lake 37 B7
Wanless 37 D5
Wanless Lake 36 D4
Wapsi Lake 42 C4
Waptus Lake 42 A3
War Club Lake 26 B2
Warburg Lake 45 A6
Ward Lake 37 D7; 70 A4; 75 A5
Wardeberg Lake 30 C1
Warpaint Lake 27 D6
Warren Lake 42 A1; 47 B8; 55 D5; 82 B1
Wasaw Creek 25 A7
Washburn Lake 44 D4; 45 C7
Washington Creek 69 B6
Washington Lake 42 A2; 70 B1; 75 A8
Washte Lake 36 B2
Washusk Lake No 1 47 B6
Washusk Lake No 2 47 B6
Washusk Lake No 3 47 B6
Wasson Lake 33 C8
Watab Lake 62 C2
Watab River 62 C2
Watap Lake 38 A1
Water Hen Creek 47 A5
Water Hen River 47 A6
Water Tank Lake 48 B2
Watercress Lake 34 C3
Waterloo Creek 87 D6
Watkins Lake 76 D3; 82 C3
Watonwan Lake 37 C5
Watonwan River 82 A2, A3; 83 A5, A6
Watson Creek 86 C3
Watson Sag 67 C5
Waukenabo Lake 55 A6
Wauswaugoning Bay 39 B5
Waverly Lake 69 C8
Wawa Lake 44 C2
Wawaswi Lake 37 B5
Wax Lake 44 C3
Weasel Lake 36 C2
Weaver Lake 70 B3
Webb Lake 44 C1
Webster Creek 22 C1
Webster Creek Pool 21 C8
Webster Lake 22 C1; 32 C1
Wedel Lake 51 C7
Wednesday Bay 36 A1
Wegwos Lake 43 D8
Weir Lake 26 B3
Weisel Creek 86 D4
Weiss Creek 36 D3
Welch Lake 32 B3
Welcome Lake 46 A1
Wells Lake 76 C4
Welshes Bay 43 B8
Wendigo Arm Bay 45 B6
Wending Lake 31 B7
Wendt Lake 52 A1
Wenho Creek 48 A2
Werk Lake 59 B8
West Lake 64 A4
West Albany Creek 78 C2
West Annalaide Lake 53 D5
West Bass Lake 47 B5
West Battle Lake 52 C2
West Bay 35 A5; 35 C8
West Branch River 22 A4
West Branch, Baptism River 48 A3
West Branch, Beaver River 48 B2
West Branch, Blue Earth River 83 D7
West Branch, Bug Creek 47 B6
West Branch, Cloquet River 47 A8, B8
West Branch, Floodwood River 46 B1
West Branch, Kettle River 56 B1
West Branch, Knife River 47 C8; 48 D1
West Branch, Onion River 37 D6
West Branch, Rum River 63 B5, C6
West Branch, Sunrise River 64 D1; 71 A5
West Branch, Twelvemile Creek 59 C6
West Branch, Warroad River 18 D4
West Branch, Zippel Creek 19 D6
West Camp Creek 36 D3
West Chub Lake 36 D1
West Cranberry Lake 42 B3
West Crooked Lake 43 C7
West Fork, Baudette River 23 A8
West Fork, Beaver Creek 68 D1; 74 A2
West Fork, Black River 24 B4
West Fork, Crooked Creek 56 D4; 64 A4
West Fork, Groundhouse River 63 A6
West Fork, Lac qui Parle River 66 C2
West Fork, Little Sioux River 81 D8
West Fork, Moose Horn River 56 B3
West Fork, Prairie River 33 D7
West Fork, Twelvemile Creek 59 C6
West Fork, Yellow Bank River 66 B2
West Four Legged Lake 30 C4
West Fox Lake 44 D3; 54 A3
West Graham Lake 81 B7
West Hunter Lake 63 D6
West Indian Creek 78 D3
West Knuckey Creek 34 C3
West Lake 41 D8; 55 A6; 68 A4
West Lake Stay 72 C3
West Leaf Lake 52 C3
West Lost Lake 52 C1
West Mason Lake 52 C2
West McDonald Lake 52 B1
West Nelson Lake 53 C8
West Olson Lake 21 C8
West Pike Lake 38 B2
West Solomon Lake 68 B1
West Spirit Lake 52 A1
West Split Rock River 48 B2
West Sturgeon Lake 34 C1
West Swan River 46 A1, A2
West Toqua Lake 59 D5
West Twin Lake 54 B2; 72 D4
West Two River 35 B6
West Two River Reservoir 34 D4
West Two Rivers 34 D3; 46 A3
West Union Lake 61 B5
Western Lake 35 A6
Westra Rapids 53 A7
Wet Lake 58 C4
Wetlegs Creek 35 D7
Wettles Lake 42 D2
Whaletail Lake 70 C1
Wheelbarrow Falls 36 A1
Wheeler Lake 68 B3
Whelp Creek 37 C5
Whipped Lake 37 B5
Whipple Lake 43 B5
Whiskey Creek 42 A1; 51 A7
Whiskey Lake 60 A2
Whisky Creek 50 B4; 51 A5, A6, C5; 53 C5
Whisky Jack Lake 27 D8
Whisky Lake 21 C8; 51 A7
Whitaker Lake 37 B8
White Bear Lake 55 D5; 71 C6
White Earth Lake 42 B1
White Earth River 42 B2
White Elk Creek 45 D6; 55 A6
White Elk Lake 45 D5
White Feather Lake 27 D8
White Fish Lake 31 C7
White Iron Lake 36 C1
White Lake 35 D5; 47 B8; 84 C3
White Lily Lake 56 D1
White Oak Lake 44 D4; 45 A5
White Pine Lake 37 D7
White Pine River 47 D5
White Porky Lake 33 D7
White Rock Lake 71 B6
White Sand Lake 54 C2
White Stone Lake 71 A6
White Swan Lake 33 C7
Whiteface Reservoir 47 A6
Whiteface River 46 B4, C3; 47 B6
Whitefish Creek 24 A2
Whitefish Lake 30 D2; 31 C5; 32 C4; 37 D5; 55 D5
Whitewater Lake 35 D6
Whitewater River 78 D3
Whitney Brook 63 B6
Whitney Creek 86 B1
Whitney Lake 68 A4
Whitney Lake Ditch (Badger Creek) 17 D7
Whopper Lake 37 B5
Whyte Creek 48 B2
Wicklund Lake 60 C2
Widow Lake 44 C2
Wigwam Bay 55 D5
Wigwam Lake 47 B8
Wilbur Brook 64 A4
Wilbur Creek 48 A3
Wilbur Lake 48 A3; 64 A4
Wilcox Lake 68 B4
Wild Rice Lake 23 D5; 47 D6; 56 A4
Wild Rice River 30 D2; 40 B3; 41 A6, B5; 42 A1, A3
Wildcat Creek 87 C7
Wilderness Lake 32 D2
Wilkins Bay 27 C5
Wilkins Lake 55 A7
Wilkinson Lake 71 B5
Willborg Lake 30 C3
William Lake 61 B6
Williams Creek 19 D6
Williams Lake 31 B6; 32 B3; 37 C7; 43 C8; 54 C4; 63 C7
Willie Lake 69 C5
Willing Lake 76 C3
Willmar Lake 68 B2
Willow Bay 26 A3
Willow Creek 19 D5; 37 C7; 52 B3, C3; 54 A2; 69 A6; 72 D2; 73 D7; 82 B4; 83 B6; 86 C3
Willow Lake 43 B7; 45 B5; 56 C3; 69 A6; 81 B5
Willow River 34 A1; 44 C4; 45 C5, C6, D7; 55 A6; 56 C3, C4
Willow Water Lake 29 C8
Wills Lake 37 C7
Wilmert Lake 83 D5
Wilmoe Lake 30 B3
Wilson Bay 54 C1
Wilson Creek 37 D5; 54 A1
Wilson Lake 33 C7; 37 D5; 42 B3; 44 B4; 47 A8, B5; 51 B8; 54 C4; 60 B1; 75 D5
Wimer Lake 52 A2
Winchell Lake 37 B7
Winchester Lake 34 A4
Wind Bay 36 B2
Wind Lake 36 B2
Windigo Creek 32 B3
Windy Lake 37 D5; 45 C5; 52 B4
Wine Lake 37 B6
Wing River 24 B2; 52 D4; 53 C6, D5
Wing River Lake 52 D4
Winkle Lake 47 B5
Winkler Lake 70 D1
Winnebago Creek 87 D6
Winnibigosh Lake 32 D2; 44 A2
Winter Road Lake 23 A5
Winter Road River 23 A7
Wintergreen Lake 53 D7
Wiregrass Marsh 71 B5
Wirt Lake 32 B4
Wise Lake 54 C2
Wisini Lake 36 B4
Wita Lake 75 D8
Witness Lake 36 B2
Wiwi Bay 75 C7
Wiyapka Lake 26 C3
Wladimiraf Lake 55 B6
Woksapiwi Creek 27 D6
Woksapiwi Lake 27 D6
Wold Lake 30 C2
Wolf Bay 35 A5
Wolf Creek 35 B5; 54 D3; 56 D4; 76 C4
Wolf Lake 30 D2; 31 C6, D8; 33 D6, D8; 35 A5; 35 B7; 42 D4; 43 A6, D7; 44 D3; 46 D1; 47 A8; 51 C8; 54 B4; 56 C4; 61 A8, C7; 69 C6
Wolf Lakes 52 B2
Wolfpack Lake 27 D6
Wollan Lake 60 C3
Wolverton Creek 50 A4, B4
Woman Lake 44 C2
Wonder Lake 37 C6
Wood Lake 36 B2; 44 D4; 70 A1; 72 C4; 73 A7; 74 D3
Wood Lake Creek 73 A7
Woodbury Creek 85 C5, D5
Woodbury Lake 56 A2
Woodcamp Lake 44 D3
Woodcock Lake 48 B1
Woodpile Creek 38 B1
Woods Creek 38 C2
Woods Lake 44 D4
Worm Lake 59 A8
Wren Lake 35 A6; 44 D4
Wright Lake 51 C8
Wringer Lake 37 D6
Wye Lake 37 D5
Wyman Creek 35 D7
Wynne Lake 35 D6

XYZ

Yabut Lake 27 C7
Yaeger Lake 53 A6
Yager Lake 69 C8
Yellow Bank River 66 B2
Yellow Medicine River 72 A4, B2, B3; 73 A6
Yodeler Lake 27 D6
York Lake 41 D7
Youman Lake 42 D1
Young Lake 37 D5
Youngs Bay 19 A6
Youngstrom Lake 68 B4
Zanders Lake 74 D4
Zebulon Pike Lake 62 B2
Zephyr Lake 37 A5
Zimbrick Brook 64 A4
Zippel Bay 19 D7
Zoo Lake 37 C8
Zorns Lake 52 B1
Zuleger Creek 62 B3
Zumbro Lake 78 D1
Zumbro River 78 C2, D1
Zumwalles Lake 62 D1

Minnesota is famously known as the Land of 10,000 Lakes, though the moniker is a bit of an understatement. There are almost 12,000 lakes larger than 10 acres in the state. Lake Superior, the largest freshwater lake in the world creates a coastline along the northeast edge of the state. Minnesota also features the headwaters for the Mississippi River. With all that water it is not hard to imagine the recreational possibilities offered to Minnesota's residents and visitors.

The western-most of the Great Lakes states, Minnesota received many of its earliest visitors by boat. Native Americans portaged around High Falls. Grand Portage is now a destination for its scenic trail and views of the falls. Duluth, at the far edge of Lake Superior, provided an entry point to settlers from the days of the fur trade to the 20th century. Many attractions in the state reflect that heritage, including preserved 19th-century estates and a restored 1892 train depot. Visitors to the region can view the boats that plied the waters of the Great Lakes since the beginning of recorded history at the Great Lakes Maritime Museum, or the re-created Viking ship that crossed the Atlantic in 1982. The coastline of Lake Superior can be explored by auto tour or by railroad excursion.

Kayakers, canoeists and paddlers of every type enjoy the rivers and lakes of Minnesota, from the tumbling rapids of the Kettle River to the placid flow of the Crow Wing. Paddlers can explore the bays and islets of Kabetogama Lake or navigate the Mississippi through the Twin Cities of Minneapolis and St. Paul. The Minnesota River traverses an area rich in migratory birds while the Canon River is paralleled by a wonderfully scenic bike path.

Minnesota's state fish is the walleye and there may be no better place to catch one than on Lake Vermilion, in the northern reaches of the state. Thousands of lakes support teeming populations of walleye, perch and pike. There are excellent fishing spots across the state, from piers on Lake Superior to isolated ponds. Add in a multitude of trout streams and the North Star State is a veritable angler's paradise.

Many of Minnesota's lakes owe their origin to the retreating glaciers of the ice age. That process left many unique features including a building-sized magnetic rock and the potholes of the St. Croix River Valley. Some of the state's largest lakes are the remnants of Lake Agassiz, an enormous prehistoric lake that once covered an area greater than all five Great Lakes during the last glacial period.

In winter, most lakes in the state freeze over and offer additional activities. Many lakes and ponds provide excellent ice fishing. Others are perfect for ice skating or hockey. Winter sports of all types are common while snowmobiling, skiing and snowshoeing are very popular. No matter the season, there is always something to do in the Land of 10,000 Lakes. As a starting point, this Gazetteer features a selection of activities for all ages and activity levels. For a more comprehensive list of destinations and activities, contact the following agencies.

RECREATION

Explore Minnesota Tourism has a wealth of information on activities in the state. From working farms to art museums and aquariums, the official tourism establishment has travelers covered. The agency provides details on outdoor activities for all seasons, including fishing spots, golf courses and ski resorts. When the day's activities are done, Explore Minnesota helps travelers find places to stay and eat. With complete listings on festivals, fairs and events of any kind, Explore Minnesota puts the state at the fingertips of travelers. Resources are available online or at any of its travel information centers, located at most major highway entrances to the state.

Explore Minnesota Tourism
www.exploreminnesota.com
(888) 847-4866

Some of the best destinations in the state are at Minnesota's state parks. The recreation begins at the water's edge in the Land of 10,000 Lakes. Most state parks offer lake access for boating, swimming and fishing. While the lakes may freeze in the winter, Minnesota's parks remain open. Many support extensive trail networks that are open all year long. Hikers, equestrians and mountain bikers will find trails from the southern prairies to the northern mountains. In the winter, those same trails are turned over to cross-country skiers and snowmobilers. A network of long-range trails connects many of the Gopher State's parks.

Department of Natural Resources
www.dnr.state.mn.us/state_parks
(651) 296-6157

Further opportunities for recreation exist on federal lands in Minnesota. Water is the main attraction at two of the North Star State's most notable destinations; Boundary Waters Canoe Area Wilderness on Lake Superior, and Voyageurs National Park on Lake of the Woods. The interconnected waterways and scattered islands make for a boater's paradise but hundreds of campsites and excellent fishing mean the paddler is not alone in the appreciation of the two northern parks. Winter snows mean many passageways freeze over; visitors bring out the skis and at Voyageurs, snowmobiles.

Elsewhere, paddlers are attracted to the Mississippi National River and Recreation Area, where visitors can camp, hike and fish just outside the Twin Cities. At Grand Portage National Monument hikers can walk the trail where for centuries Native Americans carried their canoes to avoid a waterfall. A much longer hike is offered by the North Country National Scenic Trail.

Still more opportunities to enjoy Minnesota's great outdoors can be found at two national forests. Chippewa and Superior offer impressive trail networks, popular among those who ride horses, bikes, snowmobiles and all-terrain vehicles.

National Park Service
www.nps.gov/state/MN

USDA Forest Service
www.fs.usda.gov/r9
(414) 297-3600

US Fish and Wildlife Service
www.fws.gov/midwest
(612) 713-5360

TRAVEL

The Minnesota Department of Transportation (MnDOT) assists the state's motorists in a variety of ways. The agency provides a multitude of maps, from a basic highway map to traffic volume and metro maps. Travelers also benefit from MnDOT's system of well-kept rest areas and waysides.

Drivers aren't the only ones who can take advantage of MnDOT's services. The department aids pedestrians and those using railways, airports or busses. Bicyclists can also be guided toward the extensive greenway networks present in many of Minnesota's metro areas.

No matter the method of transportation, Minnesota's many travelers can use MnDOT's 511 information system. Up-to-the-minute updates on traffic, incidents and changing weather conditions can be found on the internet or by a phone call for those already on the road.

Department of Transportation
www.dot.state.mn.us
(651) 296-3000

511 Traffic Infomation
www.511mn.org/

STATE FACTS

Admitted to the Union:
  May 11, 1858; 32nd state
Capital: St. Paul
Size: 86,943 square miles
Population: 5,707,390 (2021 estimate)
Nicknames: Land of 10,000 Lakes, Gopher State, North Star State
Motto: The Star of the North
Bird: Common Loon
Fish: Walleye
Butterfly: Monarch
Flower: Lady's slipper
Tree: Red Pine
Fruit: Honeycrisp Apple
Grain: Wild Rice
Mushroom: Morel
Beverage: Milk
Gemstone: Lake Superior Agate
Song: Hail Minnesota
Name for Residents: Minnesotans

Major Cities (with population):
  Minneapolis.............................425,336
  St. Paul 307,193
  Rochester 121,465
  Duluth..86,372
  St. Cloud 68,818
Major Interior Lakes:
  Red Lake ....288,640 acres
  Mille Lacs Lake ....132,480 acres
  Leech Lake ....111,360 acres
  Lake Winnibigosh............58,240 acres
  Lake Vermilion ....40,320 acres
Major Rivers:
  Mississippi River....................681 miles
  Red River of the North   457 miles
  Minnesota River.....................370 miles
  Rainy River ....292 miles
  Bigfork River............................220 miles
Highest Point
  Eagle Mountain....................2,301 feet

FISHING AND HUNTING

With an abundance of forests and almost 12,000 lakes, Minnesota provides many options for hunting and fishing. The Gazetteer features a selection of the state's 1,500 wildlife management areas and a sampling of fishing spots in the Gopher State. To locate hunting and fishing opportunities in this Atlas, look on the pages provided in the charts for the appropriate purple symbols on the maps. Fishing spots are identified by four-digit numbers that correspond to the bodies of water indicated in the fishing chart.

It is important to be familiar with local rules, regulations and restrictions before hunting or fishing in any area. For comprehensive guides and licensing information, contact the following agency.

Department of Natural Resources
www.dnr.state.mn.us

CAMPGROUNDS

Campgrounds with a variety of different facilities are located on state, federal and private lands. The public campground symbol, as shown in the Legend (see inside front cover), identifies campgrounds located within national forests and parks. For information on fees services and reservations at public campgrounds, contact one of the state or federal agencies listed above.

The Gazetteer also lists information on a selection of privately owned and operated campgrounds. To locate campgrounds listed in the Gazetteer, look on the given page for the purple campground symbol and corresponding four-digit number.

Family Outings

ALEXANDER RAMSEY HOUSE – St. Paul – 71 C5 French Second Empire-style mansion built in 1872, home of first territorial governor Alexander Ramsey. Fifteen period-furnished rooms featuring black walnut woodwork, marble fireplaces, dollhouse and personal mementos. Guided tours.

AMERICAN SWEDISH INSTITUTE – Minneapolis – 70 C4 Turn-of-the-century Romanesque chateau mansion built in 1908 by publisher Swan Turnblad. Features a mix of period furnishings and museum exhibits. Social and cultural Swedish-American artifacts include unique *kakelugnar*, Swedish porcelain stoves.

APPLE BLOSSOM DRIVE – Winona – 87 A7 17-mile drive through the rolling hills and apple orchards of the Mississippi River Valley. Named for the outstanding views of blossoming apple trees, prevalent in spring.

THE BAKKEN MUSEUM – Minneapolis – 70 C4 Tudor mansion houses exhibits on electricity and electric medical devices. Museum founded by Earl Bakken, inventor of the pacemaker, offers hands-on exhibits that show the role of electricity in and outside the body. Extensive library.

BELL MUSEUM – Minneapolis – 70 C4 Museum preserves the native flora and fauna of Minnesota. Collection features mounted native Minnesota birds and animals. Touch-and-see room. Wildlife artwork. Traveling exhibits.

BIRCH COULEE BATTLEFIELD – Morton – 74 B2 Site of battle and siege during 1862 Dakota War. Self-guided trail explores the site. A series of informational panels tell story of the battle from the perspectives of a US army captain and a Mdewakanton soldier.

CHARLES LINDBERGH HOUSE & MUSEUM – Little Falls – 62 A1 Three-story frame house was the childhood home of famed aviator Charles Lindbergh. Original furnishings and family mementos, including 1916 Saxon automobile. Visitor center explores Lindbergh's life and adventures. Photographs. Full scale replica of *The Spirit of St. Louis*.

COMO PARK ZOO & CONSERVATORY – St. Paul – 71 C5 Popular zoological garden features a variety of animals. Big cats, gorillas and orangutans. Aquatic animals including penguins and polar bears. Conservatory features indoor and outdoor gardens of both native and exotic styles. Bonsai and orchids. Sculpture garden and naturalist art.

THE DEPOT – Duluth – 47 D7 Several art and historic organizations in restored Union Depot built in 1892, one of the best examples of Chateauesque architecture in US. Lake Superior Railroad Museum exhibits a multitude of historic engines and railcars, along with restored period buildings. North Shore Scenic Railroad offers narrated excursions. Duluth Art Institute showcases local art. Duluth Playhouse and Minnesota Ballet over classes and entertainment.

END-O-LINE RAILROAD PARK & MUSEUM – Currie – 81 A6 Railroad museum exhibits restored steam engines, motorcars and depot. Model railroad display re-creates Currie yards as they existed in 1900. Replicas of historic buildings include courthouse, mill and coal bunker.

FARMAMERICA – Waseca – 76 D2 The Minnesota Agricultural Interpretive Center tells story of the family farms and rural people of Minnesota through living history demonstrations and exhibits. 19th-century settlement farm, town hall and blacksmith shop. 1920s–1930s dairy farm and 10-acre prairie restoration. Historic vegetable gardens and field crops re-created.

FOREST HISTORY CENTER – Grand Rapids – 45 B6 Authentically reconstructed 1900 logging camp with 2.5 miles of interpretive trails. Buildings include cook and sleep camps, filer's shack, river wanigan: a floating cook shack and bunkhouse. Visitor center. Forest service cabin. Costumed guides.

FORT RIDGELY STATE PARK – Fairfax – 74 B3 Restored stone commissary houses and exhibits depicting fort's history and role in the US-Dakota War. Cemetery. Trails.

GLENSHEEN – Duluth – 47 D7 39-room Jacobean-style manor house, former home of Chester Adgate Congdon, attorney and philanthropist. Built in 1908, with boat and coach houses, bowling green, formal gardens and gardener's cottage. Detailing exemplified by hand-carved woodwork and leaded art-glass windows.

GRAND PORTAGE NATIONAL MONUMENT – Grand Portage – 39 B5 Monument preserves walking trail linking Lake Superior with the inland waterways of Canada, created to bypass High Falls. Heritage Center hosts exhibits on historical lifestyles of the area. Recreated buildings include great hall, canoe warehouse and kitchen. Ojibwe village and dock. 17-mile path to Lake Superior. Hiking trail to Mount Rose.

GREAT LAKES AQUARIUM – Duluth – 47 D7 Aquatic habitats re-create local habitats, such as the St. Louis River and Lake Superior, and exotic locations like the Amazon. Otters, seahorses and aviary. Art gallery.

GREAT RIVER ROAD – Itasca State Park – 43 B5 Route follows the Mississippi River from its source at Lake Itasca to the Gulf of Mexico. Minnesota portion traverses the state's central lake region, offering views of agricultural and metropolitan areas. Crosses the southeastern blufflands and continues into Iowa.

GUNFLINT TRAIL – Grand Marais – 38 C1 Scenic drive encounters the forested peaks and valleys of Superior National Forest on 57-mile route from Grand Marais to Trails End Campground at the edge of Boundary Waters Canoe Area. Ascends the Sawtooth Mountains, offering scenic vistas of pristine lakes and untouched wilderness.

HARKIN STORE – New Ulm – 74 C4 Restored 1870 general store, once commercial and social center of West Newton. Originally owned by community leader Alexander Harkin. Stocked with foodstuffs and farm supplies of era, much of it unsold after the town was bypassed by the railroad.

HAWK RIDGE BIRD OBSERVATORY – Duluth – 47 D7 Observation points offer views of nineteen species of migrating hawks observed annually in September and October. Hawks fly with favorable west or northwest winds along the north shore of Lake Superior. Broad-winged hawk is the most common while the Peregrine falcon is the rarest. Traversed by network of hiking trails.

HILL ANNEX MINE STATE PARK – Calumet – 45 A8 Tours of an open pit mine. Interpretation of the site's importance to Minnesota's history and culture. Fossil hunting. Scenic overlook.

HINCKLEY FIRE MUSEUM – Hinckley – 64 A2 Exhibits relate stories of escape and tragedy of the Hinckley Fire of 1894. Reconstructed depot features freight room, beanery, women's and men's waiting rooms, depot agent's office and apartment. Relief furnishings, murals and photographs.

HISTORIC FORT SNELLING – Mendota – 71 D5 Restored 19th-century fort built on bluff overlooking Minnesota and Mississippi rivers. Fort was the center of government policy and administration prior to statehood. Costumed guides provide tours, demonstrations of period activities and skits.

HJEMKOMST CENTER – Moorhead – 40 D3 Exhibits Robert Asp's life-size model of a Viking ship, *Hjemkomst*. 1982 voyage from Duluth to Bergen, Norway, is chronicled in photographs, recordings and audio-visual presentation. Replica of a Norwegian church of the Viking era. Exhibit on the history of the Red River Valley.

JAMES J. HILL HOUSE – St. Paul – 71 C5 Restored home of Great Northern Railroad magnate James J. Hill. Hill financed the only successful trans-continental railroad. Guided tours with upstairs-downstairs glimpses showing basement apparatus and unfurnished dining and living areas.

JAY C. HORMEL NATURE CENTER – Austin – 85 C6 500 acres of hardwoods, pine forest, floodplain and native prairie cover. Interpretive building with hands-on exhibits of area wildlife using snakeskins, antlers, furs and fungus. Wood-chipped hiking trails.

JEFFERS PETROGLYPHS – Jeffers – 74 D2 Over 5,000 carvings discovered on quartzite ridge. Petroglyphs date from two archaeological periods: Late Archaic–Early Woodland (3000 B.C.–500 A.D.) and Late Woodland (900 A.D.–1750). Depictions include native animals, weapons and spiritual leaders. Exhibit shelter offers interpretive meanings for petroglyphs and describes ecology of surrounding prairie.

LAC QUI PARLE MISSION – Milan – 67 C5 Replica of pre-territorial mission on site of the original mission, which burned down. Established in 1835 by fur trader Joseph Renville and Protestant missionary and physician Thomas Williamson.

LAKE SUPERIOR ZOO – Duluth – 57 A6 Over 500 animals including large cats, bison, polar bears and monkeys. Exhibits include prairie dog village, nocturnal house, aviary and Australian Connection.

LAKE VERMILLION–SOUDAN UNDERGROUND MINE STATE PARK – Soudan – 35 B6 Historic mine tours bring visitors to the deep recesses of an iron ore pit via mine car. Various articles of machinery and implements of old mining techniques. Tours of the underground physics lab that operates onsite.

LEGACY OF THE LAKES MUSEUM – Alexandria – 60 B4 Museum exhibits historical watercraft of the Great Lakes, from early exploration to the present. Rare boats in constantly changing displays. Exhibits on history of shipbuilding in Alexandria and old-time fishing clubs.

LOWER SIOUX AGENCY – Morton – 74 B2 History center, trails and exhibits at location of the first conflict of US-Dakota War of 1862. Buildings and grounds of former fur trading community. Period gardens display authentic Dakota farming techniques.

MALL OF AMERICA – Bloomington – 70 D4 Nation's largest shopping mall offers two main attractions. Nickelodeon Universe is an indoor theme park with several coasters among traditional amusement rides and kiddie rides. Underwater Adventures Aquarium features an acrylic tunnel that allows visitors to walk through the underwater environment. Sharks, turtles and fish of Minnesota and the Amazon.

MILL CITY MUSEUM – Minneapolis – 70 C4 Remains of the Washburn A Mill, once the world's largest flour mill, hosts a museum that tells the story of milling in Minneapolis with a variety of hands-on exhibits and activities.

MILLE LACS INDIAN MUSEUM & TRADING POST – Vineland – 55 D5 Museum interprets Ojibwe history and culture. Story of the Mille Lacs band of the Ojibwe is told from the settlement of Minnesota to the present through a series of interactive exhibits. Wall of windows reflects the shoreline of Lake Mille Lacs. Restored 1930s trading post.

MINNEAPOLIS INSTITUTE OF ART – Minneapolis – 70 C4 Showcases Eastern and Western art with vast collection of over 90,000 pieces, including paintings, sculpture, drawings, textiles and photographs. World famous masterpieces highlighted by Rembrandt's *Lucretia* and Hellenistic marble sculpture *Doryphoros*.

MINNESOTA CHILDREN'S MUSEUM – St. Paul – 71 C5 Participatory museum for young children and families. Interactive displays include electromagnetic crane, television station, computers, robot and electron microscope.

MINNESOTA DISCOVERY CENTER – Chisholm – 34 D2 Museum explores history of iron industry in Minnesota and the people that migrated to work it. Exhibits on the geology and mining techniques of the iron ranges. Traveling exhibits explore various facets of pioneer cultures. Heritage park preserves a historic homestead and several culturally important buildings. Former mining community.

MINNESOTA HISTORY CENTER – St. Paul – 71 C5 Rotating and permanent exhibits illustrate events and lifestyles in Minnesota history. Extensive collection of Native American and pioneer artifacts. Audio-visual library and genealogical resources.

MINNESOTA LANDSCAPE ARBORETUM – Hazeltine – 70 D2 Natural and planned gardens on 1,200 acres, featuring over 5,000 plant species. Prairie segment preserves original tallgrass landform of Minnesota. Bog area surrounds glacial pothole. Formal flower gardens. Guided and self-guided tours on 12 miles of trails.

MINNESOTA ZOO – Apple Valley – 70 D4 480-acre zoo containing animals from near and far. Vast habitats for animals of the north, including Minnesota, Canada and Asia. Tropical and aquatic animal centers. Petting zoo. IMAX theater.

NORTH AMERICAN BEAR CENTER – Ely – 35 B8 Center educates about the nature and behavior of wild bears. Through a series of cameras, visitors can watch wild bears in their true habitat. A glass window gives a glimpse of bears in a natural enclosure. Interactive exhibits entertain children and dispel myths about the danger of bears. Interpretive trail.

NORTH SHORE DRIVE – Duluth – 47 D4 Scenic drive follows the coastline of Lake Superior for 154 miles from Duluth to the Canadian border. Views of forested hills, rocky cliffs and historic lighthouses.

NORTHFIELD HISTORICAL SOCIETY MUSEUM – Northfield – 77 B5 Actual site of Great Northfield Bank Raid of September 7, 1876. Bank has been restored to 1876 appearance, just as it was when robbed by the James-Younger gang. Only Jesse and Frank James escaped Northfield posse.

NORTHLAND ARBORETUM – Brainerd – 54 C2 Arboretum and nature reserve features extensive wildflower gardens dissected by trails for hiking and cross-country skiing. Prairie vegetation including red pine.

OLD MILL STATE PARK – Ellerth – 21 C5 Visitors explore a log cabin and steam powered flour mill, relics from the Midwest's frontier history. Interpretive displays tell the tale of life in early Minnesota.

OLIVER H. KELLEY FARM – Elk River – 70 A2 189-acre living history farm exemplifies "book farming" practices of Oliver H. Kelley, founder of the Grange society. 19th-century implements pulled by horses and oxen. Cooking, butter-churning and chore demonstrations. Nature trail through prairie to Mississippi River.

PIPESTONE NATIONAL MONUMENT – Pipestone – 80 A2 Monument preserves site where Native Americans quarried red pipestone for centuries in order to carve pipes. Cultural demonstrations allow visitors to observe quarrying and carving being done in the centuries old tradition.

ROCHESTER ART CENTER – Rochester – 86 A1 Zinc and copper building hosts exhibitions of fine arts and crafts in airy, open spaces. Focuses on art from the Midwest. Showcases national and international artists as well.

RUNESTONE MUSEUM – Alexandria – 60 B4 202-pound Kensington Runestone believed to be standard Viking ballast stone, found in 1898 by Olaf Ohman attached to roots of an aspen tree. Runic carvings suggest presence of European explorers in North America in 1362. Other collections include Native American artifacts, antiques, telephone exhibit and stockade in Fort Alexandria Agricultural Museum. Extensive mounted wildlife.

SCIENCE MUSEUM OF MINNESOTA – St. Paul – 71 C5 Science, technology and natural history museum featuring participatory exhibits. Artifacts and specimens explore anthropology and paleontology, as well as local interests such as the Mississippi River. Omni theater.

SKYLINE PARKWAY – Duluth – 57 A6 Scenic drive follows ridgeline, offering hilltop vistas of Lake Superior and the port city of Duluth. Access to hiking trails. 25 miles.

SNAKE RIVER FUR POST – Pine City – 64 B1 Authentically reconstructed British fur post on the site of the original wintering post set up by the North West Company to trade with the Ojibwe. Stocked with utensils and barter goods of the fur trade. Ojibwe encampment. Costumed guides demonstrate daily activities of voyageurs.

ST CROIX SCENIC BYWAY – Point Douglas – 71 D7 Scenic route explores the pastoral beauty of the St Croix Valley, passing several state parks and historic towns. 123-mile route features views of rolling hills and pristine lakes.

TARGET CENTER – Minneapolis – 70 C4 Indoor arena built in 1990 for the Minnesota Timberwolves of the National Basketball Association. Also home to the Minnesota Lynx of the WNBA.

TARGET FIELD – Minneapolis – 70 C4 Downtown stadium built for the Minnesota Twins of baseball's American League in 2010.

TWEED MUSEUM OF ART – Duluth – 47 D7 Extensive collection of European and American art ranging from 15th-century Italian religious pieces to 19th- and 20th-century American Impressionism. The original collection gathered by philanthropist George P. Tweed has grown to include 6,000 pieces.

US BANK STADIUM – Minneapolis – 70 C4 Enclosed multi-purpose stadium with transparent roof. Home of NFL's Minnesota Vikings. Built on former site of the Metrodome. Opened July 2016. Stadium includes Vikings history and memorilbilia. Museum and art collection.

VALLEYFAIR – Shakopee – 70 D3 Amusement park features several roller coasters and classic attractions. Shows, family rides and kiddie rides. Soak City features water attraction.

WALKER ART CENTER – Minneapolis – 70 C4 Permanent collection of 20th-century art movements. Paintings, film and sculpture by acclaimed artists including Picasso and Georgia O'Keefe. Adjacent Minneapolis Sculpture Garden features over forty large sculptures in an open city park.

WEISMAN ART MUSEUM – Minneapolis – 70 C4 Impressive collection of early 20th-century and contemporary art is housed in a deconstructivist, steel brick building designed by Frank Gehry. 19,300 piece collection features ceramics, pottery and Korean furniture. Changing exhibits.

XCEL ENERGY CENTER – St. Paul – 71 C5 Multi-purpose arena has been the home of the Minnesota Wild since the NHL team's inception in 2000.

Number, Name	Page & Grid	Rainbow Trout	Brown Trout	Brook Trout	Lake Trout	Salmon	Northern Pike	Yellow Perch	Largemouth Bass	Smallmouth Bass	Rock Bass	Muskellunge	Channel Catfish	Bullhead Catfish	Bluegill	Pumpkinseed	Black Crappie	Carp
1450 Lake Wabasso	71 C5							•	•						•	•		•
1453 Lake Waconia	70 D1	•						•	•						•		•	•
1456 Lake Washington	75 D8	•							•						•		•	
1459 Lake Winnibigoshish	32 D3	•					•	•		•					•		•	
1462 Leech Lake	44 B1	•					•	•		•					•		•	
1465 Lester River	47 D7		•	•	•	•												
1468 Linwood Lake	71 A5	•						•	•						•	•	•	
1471 Little Brule River	38 C3	•																
1474 Little Fork River	34 A1	•					•	•		•	•	•						
1477 Little Knife River	47 C8	•	•	•	•													
1480 Little Pine Lake	52 A3	•					•			•					•	•		
1483 Little Rock Lake	62 C3	•						•							•		•	•
1486 Logan Creek	78 D2		•															
1489 Long Lake	43 D6						•								•	•	•	•
1492 Long Lake	54 B4	•					•	•	•	•					•	•	•	•
1495 Long Prairie River	53 D7	•					•	•	•	•	•				•	•	•	•
1498 Loon Lake	37 A7				•					•	•							
1501 Lower Red Lake	31 A6	•																
1504 Madison Lake	76 D1	•					•	•	•						•	•	•	
1507 Manitou River	48 A4	•	•	•	•													
1510 Mantrap Lake	43 C6	•					•	•	•					•	•			
1513 Many Point Lake	42 C3	•					•	•	•					•	•	•		
1516 Maple Lake	69 B8	•					•	•	•					•	•	•		
1519 Marion Lake	52 B2	•					•	•	•	•				•	•			
1522 Marsh River	28 D3						•	•	•									
1525 Mille Lacs Lake	55 C6	•					•	•	•					•				
1528 Minnesota River	67 D6						•	•		•	•		•					
1531 Mississippi River	45 B7	•					•	•							•			
1534 Moose Lake	36 B2	•					•	•						•				
1537 Moose Lake	32 D1	•					•	•						•	•			
1540 Moose Lake	45 A6	•					•	•					•					
1543 Moose River	22 B1	•					•	•										
1546 Mustinka River	59 B5	•					•	•										
1549 Namakan Lake	26 B4	•					•	•		•	•							
1552 Newman Lake	43 A6			•														
1555 North Star Lake	33 D6	•					•	•	•	•				•				
1558 Norway Lake	68 A1	•						•						•	•		•	
1561 Oak Lake	56 C4	•						•						•			•	
1564 O'Reilly Lake	45 A7						•		•						•			
1567 Otter Tail Lake	52 C2	•					•	•	•	•			•		•			
1570 Otter Tail River	51 D5	•					•	•	•				•					
1573 Pelican Lake	34 A2						•	•	•	•	•					•		
1576 Pelican Lake	60 A1	•					•	•	•	•	•					•		
1579 Pelican Lake	54 B3	•					•	•	•	•					•	•		
1582 Pierz Lake	62 A3	•						•	•						•			
1585 Pike Bay	43 A8	•					•			•	•							
1588 Pillager Lake	54 C1	•					•			•	•				•			
1591 Pine Creek	87 B7			•														
1594 Pine Lake	30 C3	•					•	•	•						•	•	•	
1597 Pine Mountain Lake	44 D1	•					•	•	•						•	•	•	
1600 Platte Lake	54 D4						•								•	•	•	
1603 Pokegama Lake	45 B6	•					•	•	•	•					•	•	•	
1606 Pokegama Lake	64 B1							•	•		•			•	•	•	•	•
1609 Pomme de Terre Lake	60 A1	•					•	•	•					•	•			•
1612 Pomme de Terre River	66 B4						•	•		•	•							
1615 Poplar Lake	37 B8				•					•							•	
1618 Poplar River	37 D7		•		•													
1621 Portage Lake	44 A2	•					•	•							•		•	
1624 Potato Lake	43 C6	•					•	•	•	•				•	•			
1627 Prairie Lake	46 D2						•		•						•			
1630 Rainy Lake	26 A1	•					•	•		•								
1633 Red Lake River	21 D8	•					•	•						•				
1636 Red River of the North	40 C3	•					•	•						•				
1639 Red Rock Lake	60 B2	•						•	•					•	•		•	•
1642 Redwood River	73 C5			•														
1645 Rice Lake	53 D7	•					•	•						•				
1648 Rice Lake	62 A2	•					•	•										
1651 Rock River	80 A3							•	•					•				
1654 Roseau River	22 A2	•					•	•										
1657 Rum River	63 B6	•					•	•	•	•	•							
1660 Rush Creek	86 A4			•														
1663 Rush Lake	52 B3	•					•								•		•	•
1666 Rush Lake	64 C1	•						•							•		•	
1669 Saganaga Lake	37 A6				•			•										
1672 Sand Hill River	28 D3	•						•										
1675 Sand Lake	32 C4	•						•							•			

Number, Name	Page & Grid	Rainbow Trout	Brown Trout	Brook Trout	Lake Trout	Salmon	Northern Pike	Yellow Perch	Largemouth Bass	Smallmouth Bass	Rock Bass	Muskellunge	Channel Catfish	Bullhead Catfish	Bluegill	Pumpkinseed	Black Crappie	Carp
1678 Sand Point Lake	27 C5	•					•											
1681 Sauk Lake	61 B6						•								•		•	•
1687 Sea Gul Lake	37 A6	•			•			•										
1690 Sebie Lake	54 D2						•								•	•	•	
1693 Shagawa Lake	35 B8	•					•	•							•			
1696 Shallow Lake	45 B8						•	•			•			•	•	•	•	
1699 Shell Lake	42 C3						•	•							•	•	•	
1702 Shields Lake	76 C3	•					•								•	•	•	
1708 Six Mile Lake	44 A3						•	•							•	•	•	
1711 Snake River	20 C2						•						•					
1714 Snake River	55 D8	•					•	•		•	•							
1717 Snowbank Lake	36 B3				•													
1720 South Branch; Two Rivers	20 A4	•																
1723 South Fork; Root River	86 C4		•	•														
1726 Spider Lake	33 D6	•					•	•							•	•		
1729 Split Hand Lake	45 C7	•					•	•										•
1732 Split Rock Bay; Lake Superior	48 C3		•	•	•	•												
1735 Split Rock River	48 C3		•	•	•													
1738 Spring Creek	74 C3		•															
1741 Spring Lake	26 C4						•		•									
1744 St. Louis Bay; Lake Superior	57 A7	•					•	•	•	•								
1747 St. Louis River	46 D4	•		•			•	•	•	•	•	•	•	•				
1750 Stalker Lake	52 D1	•					•			•			•	•				
1753 Star Lake	52 B1		•				•	•		•			•	•	•	•	•	•
1756 Steamboat Lake	43 A8						•	•		•			•	•	•			
1759 Straight River	84 B4		•					•							•		•	
1762 Strawberry Lake	42 C2						•	•		•				•	•	•	•	
1765 Sturgeon Lake	34 C1						•	•		•				•	•	•	•	
1768 Sturgeon Lake	56 C3						•	•		•				•	•		•	
1771 Sucker Lakes	44 A1						•	•		•					•			
1774 Sugar Lake	55 C7	•					•	•		•				•	•	•	•	
1777 Sugar Lake	69 A7						•	•							•	•	•	
1783 Swan Lake	51 D8						•	•		•				•			•	
1786 Swan Lake	46 A1						•	•							•	•	•	
1787 Taconite Harbor; Lake Superior	49 A6		•	•	•	•												
1789 Tamarac River	21 B5						•											
1792 Temperance River	37 D6		•	•	•													
1795 Ten Mile Lake	51 D8						•	•		•				•	•		•	
1798 Ten Mile Lake	43 C8						•	•		•				•	•		•	
1801 Tetonka Lake	76 D2						•			•				•			•	
1804 Thief River	21 D7						•	•										
1807 Toad Lake	42 D3						•	•		•					•	•	•	
1813 Trout Lake	35 A6				•					•				•				
1816 Trout Lake	33 D6				•					•					•			
1819 Trout Lake	45 B7				•					•					•		•	
1822 Trout Run	86 A3			•	•													
1825 Turtle Lake	33 C5						•	•	•	•					•		•	
1828 Two Island Lake	37 C8				•			•		•					•			
1831 Two Rivers Lake	62 C1						•	•							•	•	•	
1834 Uhlenkolts Lake	62 C7						•								•		•	
1837 Upper Cormorant Lake	41 D7						•	•							•	•	•	
1840 Upper Red Lake	23 D7						•								•		•	
1843 Vermilion Lake	34 A4	•					•	•		•					•		•	
1846 Wabana Lake	45 A7	•					•	•		•					•		•	
1849 Warroad River	18 D4						•	•										
1852 Washburn Lake	44 D4	•					•	•	•	•					•			
1855 Washington Lake	69 C5						•	•		•					•		•	
1858 Watonwan River	83 A6						•	•					•		•			•
1861 West Battle Lake	52 C7	•					•	•	•	•			•		•	•	•	
1864 Whaletail Lake	70 C1						•	•		•					•	•	•	
1867 White Bear Lake	71 C6						•	•		•					•	•	•	
1870 White Earth Lake	42 B1	•					•	•		•					•		•	
1873 Whiteface Reservoir	47 A6	•					•	•		•					•		•	
1876 Whitefish Lake	54 A2	•					•	•		•					•		•	
1879 Whitewater Lake	3506	•					•	•		•								
1882 Whitewater River	78 D3		•	•														
1885 Wild Rice Lake Reservoir	47 D6						•	•							•	•	•	•
1888 Wild Rice River	40 A3						•	•										
1891 Wilson Lake	37 D5						•	•							•			
1894 Woman Lake	44 C2						•	•		•	•			•	•		•	
1897 Zumbro River	78 C1	•	•	•	•			•		•								•

Campgrounds

Number, Name, Location	Page & Grid	RV Sites	Tenting
4000 A-J Acres Campgrounds, Clearwater	69 A7	195	●
4003 Acorn Hill Resort, Walker	44 B1	50	●
4006 Albert Lea/Austin KOA, Albert Lea	84 C4	66	●
4009 American Legion Family Campground, Detroit Lakes	42 D1	148	●
4015 Arnold's Campground & RV Park, International Falls	25 A7	20	●
4017 Ash Riviera Resort, Ray	26 C3	18	
4021 Ashby Resort & Campground, Ashby	60 A1	15	●
4024 Aspen Resort, Cusson	26 D1	17	
4027 Bad Medicine Resort & Campground, Ponsford	42 B4	10	●
4030 Balsam Bay Resort, Remer	44 C4	18	●
4033 Balsam Beach Resort & RV Park, Bemidji	43 A6	27	
4035 Barrett Lake Resort & Campground, Barrett	60 B1	35	●
4036 Beaver Dam Resort, Cleveland	76 C1	56	
4042 Bemidji KOA, Wilton	31 D6	49	●
4045 Bent Trout Lake Campground, Barnum	56 B4	92	●
4048 Big Foot Resort, Alexandria	60 B3	80	●
4052 Big Pines RV Resort, Park Rapids	43 C6	70	
4054 Big Springs Resort & Campground, Remer	44 C4	15	●
4055 Birch Bay RV Resort, Nisswa	54 B2	125	
4057 Birch Cove Resort, Kabetogama	26 B1	14	
4063 Birchmere Resort & RV Park, Frazee	42 D3	30	●
4066 Blacks Crescent Beach Campground, Osakis	61 B5	21	
4067 Bliss Point Resort, Pennington	32 D1	40	
4069 Bluff Valley Campground, Zumbro Falls	78 C1	275	●
4072 Breeze RV Resort, Park Rapids	43 C5	136	●
4073 Breezy Pines Resort & Campground, Nevis	43 C7	9	●
4075 Bremen Woods Resort, Willow River	56 C2	126	
4081 Broken Arrow Resort, Naytahwaush	42 B2	17	
4084 Brookside Campground, Blooming Prairie	85 B6	123	●
4086 Buffalo Lake Campground, Rochert	42 C1	50	
4087 Buffalo Valley Camping, Duluth	57 A6	63	●
4090 Cabin O'Pines Resort, Orr	34 A2	25	●
4093 Camp Faribo, Faribault	76 C4	71	●
4096 Camp Holiday Resort & Campground, Deerwood	55 C5	40	●
4099 Camp Maiden Rock, Morristown	76 D3	50	●
4102 Camp S'More Campground, Long Prairie	61 A7	26	●
4105 Camp Waub-O-Jeeg, Taylors Falls	64 D4	47	●
4111 Canary Beach Resort, Villard	60 C4	57	●
4114 Cannon Falls Campground, Cannon Falls	77 B6	215	●
4117 Canoe Country Cabins & Campground, Winton	36 B2	20	●
4120 Capt Dan's Crow's Nest Resort, Mora	63 A8	57	●
4123 Cass Lake Lodge, Cass Lake	43 A8	66	●
4126 Castaways Campground, South Haven	69 A7	38	
4127 Caven's Landing Campground, Sherburn	82 C3	17	
4129 Checkers Welcome Campground, Welcome	82 C4	44	●
4135 Cloquet/Duluth KOA, Carlton	57 A5	55	●
4141 Country Campground, Detroit Lakes	42 D1	30	●
4142 Country Camping, Isanti	63 D8	100	●
4144 Cozy Corner Campground, Richmond	69 A5	200	
4145 Crooked Pines Campground, Nevis	43 C7	20	
4147 Crow Wing Lake Campground, Brainerd	54 D2	100	●
4148 Cushon's Peak Campground, Houston	87 B6	44	●
4150 Dakotah Meadows RV Park, Prior Lake	76 A3	122	
4153 Deer Creek Campground, Spring Valley	86 C1	50	
4156 Deer Trail Resort & Campground, Longville	44 C3	16	●
4165 Dunromin' Park Campground, Caledonia	87 D6	72	●
4171 Eagle Cliff Campground & Lodging, Lanesboro	86 C4	150	●
4173 Eagle View Campground, Becker	41 D8	60	
4174 Edelweiss Resort & Campground, Sturgeon Lake	56 C3	60	
4180 El Rancho Mañana Campground & Riding Stable, Richmond	62 D1	120	●
4183 Elk Horn Resort & Campground, Naytahwaush	42 B2	80	●
4186 Elks Point, Fergus Falls	51 C8	30	●
4189 Fairgrounds Campground, Cambridge	63 D8	110	●
4192 Farm Island Lake Resort & Campground, Aitkin	55 B5	39	●
4198 Fish Lake Acres Campground, Prior Lake	76 A3	140	●
4201 Fish Trap Camping & RV Resort, Cushing	53 D8	158	
4204 Fishing Springs Campground, Grand Rapids	45 B6	12	●
4210 Flying Goose Campground, Fairmont	83 C6	100	●
4213 Fond du Lac Campground & Boat Landing, Duluth	57 A6	55	●
4215 Forest Hills Golf & RV Resort, Detroit Lakes	41 D8	200	
4217 Forest River Campground & Marina, Winona	87 A6	35	●
4219 Fortune Bay Resort Casino RV Park, Tower	35 B6	36	
4223 Fox Lake Campgroound of Bemidji, Turtle River	31 C7	81	●
4225 Fritz's Resort Campground, Nisswa	54 B2	95	●
4234 Golden Acres, Stillwater	71 B7	54	●
4237 Golden Eagle RV Village, Perham	52 B3	145	●
4240 Grand Casino RV Resort, Hinckley	64 A2	271	
4243 Grand Portage Lodge & Casino, Grand Portage	39 B5	29	●
4246 Graves Lake Resort & Campground, Remer	44 B4	22	●
4249 Green Valley Resort, Nevis	43 C7	12	●
4255 Gunflint Pines Resort & Campground, Grand Marais	37 A7	14	●
4258 Ham Lake Resort, Ham Lake	70 A4	114	●
4264 Hay Creek Valley Campground, Red Wing	77 B8	142	●
4267 Head of the Lakes Resort, Osakis	61 A6	20	●
4270 Hi Banks Resort & Campground, Fredenburg	47 C6	60	
4276 Hickory Hills Campground, Albert Lea	84 D3	99	
4282 Hidden Bluffs Resort, Spring Grove	87 C5	88	●
4285 Hide-Away Campground, New London	68 A3	35	●
4288 Highview Campground & RV Park, Breezy Point	54 A3	152	
4291 Hillcrest RV Park, Lindstrom	63 D2	83	
4297 Hoodoo Point Campgrounds, Tower	35 B6	97	●
4300 Hope Oak Knoll Campground, Owatonna	84 A4	70	●
4303 Hungry Jack Lodge & Campground, Grand Marais	37 B1	14	●
4306 Island Lake Campground, Cromwell	56 A2	30	
4312 Jackpot Junction Casino Hotel RV Park, Morton	74 B2	30	
4315 Jackson KOA, Jackson	82 C1	61	●
4318 Jessie View Resort, Bowstring	33 D5	30	●
4321 Kamp Dels, Waterville	76 D2	400	●
4324 Kiesler's Campground & RV Resort, Waseca	84 A3	300	●
4330 Kitchi Landing Resort, Blackduck	32 D1	30	●
4333 Lake Edward Resort, Crosby	54 B3	29	
4336 Lake Emily Resort, Emily	54 A4	41	●
4338 Lake of the Woods Campground, Baudette	19 D8	85	●
4339 Lake Pepin Campground, Lake City	78 B2	44	
4345 Lakedale Campground, Dassel	69 B6	45	
4348 Lakeshore RV Park, Ortonville	66 A1	95	●
4351 Lamb's Resort, Schroeder	49 A6	100	●
4354 Lazy "D" Campground, Altura	86 A3	125	●
4355 Lazy Days Campground, Miltona	60 A4	100	●
4357 Le Mieux Resort, Faribault	76 C3	60	●
4360 Long Lake Campsite, Detroit Lakes	42 D1	81	
4363 Long Lake Park & Campground, Bagley	42 A4	91	●
4366 Longville Campground–Austin's Swamp, Longville	44 C2	30	●
4369 Lost Acres Resort, Blackduck	32 D1	41	●
4375 Maple Springs Campground, Preston	86 C2	50	●
4381 Minneapolis Northwest KOA, Rogers	70 B3	123	●
4384 Minneapolis Southwest KOA, Shakopee	76 A2	98	●
4387 Mission Beach Resort & Campground, Crosby	54 B3	17	
4390 Money Creek Haven Campground, Houston	87 B6	199	●
4393 Moosehorn Resort, Kabetogama	26 B1	6	
4398 Mort's Dock & RV Campground	31 A8	20	●
4399 Oak Lake Campground, Kerrick	56 C4	207	●
4400 North Star Resort, Onamia	55 D5	64	
4401 Northern Skys RV Resort - Mille Lacs, Isle	55 D7	184	
4402 Oak Park Kampground, Garfield	60 B3	59	●
4405 Oakwoods Trails Campground, Austin	85 C5	21	●
4408 Old Barn Resort, Preston	86 C3	276	●
4411 Old Wagon Campground, Hawick	68 A3	120	
4414 Olson's Campground, Silver Creek	69 A8	63	●
4417 Peaceful Valley Campground, Le Sueur	75 B8	34	●
4420 Pelican Hills RV Park, Dunvilla	51 A8	166	●
4423 Penmarallter Campsite, Two Harbors	48 D1	24	
4426 Pete's Retreat Family Campground & RV Park, Malmo	55 C7	100	●
4427 Pikedale Lodge, Whipholt	44 B2	70	
4429 Pimushe Resort, Pennington	52 D1	8	
4432 Pine Acres Resort & Campground, Orr	34 A2	50	●
4435 Pine Aire Resort, Kabetogama	26 B1	30	●
4441 Pine Mountain Campground, Grand Marais	37 C1	21	●
4444 Pioneer Campsite, Wabasha	78 C4	240	●
4447 Pipestone RV Campground, Pipestone	80 A2	78	●
4450 Pla-Mor Campground, Winona	87 A6	80	●
4453 Ponderosa Campground, Mazeppa	78 D1	98	
4456 Prairie Cove Campground & RV Park, Ashby	60 A1	22	●
4459 Prairie Island Campground, Winona	87 A5	170	●
4462 Prairie Lake Campground & RV Park, Coleraine	45 A6	55	●
4465 Quadna Mountain Park Campground, Hill City	45 C6	50	●
4468 Quietwoods Resort, Hackensack	43 C8	23	●
4471 Red Fox Campground & RV Park, Moose Lake	56 B3	40	●
4474 Ripple River Motel & RV Park, Aitkin	55 B5	19	
4477 River View Campground, Owatonna	84 A4	155	●
4483 River View RV Park, Pine River	62 D1	26	●
4486 Roberds Lake Resort & Campground, Faribault	76 C4	62	
4489 Rochester/Marion KOA, Eyota	86 A1	51	●
4492 Rogers Resort & Campground, Kelliher	23 D8	24	
4495 Rose Ridge Resort, Frazee	52 A1	7	●
4498 Round Bay Resort, Park Rapids	43 D7	50	●
4504 Ruttger's Pine Mountain Resort, Backus	44 D1	24	●
4507 RV Resort Village, Pequot Lakes	54 B2	62	
4513 Schreier's on Shetek Campground, Currie	73 D6	120	●
4516 Shades of Sherwood Campground & Waterpark, Zumbrota	77 C7	350	●
4519 Shady Hollow Resort & Campground, Brainerd	54 C2	7	
4522 Shady Oaks Campground, Garden City	83 A7	77	●
4528 Shores of Leech Lake Marina, RV Sites & Cottage, Walker	43 B8	46	●
4531 Sissebagamah RV Resort on Bay Lake, Deerwood	54 C4	36	
4534 Sleeping Fawn Resort, Park Rapids	43 C6	30	●
4537 South Isle Family Campground, Isle	55 D7	130	
4540 Spirit Mountain Campground, Duluth	57 A6	73	●
4543 Spruce Hill Campground, Park Rapids	43 D6	47	
4546 St. Cloud Campground & RV Park, Sauk Rapids	62 D3	102	●
4547 St. Croix Haven Campground, Danbury	65 A5	128	
4552 St. Cloud/Clearwater RV Park, Clearlake	62 D3	102	●
4555 Stony Point Resort, Cass Lake	43 A8	175	●
4558 Sugar Bay Campground, Grand Rapids	45 B6	10	●
4561 Sullivans Resort & Campground, Brainerd	54 B2	50	
4564 Summer Haven RV Resort, Ten Strike	31 C7	121	
4570 Sundown Campground, Ogilvie	63 B7	30	
4576 Sunset Beach Resort, Battle Lake	52 C2	30	
4579 Swan Lake Resort & Campground, Fergus Falls	51 D8	10	●
4582 Timber Trails Resort, Remer	44 B3	12	●
4585 Timberline RV Resort, Sturgeon Lake	56 C3	224	
4588 Town & Country Campground, Savage	70 D3	80	●
4591 Trails RV Park, Walker	43 B8	106	
4594 Treasure Island Resort & Casino RV Park, Red Wing	77 A8	82	●
4597 Twin Lake Resort, Battle Lake	52 C1	15	
4600 Two Rivers Campground & Tubing, Royalton	62 B2	221	●
4601 Up a Creek Campground, Fifty Lakes	54 A3	83	●
4602 Upper Cullen Resort & Campground, Nisswa	54 B2	54	●
4603 Vagabond Village Campground, Park Rapids	43 C6	115	●
4606 Valhalla Island Campground, Currie	73 D6	104	●
4609 Valley View Campground, Preston	86 C3	49	
4610 Voyageurs View Tubing & Camping	29 B6	112	●
4612 Waldheim Resort, Finlayson	56 D1	30	
4627 Wilderness of Minnesota Campground, Garrison	55 C5	99	●
4630 Wildhurst Lodge & Campgrounds, Finland	48 A4	8	●
4633 Wildwood RV Park & Campground, Taylors Falls	71 A7	170	●
4642 Woodlawn Resort & Campground, Glenwood	60 C3	30	●
4645 Woodsong Campground, Ogilvie	63 B7	134	
4646 World Famous Camperville, Mora	63 A8	150	
4648 Yogi Bear's Jellystone Park Camp-Resort, Austin	85 C7	241	●

Unique Natural Features

AGATE BEACH – Gooseberry Falls State Park – 48 C3 Lake Superior agate, the official Minnesota state gemstone, is commonly found on beach and along the north shore of Lake Superior. Agates are recognized by reddish-orange color with white bands. No collecting in park.

BARN BLUFF – Red Wing – 77 B8 Former island in Mississippi River channel before natural course change. Now a high bluff overlooking river and town of Red Wing. Offers spectacular views of Lake Pepin, Mississippi River and Red Wing fault.

BIG SPRING – Forestville State Park – 86 C2 Underground Canfield Creek forms a spring at its emergence from cave. Access by hiking–horseback trail.

BIG WOODS – Nerstrand Big Woods State Park – 77 C5 Exceptional remnant of large deciduous trees, including oak, hard maple, elm and basswood, which covered south-central Minnesota prior to settlement. Also found in Sakatah Hills State Park.

BLUE MOUNDS – Blue Mounds State Park – 80 C3 Outcropping of Sioux quartzite forms a cliff 1-mile long and over 100 feet high. Appeared blue to settlers as the sun set behind it.

BLUESTEM PRAIRIE – Buffalo River State Park – 41 D5 Prairie lies along beach ridge of glacial Lake Agassiz. The Nature Conservancy protects over 307 native plant species and 54 native prairie grasses. Nesting and booming grounds for greater prairie chicken.

BOULDER HILL – Bena – 44 A2 40–50-foot-high glacially deposited hill in generally flat area of Chippewa National Forest. Lookout tower.

BRAIDED DELTA ESKERS – Marcell – 33 D8 Delta formed by meltwaters of two glacial lobes. Rugged topography includes braided eskers, caused by intertwining glacial stream. Many kettle lakes in vicinity.

CASCADE FALLS – Cascade River State Park – 37 D8 Numerous cascading waterfalls seen on Cascade River. Formed from basalt and eroding sedimentary rock. Hiking trails provide access.

CHASE POINT ESKER – Scenic State Park – 33 C6 One of the most prominent examples of eskers in Minnesota. Interpretive trail follows esker between Coon and Sandwick lakes. Scenic overlook at Chase Point. Interpretive center.

CHIMNEY ROCK – Whitewater State Park – 86 A3 40-foot-high chimney-shaped sandstone rock. Carved by erosive waters that are typical of southeastern Minnesota.

COTEAU DES PRAIRIES – Pipestone National Monument – 80 A2 "Highland of the Prairie" consists of glacial drift and Sioux quartzite. Rises between ancient river basins in southwestern Minnesota. Many native prairie grasses.

DEVIL'S KETTLE – Judge C. R. Magney State Park – 38 C3 Unusual waterfall segment on Brule River. Jutting rock mass divides river into two sections. Eastern section drops 50 feet into pool below, while western section plunges into huge pothole and, according to legend, disappears forever.

DRIFTLESS AREA – Great River Bluffs State Park – 87 A7 Example of preglacial Minnesota left untouched by glacial debris. Land covered with blanket of windblown soil provides good farming opportunities. Erosive waters dissect countryside and carve sandstone cliffs from blufflands.

EAGLE MOUNTAIN – Grand Marais – 37 C8 Highest point in Minnesota at 2,301 feet. Views of Laurentian Range and numerous ponds. Hiking access through Pat Bayle State Forest.

ELY GREENSTONE – Ely – 35 B8 Pillow rock outcropping, composed of molten rock cooled below primeval ocean. Estimated at 2.7 billion years old. Gray-green in color. Fenced enclosure. Also seen in road-cuts in Ely area.

GOAT PRAIRIES – Great River Bluffs State Park – 87 A7 King's and Queen's Bluff provides habitat for unique plant community growing on 40–50-degree slopes facing south to southwest—so steep that only goats can graze on it.

GOOSEBERRY FALLS – Gooseberry Falls State Park – 48 C3 Bedrock waterfalls of the Gooseberry River are examples of glacial scouring and ancient lava flows along north shore of Lake Superior. Five separate falls with plunges ranging from 30–60 feet.

GRANITE GNEISS – Granite Falls – 67 D7 Oldest-known exposed rocks in the world—dating back 3.8 billion years. Formations consist of quartz, feldspar and crystals. Colors range from gray to pink and dark red.

HIGH FALLS – Grand Portage State Park – 39 B5 120-foot waterfall plummets from rock outcropping on the Canadian border to Pigeon River. Accessed by a 0.5-mile trail and viewed from boardwalk.

IRONWOOD TREE – Maplewood State Park – 51 B8 Largest ironwood tree in Minnesota stands 22 inches wide and 35 feet tall. Average ironwood 6 inches wide and 16 feet tall.

KARST TOPOGRAPHY – Fountain – 86 C2 Landscape dotted with sinkholes filled with rocks, water or living trees formed as limestone caves dissolved and collapsed. Many sinkholes viewed from SR 80 between Wykoff and Fountain.

LAKE AGASSIZ – Old Mill State Park – 21 C5 Prehistoric glacial lake. Remains include beach ridges that developed when new outlets formed and lake level dropped in stages. Upper and Lower Red Lakes and Lake of the Woods, in US, and Lake Manitoba, in Canada, are remnants of Lake Agassiz.

LAKE ITASCA – Itasca State Park – 43 B3 Source of Mississippi River charted by Henry Schoolcraft in 1891. Interpretive center and trail.

LAKE SUPERIOR – Split Rock Lighthouse State Park – 48 C3 Largest freshwater lake in the world at 350 miles long and 160 miles wide. Bordered by Minnesota, Wisconsin, Michigan and Canada. Excellent vantage point at Split Rock Lighthouse.

LAURENTIAN DIVIDE – Virginia – 34 D4 Ridge of low, rugged hills is a three-way continental divide, where headwaters of streams flow north to Hudson Bay, east to St. Lawrence River and south to the Gulf of Mexico.

LOST FORTY – Dora Lake – 32 B3 Stand of virgin red and white pine left untouched by early loggers due to mapping error showing area underwater.

MAGNETIC ROCK – Grand Marais – 37 A6 Building-sized rock, relic from the last glaciation, possesses a strong magnetic field. Compass demonstrates magnetism of rock, but may be damaged by prolonged exposure. Access by Gunflint Trail.

MINNEHAHA FALLS – Minneapolis – 70 D4 53-foot-high waterfall in city park. Mentioned in Longfellow's poem "Song of Hiawatha."

MYSTERY CAVE – Forestville/Mystery Cave State Park – 86 C2 Longest cave in Minnesota with over 13 miles of natural passages. Guided tours through representative portions of cave. Average year-round temperature of 48 degrees Fahrenheit. Used by four species of hibernating bats.

NIAGARA CAVE – Harmony – 86 D3 Limestone cave features 60-foot-high waterfall, stalactite room, bridal path, wishing well and wedding chapel. Temperature 48 degrees Fahrenheit. Guided tours.

NORWAY DUNES – Halma – 21 A5 Sand dunes provide habitat for oak savanna with bur oak and rare clustered broomrapes, a type of vegetation abundant before settlement. Accumulated on eastern side of glacial Lake Agassiz.

PENNINGTON BOG – Pennington – 32 D1 Bog contains an abundance of orchids amidst a variety of plant species. Permit required.

POTHOLES – Interstate State Park – 71 A8 Potholes formed after waters of glacial Lake Duluth roared south, carving the St. Croix River Valley. Park contains over 100 potholes including the widest and deepest recorded in the world. "The Caldron" is over 20 feet wide and "Bottomless Pit" is over 60 feet deep. Trail to potholes begins at interpretive center.

SHOVEL POINT – Tettegouche State Park – 48 B4 Tilting bedrock formed when basaltic lava poured out of continental rift, creating Sawtooth Mountains and the bedrock of Lake Superior's North Shore. Release of lava from beneath lake caused flows to tilt southeasterly 20–30 degrees.

TEMPERANCE RIVER GORGE – Temperance River State Park – 49 A6 Narrow gorge formed as lava potholes became larger and connected with each other. Dry potholes left on both sides of gorge as stream changed course or grew smaller. Trails on both sides.

TINTA-INYA-OTA – Minneopa State Park – 75 B7 Numerous granite erratics. Dakota people name means "prairie with many rocks."

ZIMMERMAN PRAIRIE – Ulen – 41 B7 Black soil prairie dominated by big bluestem, indian grass, prairie cord grass and rare sedge. Natural prairie vegetation escaped the settler's plow. Marbled godwit, upland sandpiper and greater prairie chicken.

Outdoor Adventures

HIKING

AFTON STATE PARK – Afton – 71 D7 Trail network in wilderness environment of wooded bluffs and prairie along lower St. Croix. Trails follow wooded ravines, along hillsides and meadows. 20-mile system allows a variety of trail difficulties and lengths.

ANGLEWORM TRAIL – Ely – 35 A8 Trail forms 14-mile loop around Angleworm, Home and Whiskey Jack lakes. Rugged terrain with stand of white and red pines and high rock ridges with scenic overlooks. Camping restricted to nine designated sites. Trailhead off of Echo Trail.

ARROWHEAD STATE TRAIL – Peyla – 35 B5 Naturally surfaced, 135-mile trail features rolling hills with numerous lakes and streams amongst mixed conifer and hardwood forest. Many wet areas in summer. Southern portion used primarily for snowmobiling.

BANNING STATE PARK – Sandstone – 56 D2 Trails follow along wild and scenic sections of Kettle River and through ruins of historic Banning quarry. Trails vary in length with many loops and cutoffs. 17-mile system explores rocky and rugged terrain with wooded areas and numerous scenic vistas. Self-guided Banning Quarry Trail along abandoned quarry railroad grade.

BASS LAKE TRAIL – Ely – 35 B8 Well-marked trail leads around Bass Lake and through various ecological zones. Trail sections cross old lake bottoms. Return same route. Trailhead off Echo Trail/CR 116 in Superior National Forest. 12 miles.

BEAR HEAD LAKE STATE PARK – Soudan – 35 B7 Trail network provides scenic northwoods setting with rolling forested hills. Series of marked trails with loops and cutoffs circling several remote lakes. Intersects with Taconite State Trail. Wildlife includes timber wolf and bear. 17 miles.

BLUE MOUNDS STATE PARK – Luverne – 80 C3 Loop trails offer opportunities to view Minnesota's prairie environment, complete with grazing Buffalo herd. 13-mile trail networktraverses prairie and on top of unique rock outcropping of Sioux quartzite.

BORDER ROUTE TRAIL – Grand Marais – 38 B4 Rugged 65 mile long trail for experienced hikers parallels canoe routes of Native Americans and voyageurs in BWCA Wilderness. Follows along high cliffs with views of forests and lakes. Crosses several canoe portages. Wildlife includes deer, moose, wolf and loon. 40-mile route ends at Arrowhead Trail.

BUFFALO RIVER STATE PARK – Glyndon – 41 D5 Trail network meanders alongside the Buffalo River and into the vast expanse of one of Minnesota's largest remaining virgin prairies. Savanna Cutoff interpretive trail. Level terrain for easy walking. 12 miles.

CAMDEN STATE PARK – Lynd – 72 C4 Network of loops across open prairie and through wooded valley of the Redwood River. Several scenic vistas and historic sites highlight 16-mile trail system. Prairie, woodland plants and wildlife. Easy hiking with some steep areas.

CASCADE RIVER STATE PARK – Grand Marais – 37 D8 Trail network along both sides of the Cascade River Gorge and Lake Superior shoreline and up to Lookout and Moose mountains. Panoramic view of Lake Superior, Sawtooth Mountains and river gorge. 15-mile network of loops provides short walks and long hikes with varied terrain.

CRUISER LAKE TRAIL – Voyageurs State Park – 26 B3 Trail crosses Kabetogama Peninsula to Anderson Bay on Rainy Lake. Seven lakes along trail and connecting spurs include Cruiser Lake at midway point. Trail loops at each bay. Scenic overlooks, granite outcroppings and a variety of plants and wildlife. Return by same route. Numerous campsites along trail. 9-mile route is accessible by water only. Trailhead on north-east edge of Lost Bay on Kabetogama Lake.

CUT FOOT SIOUX TRAIL – Inger – 32 D3 Loop trail with many offshoots along continental divide. 22-mile route passes through hardwood and large pine forest in hilly area with small lakes. Connects with Simpson Creek Trail, 13-mile system through large red pine forest on a peninsula on Lake Winnebigoshish. Two designated campsites. Good views of osprey, eagle and loon. Plentiful fishing and berry picking in area.

EAGLE MOUNTAIN TRAIL – Grand Marais – 37 C8 Trail extends north 7 miles to Eagle Mountain, the highest point in Minnesota at 2,301 feet. Gently rolling terrain through birch, spruce and fir forest includes Lake Superior. Trailhead at junction of FR 153 and FR 158. Return by same route.

FORESTVILLE/MYSTERY CAVE STATE PARK – Preston – 86 C2 Trails wander through hardwood forests and steep ravines of Root River Valley. Stream-dissected terrain includes springs, caves and underground rivers. Variety of trails, some shared with horseback riders. 17-mile network.

FORT RIDGLEY STATE PARK – Fairfax – 74 B3 8-mile trail network passes over rolling prairie and wooded ravines of the Minnesota River Valley and through site of Dakota Conflict of 1862. Historic buildings and museum.

GEORGE H. CROSBY MANITOU STATE PARK – Schroeder – 49 A5 Trail network provides scenic routes along Manitou River, past waterfalls and Lake Superior and through yellow birch forest. Hilly terrain with steep and rocky areas. 24-mile network includes excellent backcountry trails.

GLACIAL LAKES STATE PARK – Starbuck – 60 D3 Trails loop through high, open hills and glacial ridges surrounding Signalness Lake. Panoramic views. Vegetation ranges from virgin prairie to oak forest. 16-mile network.

GRAND PORTAGE TRAIL – Grand Portage National Monument – 39 B5 Route follows historic portage of fur traders to the site of Fort Charlotte. 8-mile trail through varied terrain with rolling hills and rugged, wet and muddy places. Short spur to The Cascades waterfall at trail end.

GREAT RIVER BLUFFS STATE PARK – Dakota – 87 A7 Network of easy loop trails in an exceptionally beautiful area. Blufflands with limestone cliffs, ravines, wooded eastern slopes and grass-covered western slopes. King's Bluff Nature Trail offers panoramic view of Mississippi River Valley. 7-mile system includes several short, but steep trails.

HAY CREEK TRAILS – Red Wing – 77 B8 Trail loops through the rugged, steep hills and valleys of Richard J. Dorer Memorial Hardwood State Forest. 17-mile route through dense hardwood forest provides views of sparsely developed valley. Wildlife includes wild turkey. Picnic area.

HAYES LAKE STATE PARK – Winner – 22 A3 Trails loop around lake and Roseau River in pristine northwoods setting. 13 miles of easy hiking with scenic views. Abundant wildlife includes heron, grebe and some of Minnesota's less common waterbirds.

HERRIMAN LAKE TRAIL – Crane Lake – 27 C5 Trail network boasts 15 miles of short and long loops. Major trails lead to Dovre and Little Vermilion lakes or south along Echo River. Difficult climb to scenic ridgetop overlooking Baylis Lake. Three designated campsites. Trailhead off of CR 424 in Superior National Forest.

HOGBACK LAKE TRAIL – Isabella – 36 D4 Trailhead at Hogback Lake Picnic Area off of FR 172 in Superior National Forest. Loops around Scarp Lake to Lupus Lake. Four wilderness campsites along maintained trail. 5 miles.

ITASCA STATE PARK – Lake George – 43 B5 Trail network offers variety of difficulty levels. 49 miles of trails explore 30,223 acres of lakes and virgin pine forest. Rolling terrain with some steep hills. View of forest from fire tower.

JAY COOKE STATE PARK – Brownell – 57 A5 Extensive, 50-mile trail network with long loops for experienced hikers and short trails for beginners. Trail crosses rugged and spectacular terrain in hardwood and pine forest with the St. Louis River running through a picturesque gorge. Suspended swinging bridge and historic St. Louis River portage. Several scenic vistas.

KILEN WOODS STATE PARK – Lakefield – 82 C1 Series of walking trails in Des Moines River Valley. Trails pass through oak savanna, meadows, woods and prairie amid rolling farmland. Park features abundant wildlife and rare plants. 5-mile network.

KRUGER TRAIL – Wabasha – 78 C3 Loop trail through steep, rugged hardwood forest with excellent views of Zumbro River valley. 8-mile route begins off of CR 81.

LAKE BRONSON STATE PARK – Lake Bronson – 20 A4 Trails loop through short-grass prairie, marshes and rolling hills of Red River Valley area. Wildlife includes upland sandpiper and moose. 14-mile network.

LAKE MARIA STATE PARK – Monticello – 69 A8 Widely varied hiking trails on 14 miles of wooded and rolling land with deciduous tree cover surrounding several lakes, ponds and marshes. Spring wildflower bloom. Terrain characteristic of terminal moraines left by last glaciers. Bird-watching.

LOCATOR LAKE TRAIL – Voyageurs National Park – 26 B1 Nature trail crosses a variety of plant and animal environments including granite ridges, damp lowlands and beaver flowages. Moderately difficult, 2.5-mile route with many hills. Exceptional scenic views. Trailhead on Kabetogama Peninsula near La Bontys Point on Kabetogama Lake.

LOST FORTY TRAIL – Dora Lake – 32 B3 Trail loop winds through majestic pines of Lost Forty. Trees are up to 350 years old. Trailhead off of FR 2240 in Chippewa National Forest. 0.5 miles.

MAGNETIC ROCK TRAIL – Grand Marais – 37 A6 Easy, 3-mile hike , part of the Border Route Trail, passes bare rock, a bog and Larch Creek. Enters area of 1974 forest fire. Blueberry picking. Wildlife features beaver and moose.

MAPLEWOOD STATE PARK – Pelican Rapids – 51 B8 25-mile trail system loops through maple-covered hills with striking vistas of small, clear lakes nestled in deep valleys and surrounding farmland. Outstanding fall foliage. Some trails steep and strenuous. Self-guided Grass Lake Interpretive Trail.

MILLE LACS KATHIO STATE PARK – Vineland – 55 D5 Network of hiking trails among hills, meadows and forest on west side of Mille Lacs Lake. Two self-guided walks near interpretive center. Spectacular views of Mille Lacs area from 100-foot tower. 35 miles.

MINNESOTA VALLEY STATE PARK – Belle Plaine – 76 A1 Secluded backcountry trail close to urban area. 36-mile path runs along floodplain marshes and meadows of Minnesota River Valley. Historic route of Native Americans, explorers and settlers. Prolonged flooding in spring. Camping available. Trailhead at St. Lawrence State Wayside off of CR 57.

MYRE–BIG ISLAND STATE PARK – Albert Lea – 84 C4 Three self-guided trails of varying lengths. Glacial evidence dots park in vast prairie pothole region. Gathering ground for thousands of white pelicans in spring and fall. Camping available. 16 miles.

NERSTRAND BIG WOODS STATE PARK – Nerstrand – 77 C5 13-mile trail explores outstanding example of "big woods." Gently rolling, wooded hills and secluded valleys. Colorful fall foliage. Picturesque creek and waterfall. Wildflowers. Some trails shared with horseback riders. Variety of trail lengths. Camping available.

NORTH COUNTRY NATIONAL SCENIC TRAIL – Walker – 43 C8 Long range trail threads through numerous lakes and wetlands in pine and hardwood forest. Relatively level terrain on eastern portion while western end becomes rolling. Wildlife includes bald eagle. Spring wildflower bloom. Seven primitive campsites. 68 miles in state.

NORTH DARK RIVER TRAIL – Virginia – 34 C3 Trail follows east bank of the Dark River through jack pine plantation, looping back on an old logging road. Views of river gorge and sandy valley. Return by same, 1.3-mile route.

NORTH SHORE STATE TRAIL – Finland – 48 A4 Trail traverses northeastern Minnesota, winding through forested bluffs overlooking Lake Superior. Remote, natural and undeveloped setting. Wildlife includes timber wolf, moose, waterfowl and raptors. Campsites available along trail. Popular among snowmobilers. 70 miles.

NORWAY TRAIL – Lake Jeanette State Forest – 27 D6 Trail leads 8 miles to Trout Lake in BWCA Wilderness and crosses Norway Creek. Useable in winter for cross-country skiing. Trailhead off of CR 116.

POWWOW LAKE TRAIL – Forest Center – 36 C3 55-mile route through BWCA Wilderness. Trail uses old logging roads and passes through a variety of land types featuring high pine-covered ridges, wet brushy lowlands, grassy meadows and stands of old growth pine. Crossing streams and low, boggy areas may be necessary. Passes through part of Rice Lake Fire of 1976.

SAVANNA PORTAGE STATE PARK – Balsam – 46 D1 Looped trails in varied wilderness of rolling hills, lakes and bogs. Hardwood forests harbor abundant wildlife. 17-mile network includes Historic Savanna Portage Trail, once vital link for voyageurs between the Mississippi River and Lake Superior.

SCENIC STATE PARK – Bigfork – 33 C6 Trail network includes interpretive trail to Chase Point Esker. Main trail circles pristine lakes with several loops. Virgin red and white pine stand. Abundant wildlife includes deer and wolf. 14 miles.

SHINGOBEE RECREATION AREA TRAIL SYSTEM – Walker – 43 C8 6-mile trail loops through mixed aspen, birch and pine forest along two small lakes and the Shingobee River valley of Chippewa National Forest. Scenic vista. Some trails wet in spring and summer. Intersection with North Country National Scenic Trail.

SIBLEY STATE PARK – New London – 68 A2 Trails wind through hardwoods covering rolling glacial moraine hills and the long sandy shore of Lake Andrew. Trail loops feature scenic overlooks of surrounding forest, prairie knolls, lakes and farmland. 2-mile, self-guided interpretive trail. 18-mile network.

SIOUX–HUSTLER TRAIL – Superior National Forest – 27 D7 Difficult loop follows FT 165 off of FR 467. Minimally maintained trail with many streams to wade. 32-mile route penetrates some remote areas of BWCA Wilderness and returns to Echo Trail. Wilderness campsites.

SNOWBANK–OLD PINES HIKING TRAILS – Winton – 36 B3 22-mile loop passes between Parent and Disappointment lakes and around Snowbank Lake. Terrain features high rock ridges with scenic overlooks. Sixteen designated campsites. Old Pines Trail cuts off from Snowbank 5 miles from trailhead, extending 19 miles in two loops around numerous lakes. Several scenic overlooks and virgin stand of white pine over 300 years old.

SOUTH LAKE TRAIL – Grand Marais – 37 A8 Trail passes through old growth timber and stands of red and white pine. Portion between Partridge and South lakes located in Boundary Waters Canoe Area Wilderness. Intersects with Border Route Trail. Moderately difficult, 7-mile route.

ST. CROIX STATE PARK – Pine City – 64 A4 Extensive trail system follows several scenic creeks and the St. Croix River. Also loops through aspen–birch forest with some jack pine savanna. Gently rolling hills. Many trails ideal for short walks or long distance hiking. Self-guided interpretive walk. 127 miles.

STURGEON RIVER TRAIL – Chisholm – 34 C2 22-mile trail system offers unique vegetation and varied terrain, featuring high bluffs along the Sturgeon River. Travels through mature timber stands, clear-cut areas and grassy openings. Groomed for skiing in winter. Trailhead off of CR 65.

SUPERIOR HIKING TRAIL – Two Harbors – 48 C2 Rugged trail with impressive views of Lake Superior and the Sawtooth Mountains. 180-mile route features campsites every 5 to 8 miles. Trail will eventually extend 300 miles, from Duluth to Canada, linking eight state parks.

TACONITE STATE TRAIL – Grand Rapids – 45 A7 Long range trail winds 165 miles through picturesque forest of aspen, birch and pine and leads to many isolated lakes and streams. Points of interest include Star Lake logging camp and several old trapper's shacks. Interesting side trips available in various state parks and forests along trail. Camping available. Natural surface.

TETTEGOUCHE STATE PARK – Silver Bay – 48 B4 Series of loops from Lake Superior to spring-fed lakes and waterfalls of Baptism River. 23-mile network explores semi-mountainous terrain in heavily forested area providing scenic views of Lake Superior. Easy walk along sheer cliff to Shovel Point.

UPPER SIOUX AGENCY STATE PARK – Granite Falls – 73 A7 Trails weave over wooded slopes, meadows and prairie knolls and along Yellow Medicine River. Scenic views of Minnesota and Yellow Medicine

rivers from bluffs. 34-mile network includes several shared use equestrian trails.

WHITEWATER STATE PARK – St. Charles – 86 A3 Trail network through ravines and over limestone cliffs within hardwood forest. Caution should be used along steep ledges. Trout streams in mosquito-free area. Colorful fall foliage. Two self-guided, interpretive trails and 2 miles of barrier free trail. 12 miles total.

WILD RIVER STATE PARK – Almelund – 64 D3 Network of woodland trails follows the wild and scenic St. Croix River. Some wet areas and horseback riders. Self-guided nature trail around Amiks Pond. 35-mile system allows hikes of varied lengths and difficulties.

WILLIAM O'BRIEN STATE PARK – Marine on St. Croix – 71 B7 Trails wind through bluffs of wild and scenic St. Croix River Valley. Terrain of 12-mile network varies from wooded river floodplain to high, dry, rolling prairie with open areas and oak forest.

ZIPPEL BAY STATE PARK – Williams – 19 D3 Trails loop through wooded terrain and along marshes. Sandy beach stretches for miles along shore of ocean-like Lake of the Woods. Abundant wildlife, particularly shorebirds. Habitat for endangered piping plover. 6 miles.

BIKING

CANNON VALLEY TRAIL – Cannon Falls – 77 B6 Multi-use rail-trail follows Cannon River from Cannon Falls to Red Wing. 20-mile route features crushed limestone with 5 miles of asphalt surfacing. Terrain changes from steep rocky cliffs to hardwood forests and marshland.

DOUGLAS STATE TRAIL – Rochester – 85 A8 Old railroad grade is a multi-use trail between Rochester and Pine Island. Paved surface with separate path for horseback riders. 12.5 miles.

GATEWAY STATE TRAIL – St. Paul – 71 C5 Rail-trail follows 18-mile route from St. Paul northeast to Pine Point Park in Stillwater. Paved trail passes through urban areas, dense woods, lakes, ponds, wetlands and open prairie.

GLACIAL LAKES STATE TRAIL – Willmar – 68 B2 Asphalt trail on old rail line from Willmar to Harwick. 22-mile, multi-use trail passes farmland and glacially created lakes. Parallel grass path for equestrian use.

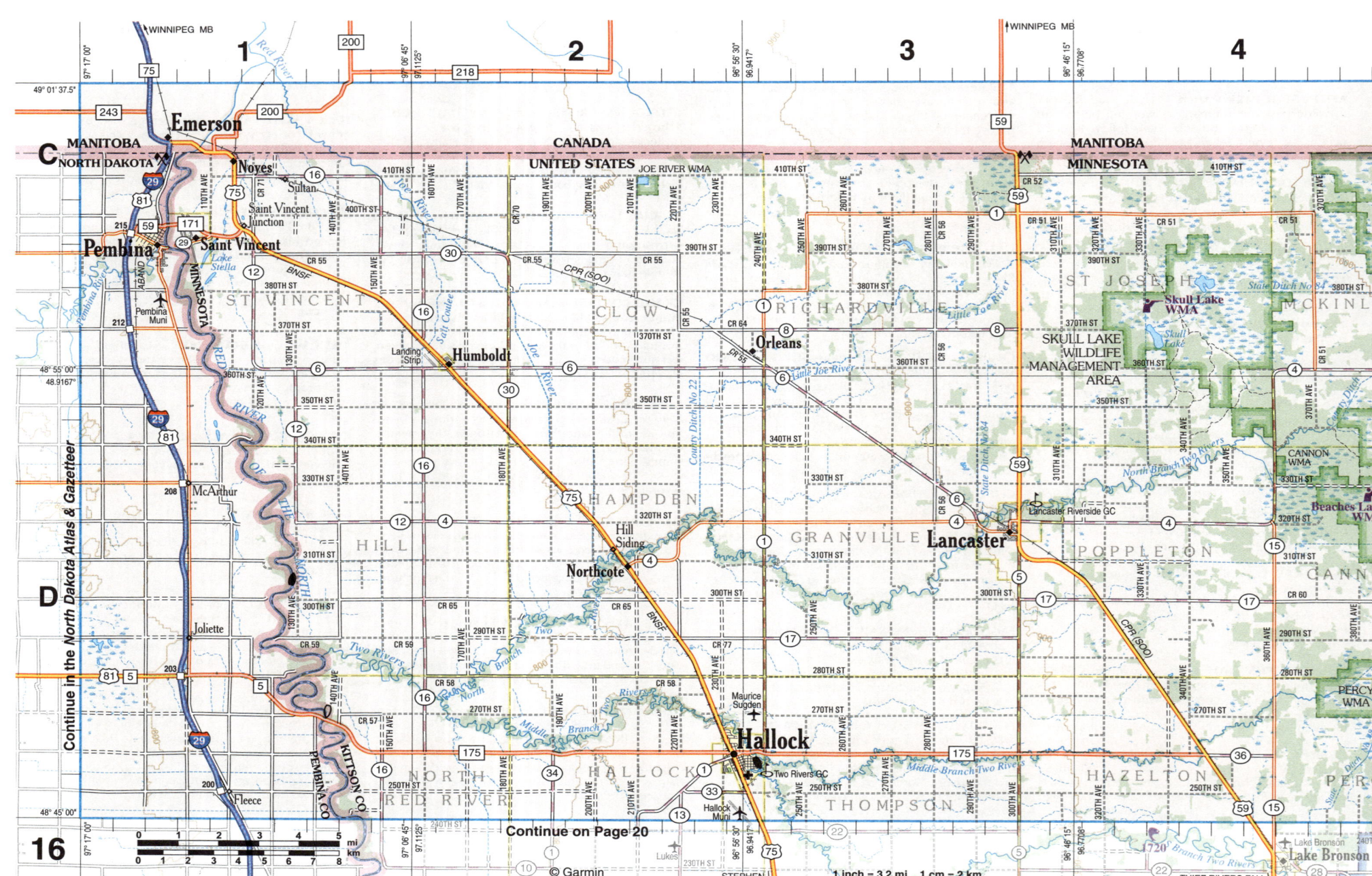

Continue on Page 20

GUNFLINT TRAIL – Grand Marais – 37 B8 Touring route passes glacial lakes, scenic vistas and abundant wildlife. 116-mile route serves as the eastern entrance to Boundary Waters Canoe Area Wilderness.

HARMONY–PRESTON VALLEY STATE TRAIL – Harmony – 86 D3 18 mile paved multi-use trail from Harmony through Preston to Root River State Trail. Southern segment descends into valley. Steep, hilly terrain. Northern segment follows old railroad grade along streams and passes through woodlands and agricultural areas. 18 miles.

HEARTLAND STATE TRAIL – Park Rapids – 43 C5 Follows old railroad grade from Park Rapids to Cass Lake. 49-mile route passes through farmlands, wooded areas, rolling hills, Paul Bunyan State Forest and Chippewa National Forest. Paved surface with grade less than 5 percent.

LAKE WOBEGON TRAIL – Sauk Centre – 61 C6 Former rail corridor is now a 46-mile bituminous trail. Heavy use from bicyclists and hikers in summer and snowmobiles in winter. Flat route features many access points for shorter trips.

LUCE LINE STATE TRAIL – Plymouth – 70 C3 Old railroad grade runs 63 miles from Plymouth to Cosmos. Trail once used by Dakota people crosses Crow River, woodlands and rural croplands and pastures. Crushed limestone surface between Plymouth and Winsted. Natural surface to Cosmos.

PAUL BUNYAN STATE TRAIL – Baxter – 54 C2 Multi-use trail primarily located on old railroad grade. Paved, 110-mile route terminates at Lake Bemidji State Park.

ROCHESTER TRAIL SYSTEM – Rochester – 86 A1 Urban trail network boasts 85 miles of concrete and bituminous paths through urban areas and city parks. Loops of varied lengths are possible.

ROOT RIVER STATE TRAIL – Fountain – 86 C3 Trail developed on abandoned railroad grade from Fountain to Houston. 42-mile route parallels Root River's limestone bluffs. 100-foot-wide right-of-way contains 48 railroad bridges. Abundant wildlife includes wild turkey, deer, hawk and turkey vulture. Rattlesnakes occasionally sighted near rock outcroppings.

SAKATAH SINGING HILLS STATE TRAIL – Mankato – 75 B8 Follows old railroad grade 39 miles from Mankato to Faribault. Multi-use trail with crushed asphalt surface. Passes through transition zone from "big woods" to prairie.

SUOMI HILLS TRAIL – Marcell – 33 D6 Mountain bike trail loops through rugged, heavily timbered terrain with numerous lakes in Chippewa National Forest. 21 miles of trail explore hardwood forest. Exceptionally scenic during fall foliage.

WILLARD MUNGER STATE TRAIL – Hinckley – 64 A2 Rail-trail also known as Hinckley Fire Trail, used as escape route for Hinckley citizens during fire of 1894. 63-mile trail on paved surface with grade less than 3 percent.

DOWNHILL SKIING

AFTON ALPS – Basswood Grove – 71 D7 MOUNTAIN: 17 chairlifts, 2 tow, 2 people movers. 48 trails: 25% beginner, 50% intermediate and 25% advanced. VERTICAL DROP: 350 ft. FACILITIES: Ski school, restaurants, ski shop, rentals, terrain parks, night-skiing, snowtubing.

ANDES TOWER HILLS – Holmes City – 60 B2 MOUNTAIN: 3 chairlifts and 1 tow. 15 trails: 55% beginner, 40% intermediate and 5% advanced. VERTICAL DROP: 290 ft. FACILITIES: Ski school, restaurant, ski shop, rentals, terrain park, snowtubing, snowshoeing. 16 km of Nordic trails.

BUCK HILL – Orchard Garden – 76 A4 MOUNTAIN: 3 chairlifts and 4 tow, 2 people movers. 16 trails: 37% beginner, 18% intermediate and 45% advanced. VERTICAL DROP: 262 ft. FACILITIES: Ski school, rentals, terrain parks, night-skiing, snowtubing.

BUENA VISTA SKI AREA – Puposky – 31 C7 MOUNTAIN: 4 chairlifts, 1 rope tow. 16 trails: 20% beginner, 55% intermediate and 25% advanced. VERTICAL DROP: 230 ft. FACILITIES: Ski school, restaurant, rentals, terrain parks, night-skiing, snowtubing. 25 km of Nordic trails.

COFFEE MILL SKI AREA – Wabasha – 78 C3 MOUNTAIN: 2 chairlifts and 1 tow. 10 trails: 40% beginner, 30% intermediate and 30% advanced. VERTICAL DROP: 425 ft. FACILITIES: Ski school, rentals, terrain parks, night-skiing.

GIANTS RIDGE – Pineville – 35 D6 MOUNTAIN: 5 chairlifts and 2 tows. 35 trails: 33% beginner, 42% intermediate and 25% advanced. VERTICAL DROP: 500 ft. FACILITIES: Ski school, restaurant, rentals, terrain parks, night-skiing. 60 km of Nordic trails, snowtubing.

HYLAND SKI & SNOWBOARD AREA – Atwood – 70 D3 MOUNTAIN: 3 chairlifts and 2 tows. 11 trails: 28% beginner, 45% intermediate and 27% advanced.

VERTICAL DROP: 175 ft. FACILITIES: Ski school, rentals, terrain park, night-skiing.

LUTSEN MOUNTAINS – Lutsen – 37 D7 MOUNTAIN: 7 chairlifts and gondola. 94 trails: 20% beginner, 47% intermediate and 33% advanced. VERTICAL DROP: 825 ft. FACILITIES: Ski school, restaurants, rentals, terrain park, snowshoeing. 3 km of Nordic trails.

MOUNT KATO – Skyline – 75 D8 MOUNTAIN: 8 chairlifts and 2 tows. 19 trails: 21% beginner, 38% intermediate and 41% advanced. VERTICAL DROP: 240 ft. FACILITIES: Ski school, rentals, terrain park, snowtubing.

POWDER RIDGE – Kimball – 69 A6 MOUNTAIN: 3 chairlifts and 3 tows. 16 trails: 25% beginner, 19% intermediate and 56% advanced. VERTICAL DROP: 300 ft. FACILITIES: Ski school, restaurant, rentals, terrain park, night-skiing, snowtubing.

SPIRIT MOUNTAIN – Smithville – 57 A6 MOUNTAIN: 5 chairlifts and 2 tows. 22 trails: 35% beginner, 40% intermediate and 25% advanced. VERTICAL DROP: 700 ft. FACILITIES: Ski school, rentals, terrain park, night-skiing. 22 km of Nordic trails.

WELCH VILLAGE – Red Wing – 77 B7 MOUNTAIN: 8 chairlifts, 3 people mover. 50 trails: 30% beginner, 21% intermediate and 49% advanced. VERTICAL DROP: 360 ft. FACILITIES: Ski school, restaurants, rentals, terrain park, night-skiing.

WILD MOUNTAIN – Almelund – 64 D3 MOUNTAIN: 4 chairlifts and 3 tows. 21 trails: 30% beginner, 30% intermediate and 40% advanced. VERTICAL DROP: 300 ft. FACILITIES: Ski school, rentals, night-skiing, snowtubing.

PADDLING

BIG FORK RIVER – Dora Lake – 32 C3 Quiet flow through wild rice marsh and tamaracks punctuated with class I–II rapids along densely wooded banks and rock outcroppings. Two mandatory portages. Camping. Put-in at Dora Lake. Takeout 165 miles downstream near Canadian border at SR 11 bridge or continue to Rainy River.

CANNON RIVER – Waterville – 76 D3 River winds through a variety of scenery including rolling farmlands, wooded valleys and a deep picturesque gorge with 250-foot-high rocky bluffs. Three man-made lakes. Many dams to portage. 80-mile route is suitable for beginners except during high water. Camping. Put-in at Sakatah Lake. Takeout on Mississippi River.

CLOQUET RIVER – Brimson – 47 A8 Intermittent class I–III rocky rapids through dense pine, birch and aspen forests. Portages at Island Lake Dam and most rapids. Segment below Island Lake Reservoir is suitable for beginners with some class I rapids. Camping. Put-in at Indian Lake near campground. Takeout 75 miles downstream.

CROW WING RIVER – Park Rapids – 43 C7 Popular sandy-bottomed river for beginners. Chain of lakes in headwaters gives way to lush forests and marshes. Numerous campgrounds along 110-mile route. Put-in on Tenth Crow Wing Lake. Takeout at Sylvan Dam or continue to Mississippi River.

DES MOINES RIVER – Dundee – 81 B7 Calm waters with some class-II character field rapids. Beginner-level, 70-mile route. Popular and scenic section from Windom to Jackson. River flows through low hills, woods, farmland and 100–200-foot-high bluffs. Camping. Portages two dams. Takeout in Petersburg near Iowa border.

INGUADONA RIVER – Remer – 44 C3 Slow-moving river flowing through Chippewa National Forest on historic Native American route. 23-mile route passes wild rice beds, Ojibwe Village and old logging camp. Put-in at Inguadona Lake off of CR 7.

KABETOGAMA LAKE – Voyageurs National Park – 26 B1 Flatwater paddle on large lake offers many bays and islands to explore. Connecting Namakan and Rainy lakes also offer miles of canoeing. Campsites available on park islands and shorelines. Put-in at Wooden Frog Campground.

KETTLE RIVER – Willow River – 56 C3 Wild and scenic river with densely forested banks. 47-mile route features intermittent, class I rapids above Banning State Park suitable for beginners. Middle section of challenging whitewater with class II–IV rapids for experienced paddlers only. Mild, class I–II rapids from Sandstone on. Put-in on Zalesky Lake. Takeout at St. Croix River.

LITTLE FORK RIVER – Linden Grove – 34 B2 Short and sharp, class I–II rapids separated by long stretches of quiet river. Farmland flanks upper and lower reaches of river. Other stretches are remote and primitive with thick forests and tamarack bogs. Abundant wildlife. Put-in off of SR 73. Takeout 135 miles downstream in Little Fork.

MINNESOTA RIVER – Milan – 67 C5 Broad channel flows through floodplain forest and wide valley, granite boulders, outcrops and wooded bluffs interspersed with farmland. 235-mile route is suitable for

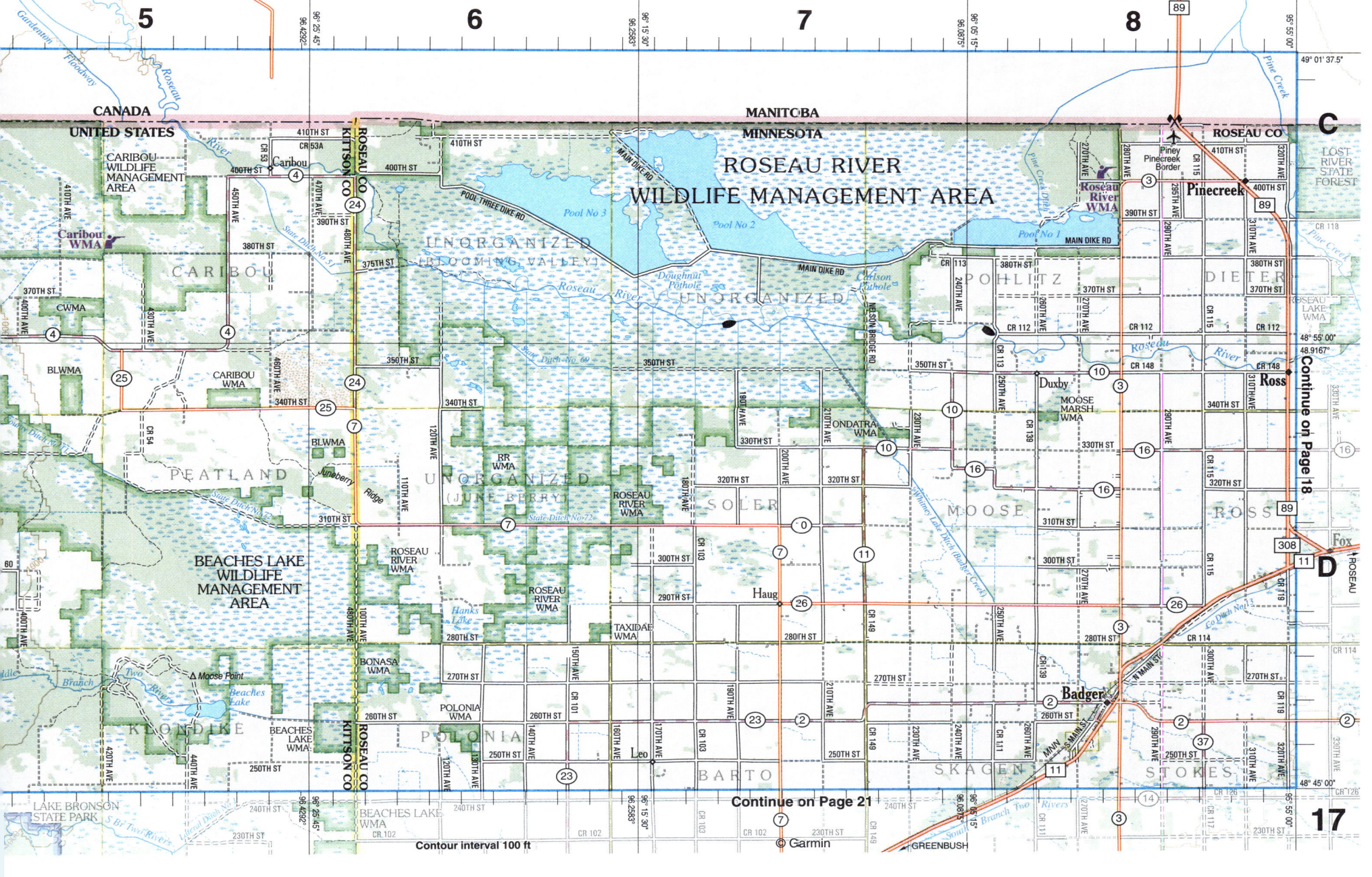

Continue on Page 21
Continue on Page 18

Contour interval 100 ft

© Garmin

beginners. Portages. Camping. Put-in below dam at Lac qui Parle Lake. Takeout at Belle Plaine.

MINNESOTA RIVER – Belle Plain – 76 A1 River passes through marshes, meadows and bottom-land forest. 50-mile stretch is wide and muddy, with sandy, eroded riverbanks. Beginner-level paddle traverses a songbird and waterfowl migratory area. Suitable for beginners, but with caution in high traffic areas near Twin Cities. Camping. Put-in at Belle Plaine. Takeout at Mississippi River confluence.

MISSISSIPPI RIVER – Anoka – 70 B3 Wooded bluffs line river downstream from Minneapolis. Passes Pig's Eye Lake, the largest rookery for black-crowned night herons. Canoes allowed passage through locks at St. Anthony Falls, Ford Dam and Hastings. Put-in on Rum River upstream from confluence with Mississippi River. Takeout 57 miles downstream.

MISSISSIPPI RIVER – Hastings – 71 D6 River broadens south of Twin Cities area, flowing through wooded bluffs and sharp cliffs and passing several historic towns. At Lake City, river expands into Lake Pepin, widest point in the river. Heavy barge and boat traffic in main channels. Backwaters easily canoed, though unmarked and unmaintained. Six locks and dams. Camping. Put-in at Hastings. Takeout 140 miles downstream at Iowa Border near Jefferson. Numerous access sites.

MISSISSIPPI RIVER – Lake Itasca – 43 B5 River winds through wilderness with variety of wildlife. Ideal for novice canoeists with few rapids. Flows through large lakes and alternates between large marshes and pine-lined corridors. Steep bluffs, forested shores and islands near Brainerd. Camping. Put-in on Lake Itasca. Takeout in Anoka upstream on Rum River. 536 miles.

NORTH FORK OF THE CROW RIVER – Payneville – 68 A4 Trip down North Fork of the Crow River to main channel and confluence with Mississippi River. Small, shallow river winding 130 miles through prairie, farmland and wooded lowlands. Lower portion of river is broader, meandering through wooded floodplain. Camping. Portages dam. Put-in on Lake Koronis. Takeout on Mississippi River near Dayton.

PINE RIVER – Pine River – 54 A1 River bordered by hardwood and pine forests, farmland and marsh. 36-mile route flows through Whitefish chain of lakes. Generally good for beginners with occasional class I rapids, but large lakes may require intermediate experience. Portages dams. Camping. Put-in at Norway Lake. Takeout on CR 11.

RED LAKE RIVER – River Valler – 30 A2 Open prairies in upper reaches change to wooded banks and pastures downstream. Mostly suited for beginners. Portages dams. Camping. Put-in off of CR 27. Takeout 173 miles downstream before dam at East Grand Forks.

RICE RIVER – Marcell – 33 C6 Slow-moving river flowing north through Chippewa National Forest. Occasional downed trees, but suitable for beginners. Route passes through lakes and down Rice River to Big Fork River. Camping. Put-in at Clubhouse Lake. Takeout 18 miles downstream at canoe access in Big Fork.

ROOT RIVER – Chatfield – 86 B2 Hardwood forests, limestone bluffs and wooded pastures line scenic route. 90-mile path suitable for beginners, with class I rapids. Camping. Historic sites near Lanesboro. Put-in on North Branch of the Root River in Chatfield and continue to Root River. Takeout on Mississippi River south of La Crescent.

RUM RIVER – Mille Lacs Kathio State Park – 55 D5 145-mile route passes through Shakopee Lake and Lake Onamia. Upper stretches flow through dense hardwood forests with some pines. Intermediate skills required due to periodic class I–II rapids. Below Princeton, low, slow-moving water is excellent for beginners. Portages dams. Put-in at Mille Lacs Kathio State Park. Takeout above Anoka.

SNAKE RIVER – McGrath – 55 D8 Route passes thick forests, Pokegama Lake outflow and flows through Cross Lake. Significant differences between upper and lower sections in river difficulty: from put-in to CR 3, expert skills are required to negotiate class II–IV rapids; below CR 3, river is accessible to beginners. Portages dam. Put-in off of Silver Star Road. Takeout 78 miles downstream at confluence with St. Croix River.

ST. CROIX RIVER – Danbury – 65 A5 145-mile stretch offers wilderness-like canoeing near Twin Cities area. Upper St. Croix north of Taylors Falls provides clear, shallow waters flowing swiftly past wooded banks. Portages around St. Croix Falls Dam. 2-mile river section includes scenic cliffs in St. Croix Dalles gorge area. Winding side channels good for fishing and exploration. Camping. Put-in off of SR 48 on Wisconsin side. Takeout at William O'Brien State Park.

ST. CROIX RIVER – Copas – 71 B7 Broad, placid river of sandy islands, quiet backwaters and wooded hillsides. 40-mile stretch is suitable for beginners. Many sandbars for swimming and picnicking. Heavy traffic on weekends. Last 25 miles widen out to Lake St. Croix. Put-in at park. Takeout upstream on Mississippi River in Hastings.

ST. LOUIS RIVER – Forbes – 46 A4 Calm waters with some fast-moving rocky areas flowing through Superior National Forest. Class I–II rapids with easy portages. Meanders through lowland brush, aspen and birch. Occasional moose sightings. Camping. Put-in near railroad bridge south of Forbes. Takeout at Cloquet before Knife Falls Dam. 83 miles.

STRAIGHT RIVER – Owatonna – 84 A4 River winds slowly through 30 miles of wooded farmland. Suitable for beginners, with class I rapids near Clinton Falls. Put-in below dam in Owatonna. Takeout on Cannon River in Faribault.

TURTLE RIVER – Birchmont – 31 C7 Slow-moving river flowing through numerous lakes in Chippewa National Forest. Small rapids with no required portaging. Wild rice beds. Wildlife includes shorebirds, heron and deer. Camping. Put-in on Turtle Lake off of CR 15. Various takeouts in Cass Lake.

VERMILION RIVER – Buyck – 35 B5 Long quiet stretches interrupted by rapids ranging from class I–IV with 12 portages ranging from short distances to over 1 mile. 42-mile route through wilderness areas with pine forests and marshy shores. Scenic falls and gorge areas. Several active eagle nests. Old homesteads and historic trading post along route. Camping. Put-in at Oak Narrows on Vermilion Lake. Takeout on Crane River near town of Crane Lake.

ZUMBRO RIVER – Cedar Beach – 78 D1 80-mile run suitable for beginners, with small, class I rapids. High limestone bluffs, thick forests and farmland line banks. From Oronoco to Theilman water flows through narrow gorges. Portages around dam. Put-in on Zumbro Lake. Takeout in Kellogg or continue down Mississippi River.

XC SKIING

ELM CREEK PARK RESERVE – Maple Grove – 70 B3 Network of groomed trails features lights for night-skiing. 30 km at Elm Creek, a further 80 km are available at other parks in the Three Rivers Park district. Lessons available.

MAPLELAG – Richwood – 42 C1 70-km groomed trail network of all possible difficulties. Various loops and combinations of trails make trips of many lengths available.

SNOWFLAKE NORDIC CENTER – Duluth – 47 D7 13 km of groomed trails through lightly wooded terrain. Lessons and rentals available at full service chalet. Biathlon range.

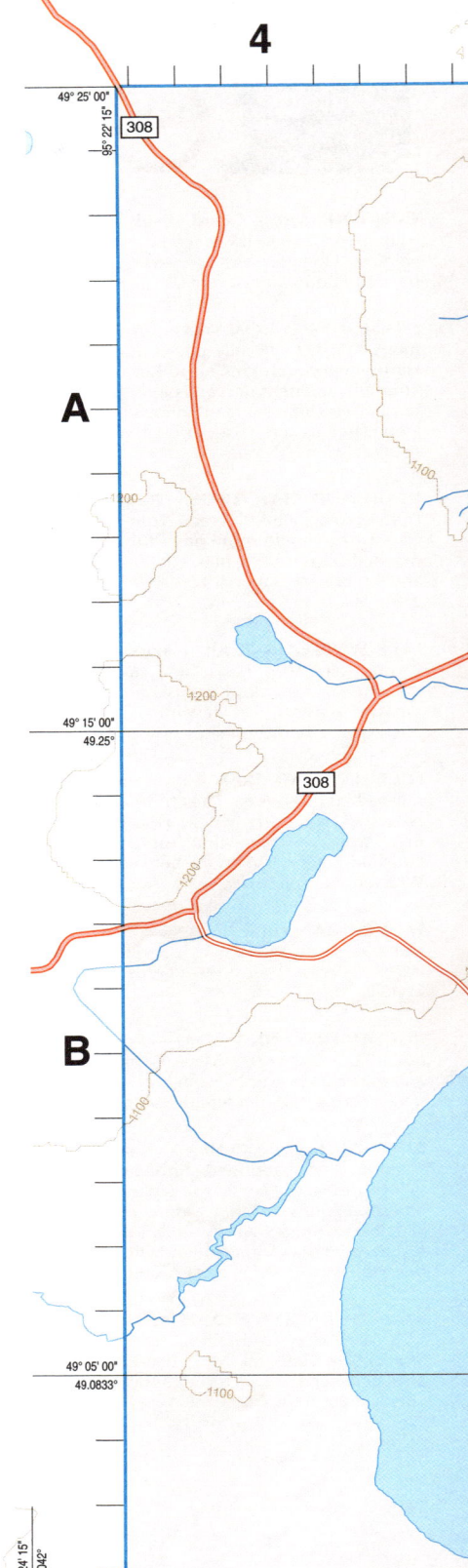

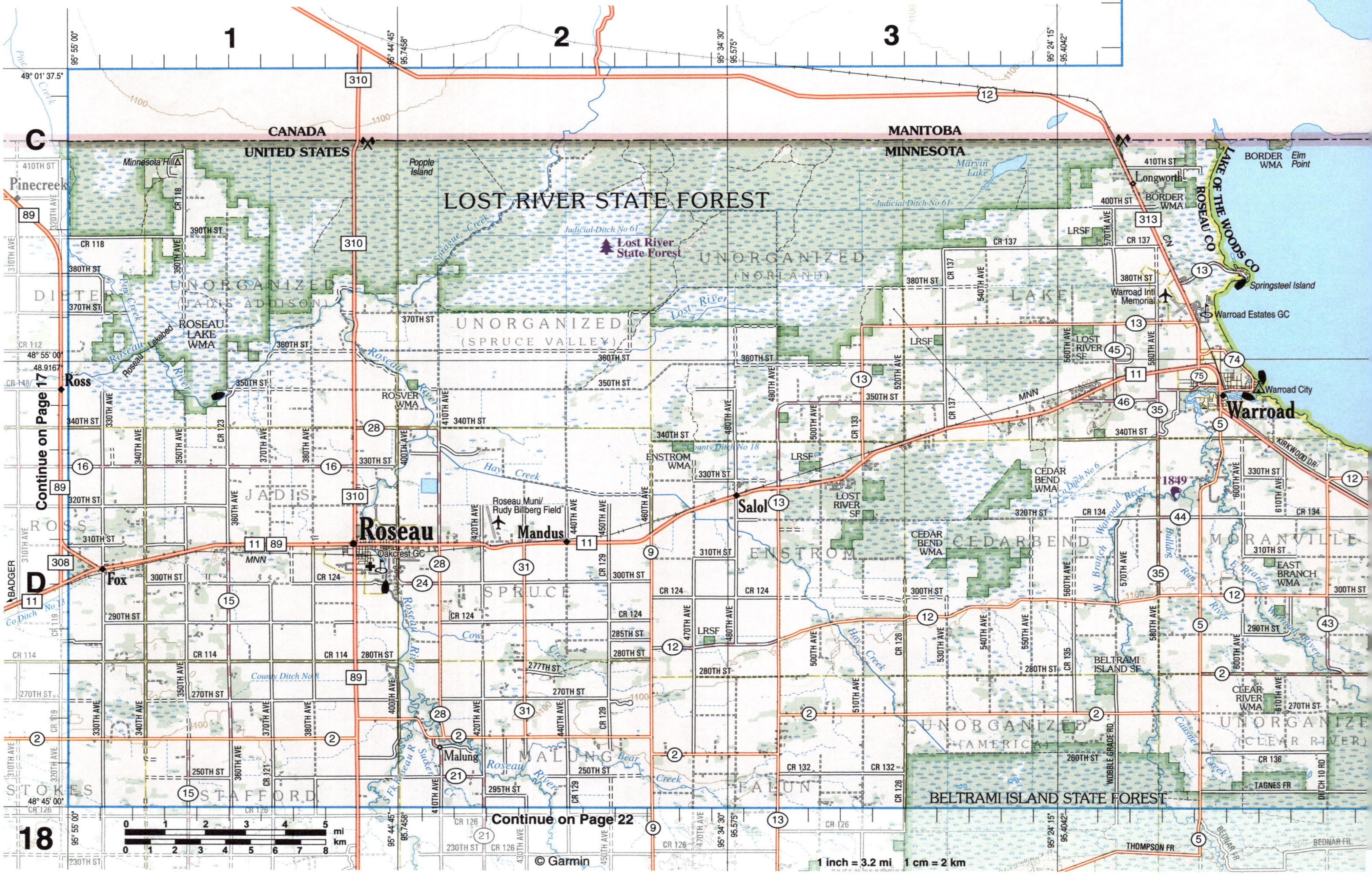

© Garmin

Continue on Page 22

1 inch = 3.2 mi   1 cm = 2 km

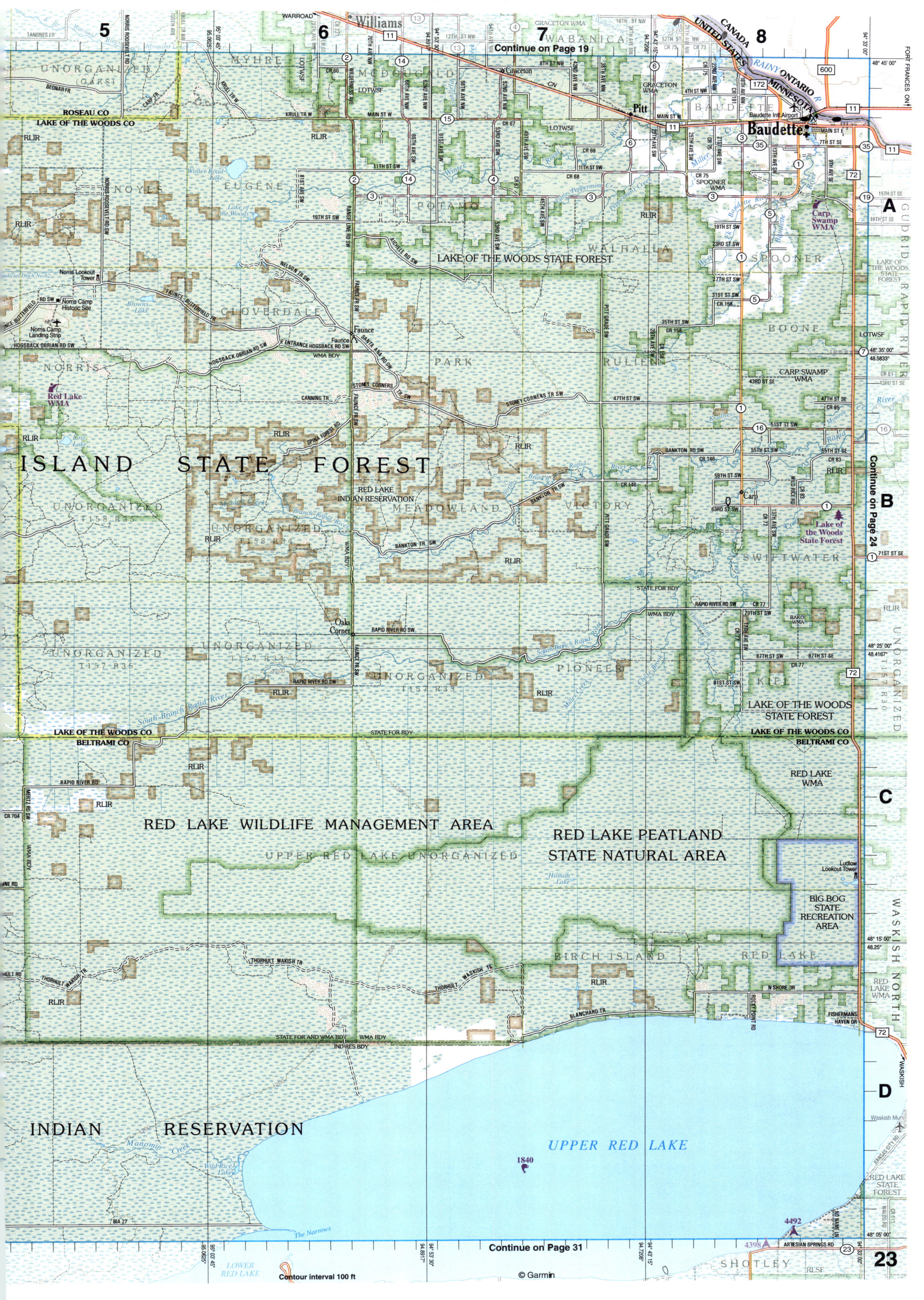

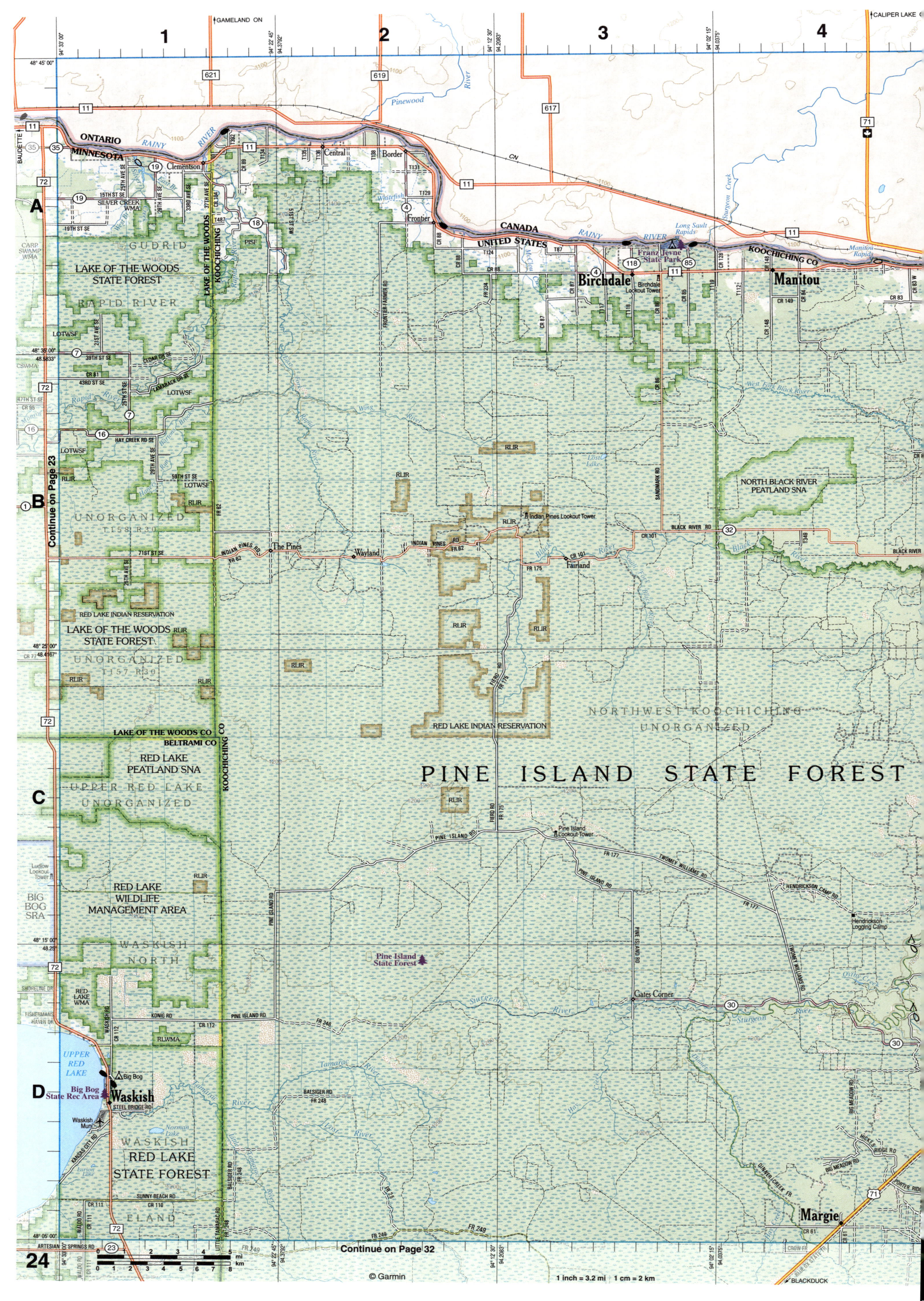

Column headers (top): 1, 2, 3, 4

Row labels (left): A, B, C, D

Key place names and features visible on the map:

- GAMELAND ON, CALIPER LAKE
- Pinewood River, Rainy River
- ONTARIO, MINNESOTA, CANADA, UNITED STATES
- Clementson, Central, Border, Frontier, Birchdale, Manitou
- Franz Jevne State Park, Long Sault Rapids, Manitou Rapids
- Birchdale Lookout Tower
- KOOCHICHING CO
- BAUDETTE
- SILVER CREEK WMA, CARP SWAMP WMA
- LAKE OF THE WOODS STATE FOREST
- RAPID RIVER
- GUDRID
- LOTWSF, RLIR, RLWMA
- North Black River Peatland SNA
- Indian Pines Lookout Tower
- The Pines, Wayland, Fairland
- RED LAKE INDIAN RESERVATION
- UNORGANIZED T158 R30, UNORGANIZED T157 R30
- NORTHWEST KOOCHICHING UNORGANIZED
- PINE ISLAND STATE FOREST
- Pine Island Lookout Tower, Pine Island State Forest
- Twomey Williams Rd, Hendrickson Camp Rd, Hendrickson Logging Camp
- LAKE OF THE WOODS CO / BELTRAMI CO
- RED LAKE PEATLAND SNA
- UPPER RED LAKE UNORGANIZED
- RED LAKE WILDLIFE MANAGEMENT AREA
- Ludlow Lookout Tower
- BIG BOG SRA
- WASKISH NORTH
- RED LAKE WMA
- Gates Corner, Sturgeon River
- UPPER RED LAKE
- Big Bog State Rec Area, Waskish, Big Bog, Waskish Muni
- WASKISH RED LAKE STATE FOREST
- ELAND
- Margie
- Tamarac River, Lost River, Sturgeon River

Continue on Page 23

Continue on Page 32

24

© Garmin

1 inch = 3.2 mi   1 cm = 2 km

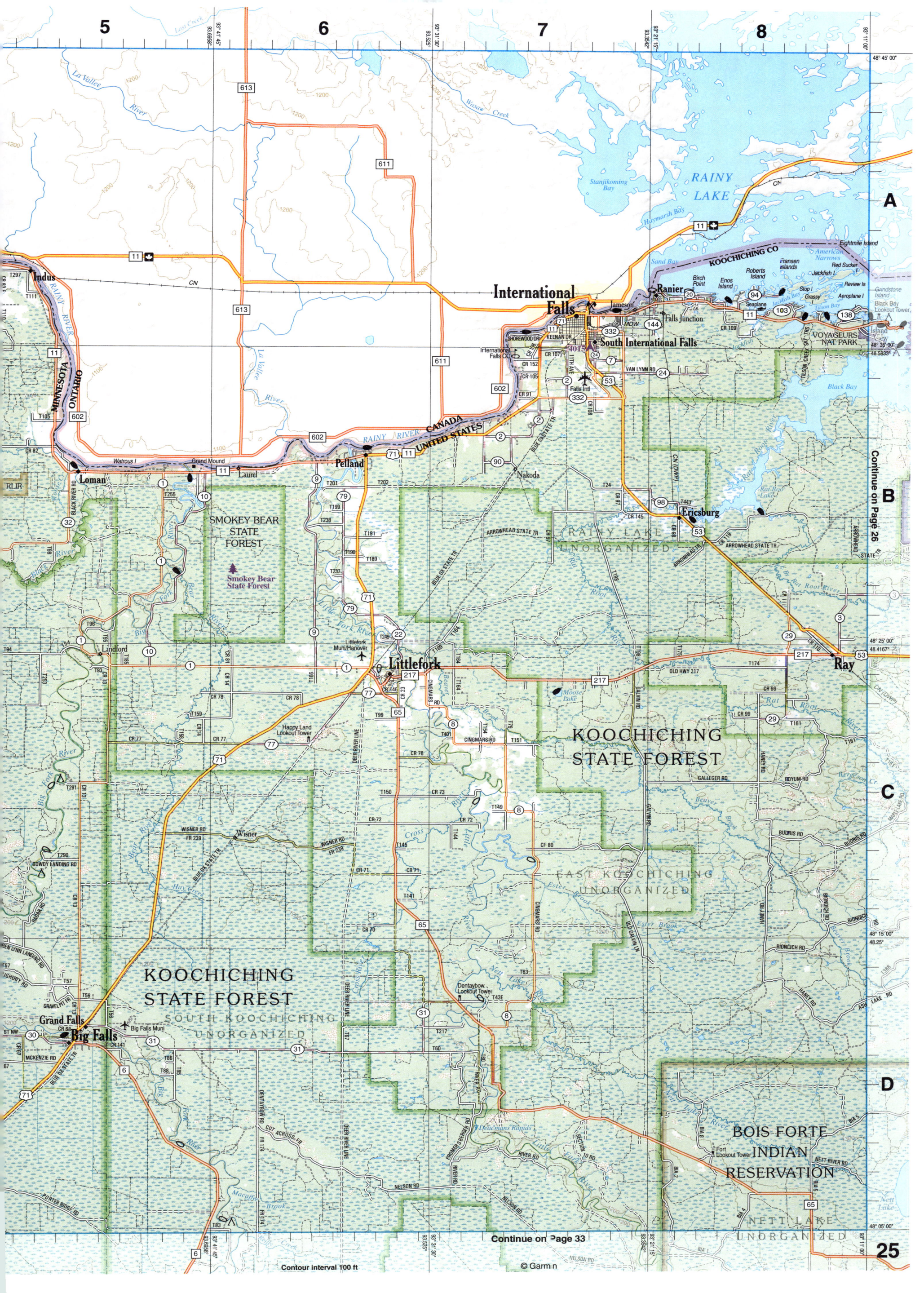

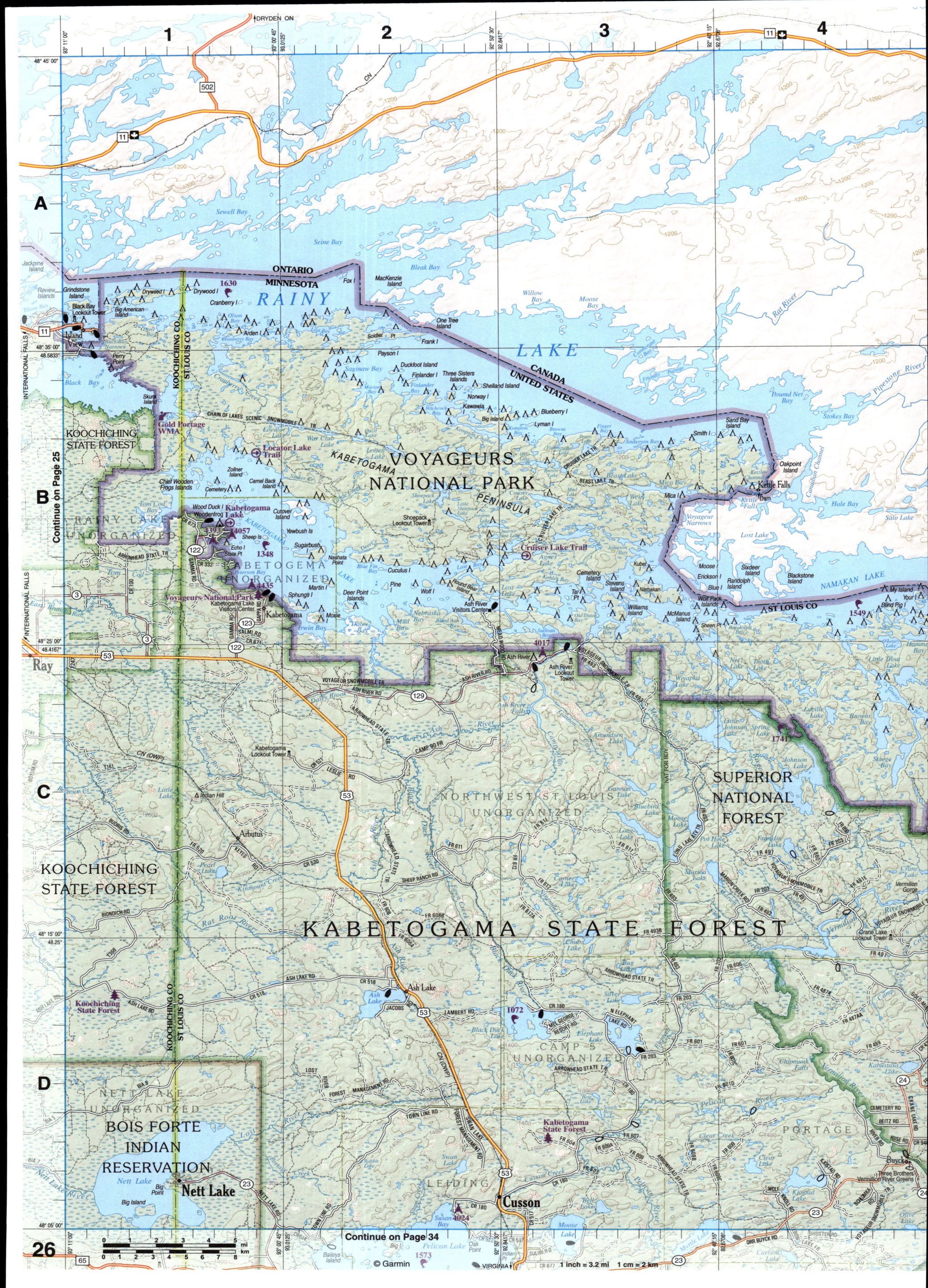

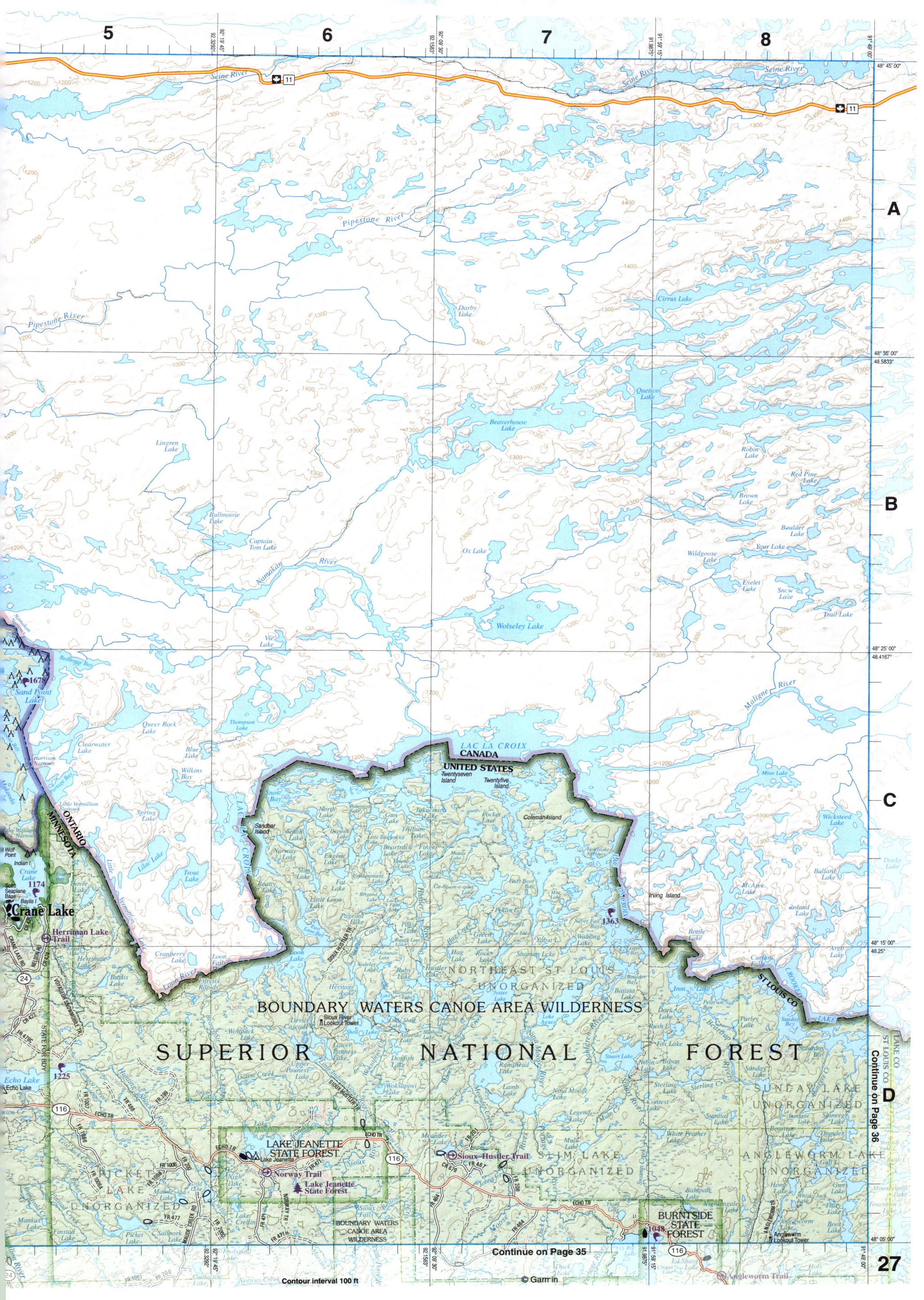

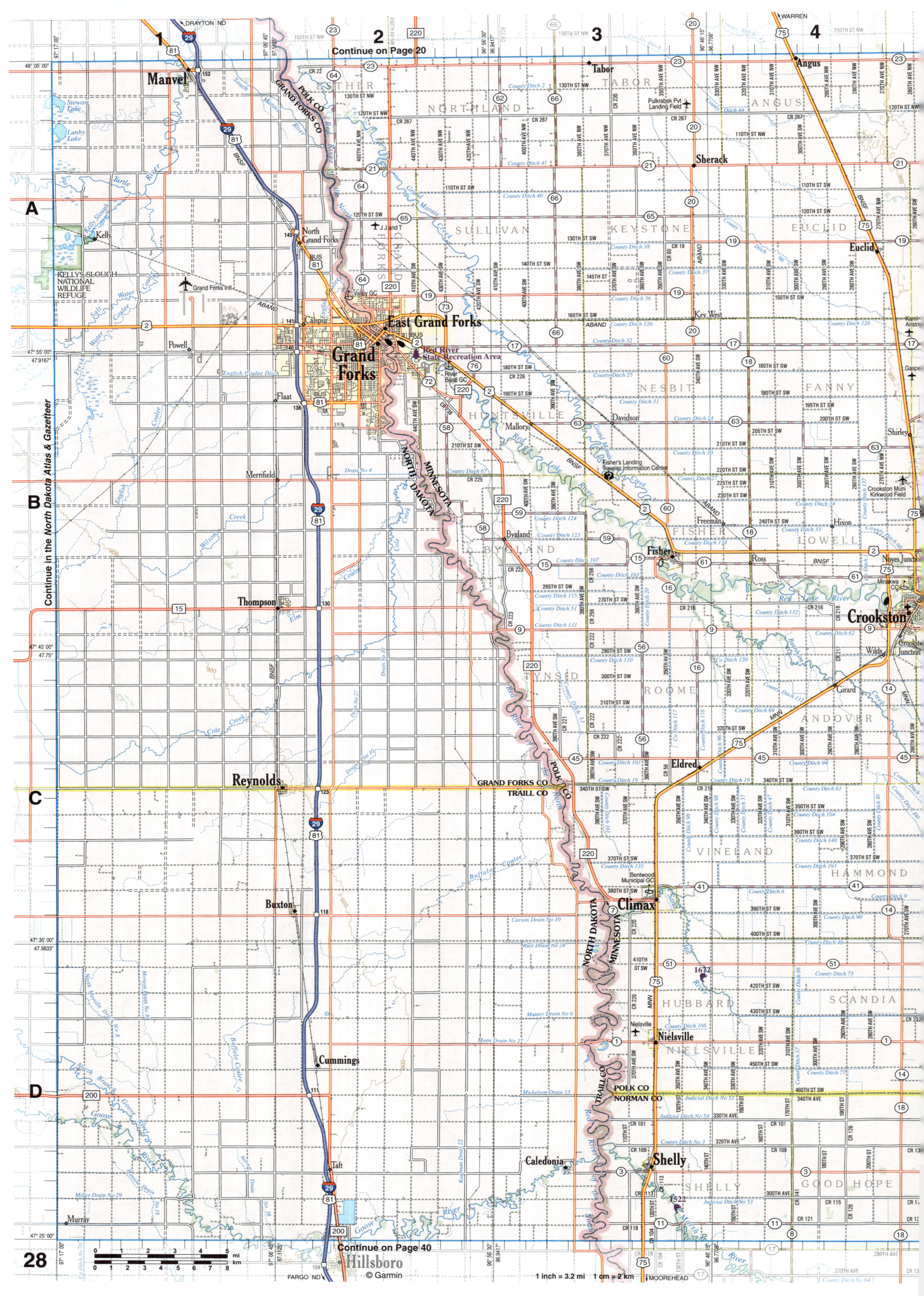

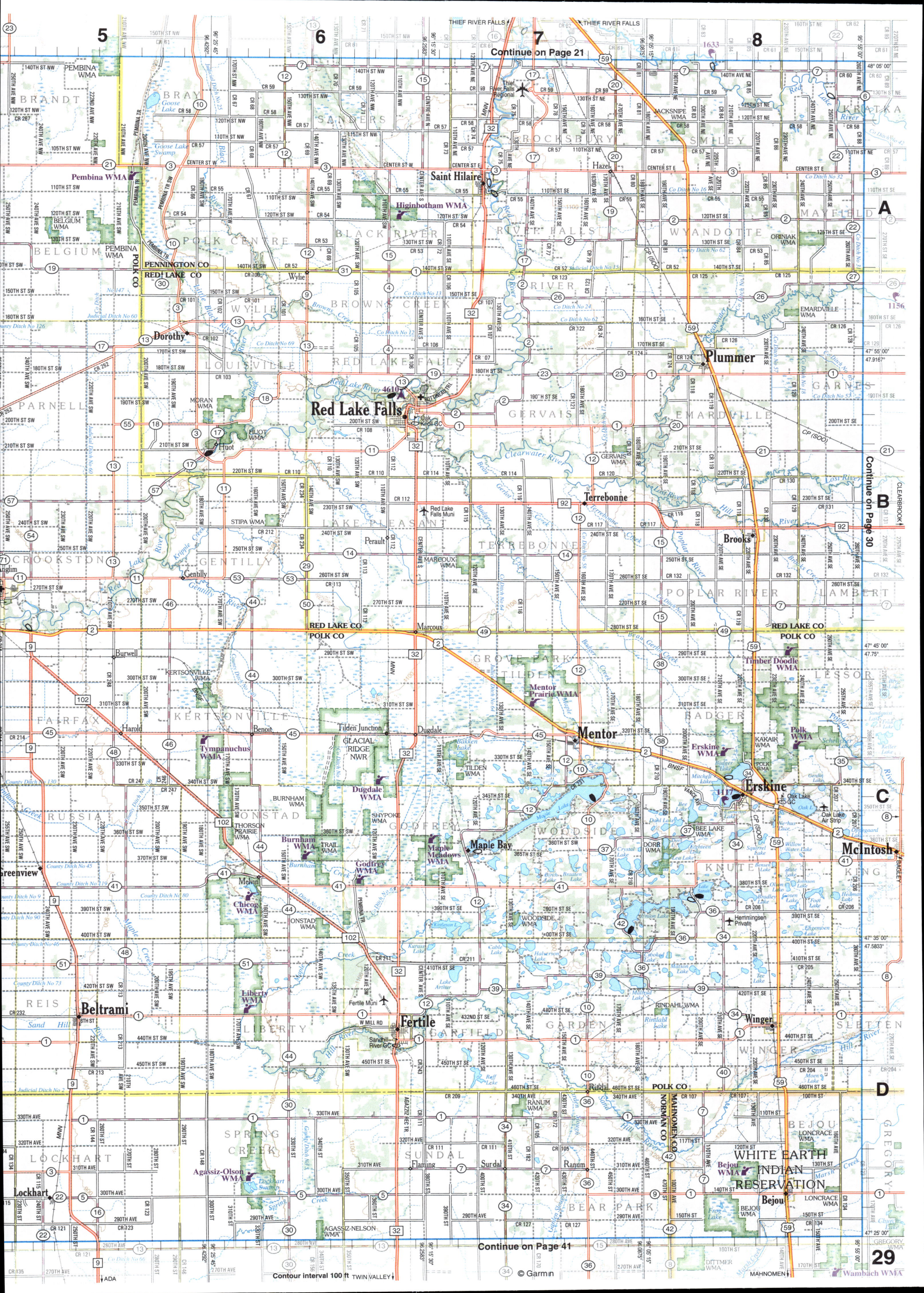

Continue on Page 21

Continue on Page 30

Continue on Page 41

Contour interval 100 ft

© Garmin

29

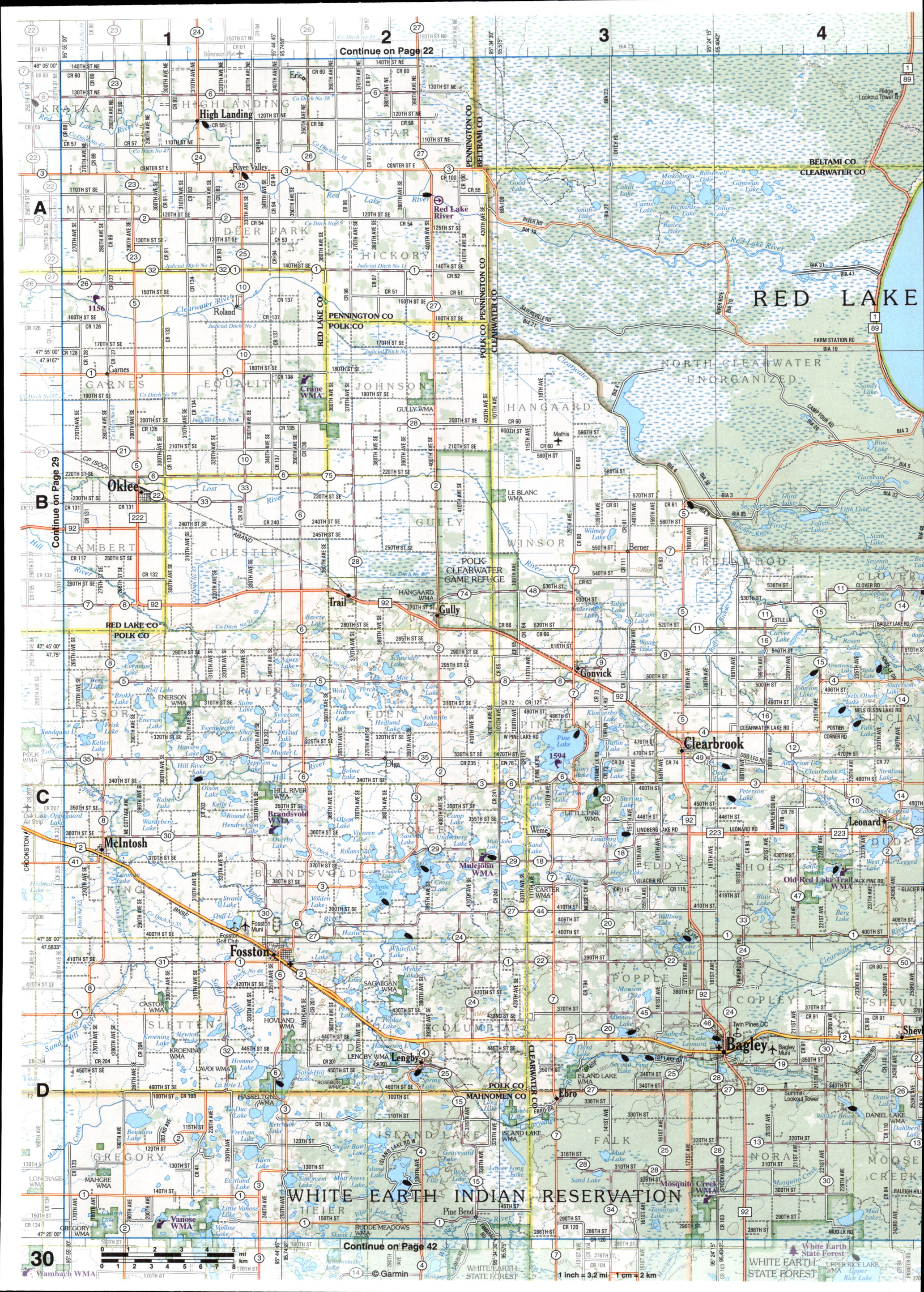

Continue on Page 23

UPPER RED LAKE

Ponemah

LOWER RED LAKE

INDIAN RESERVATION

1501

A

RED LAKE STATE FOREST

SHOTLEY

Shotley

Saum

WOODROW

Battle River

QUIRING

CORMANT

Red Lake
Redby
Little Rock

B

Continue on Page 32

O'BRIEN

LANGOR

Langor

Island Lake

ALASKA

NEBISH

Nebish

Blackduck

Blackduck

MAPLE RIDGE

ROOSEVELT

Aure

Debs

Puposky

DURAND

HAGALI

C

Tenstrike

CHIPPEWA

BLACKDUCK

Hines

HINES

Pinewood

BUZZLE

LIBERTY

Werner

Turtle River

PORT HOPE

Turtle River

TAYLOR

NATIONAL

ECKLES

Lake Bemidji
State Park

BUENA VISTA STATE FOREST

FOREST

TURTLE
RIVER

D

LAMMERS

Solway

Wilton

Lavinia

BEMIDJI
GAME REFUGE

SUGAR
BUSH

1051

JONES

Bemidji

NORTHERN

FROHN

TEN LAKE

MISSISSIPPI
HEADWATERS
STATE FOREST

GRANT
VALLEY

LEECH LAKE
INDIAN RESERVATION

BELTRAMI CO
HUBBARD CO

Continue on Page 43

HUBBARD CO / CASS CO
BELTRAMI CO

Contour interval 100 ft

© Garmin

31

Continue on Page 24

Continue on Page 31

PINE ISLAND STATE FOREST

NORTHWEST KOOCHICHING UNORGANIZED

NORTHOME UNORGANIZED

RED LAKE STATE FOREST

WASKISH

Margie

INTERNATIONAL FALLS

Kelliher

Mizpah

Gemmell

Northome

Shooks

Blackduck

Funkley

Alvwood

Bernville

Big Fork

BIG FORK STATE FOREST

POMROY

GRATTAN

ARDENHURST

KINGHURST

Wirt

CHIPPEWA NATIONAL FOREST

BLACKDUCK STATE FOREST

Squaw Lake

LEECH LAKE INDIAN RESERVATION

Max

Oslund

Inger

BUENA VISTA STATE FOREST

MOOSE LAKE FOREST

Pennington

BOWSTRING LAKE UNORGANIZED

BOWSTRING

LEECH LAKE INDIAN RESERVATION

WINNIBIGOSHISH LAKE

BOWSTRING DEER YARD WMA

BROOK LAKE UNORGANIZED

Continue on Page 44

NORTH CASS UNORGANIZED

32

© Garmin

1 inch = 3.2 mi   1 cm = 2 km

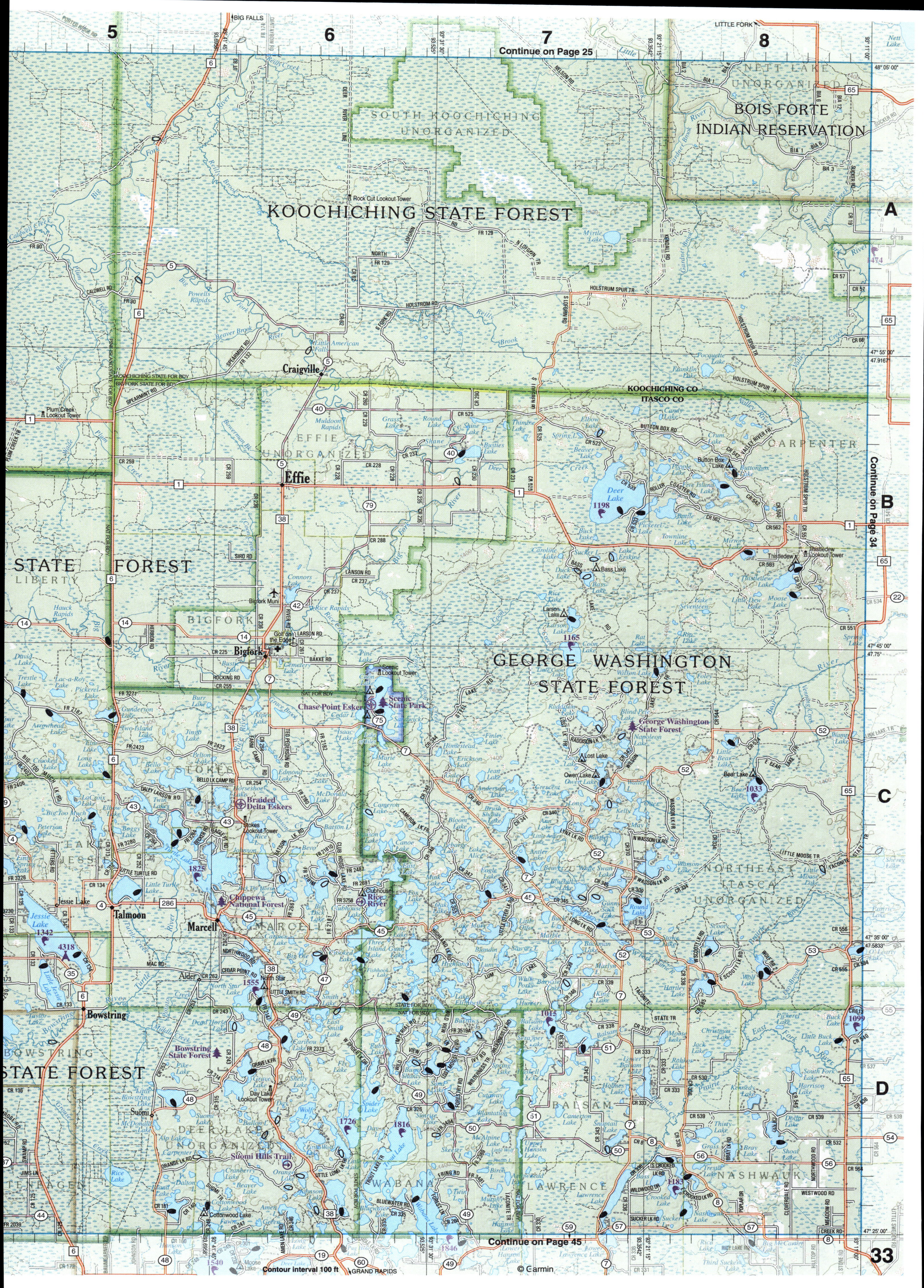

BIG FALLS   LITTLE FORK

Continue on Page 25

NETT LAKE UNORGANIZED

**BOIS FORTE
INDIAN RESERVATION**

SOUTH KOOCHICHING
UNORGANIZED

A

KOOCHICHING STATE FOREST

Rock Cut Lookout Tower

Craigville

**KOOCHICHING CO
ITASCO CO**

CARPENTER

EFFIE
UNORGANIZED

Effie

B

Continue on Page 34

Deer
Lake
1198

Bass Lake

STATE FOREST
LIBERTY

BIGFORK

Bigfork

**GEORGE WASHINGTON
STATE FOREST**

1165

Scenic
State Park

Chase Point Eskers

George Washington
State Forest
Napoleon

75

Lost Lake

Owen Lake

C

Braided
Delta Eskers

Little
Bear
Lake
1033
Bear Lake

LAKE
JESSIE

NORTHEAST
ITASCA
UNORGANIZED

1826

Jessie Lake
1342

Chippewa
National Forest

Talmoon

4318

Marcell

MARCELL

1555

Alder

Bowstring

Bowstring
State Forest

BALSAM

Buck
Lake
1099

1015

Suomi

Suomi Hills Trail

**BOWSTRING
STATE FOREST**

1726

1816

DEER LAKE
UNORGANIZED

WABANA

LAWRENCE

1846

NASHWAUK

D

Continue on Page 45

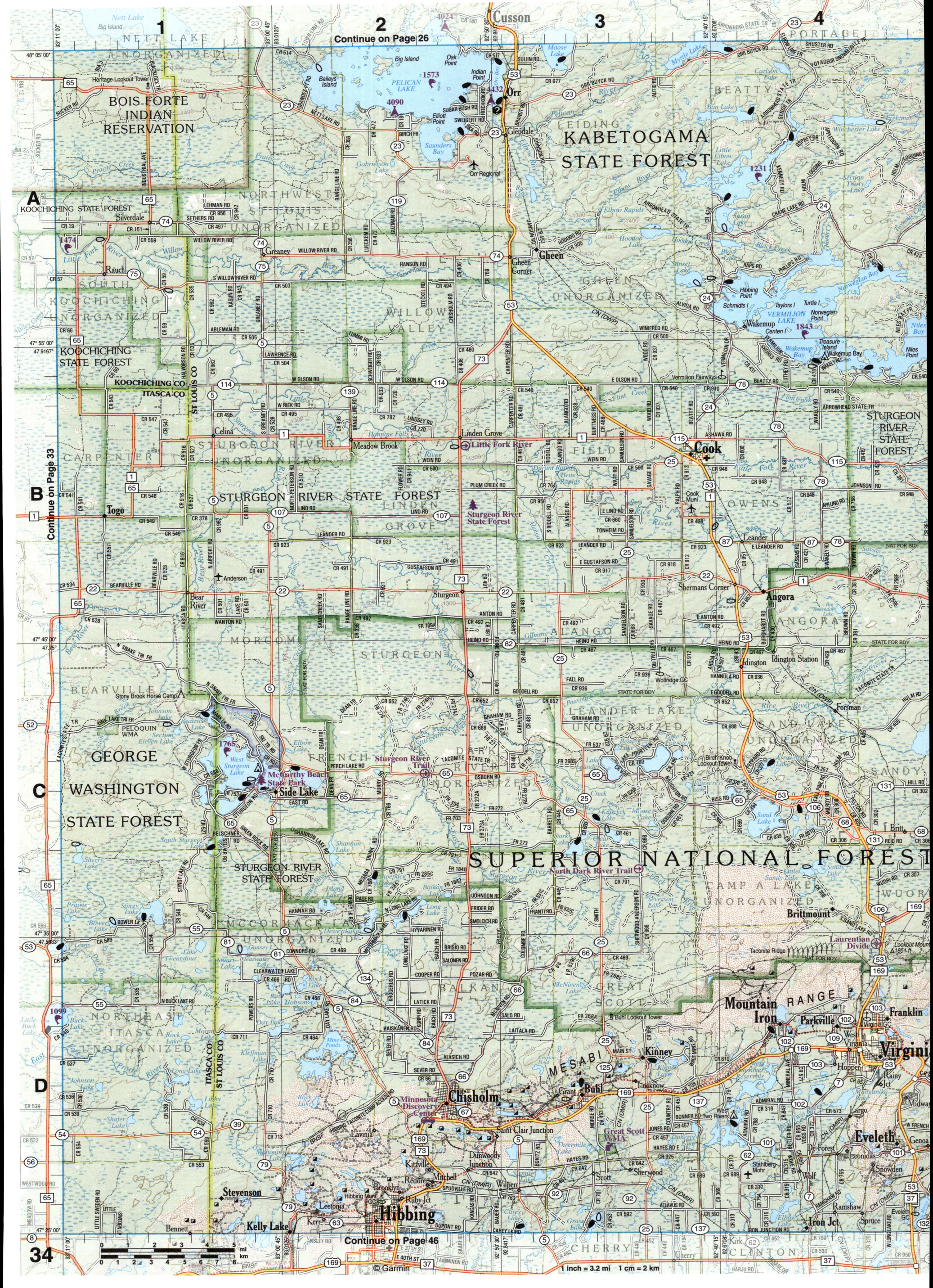

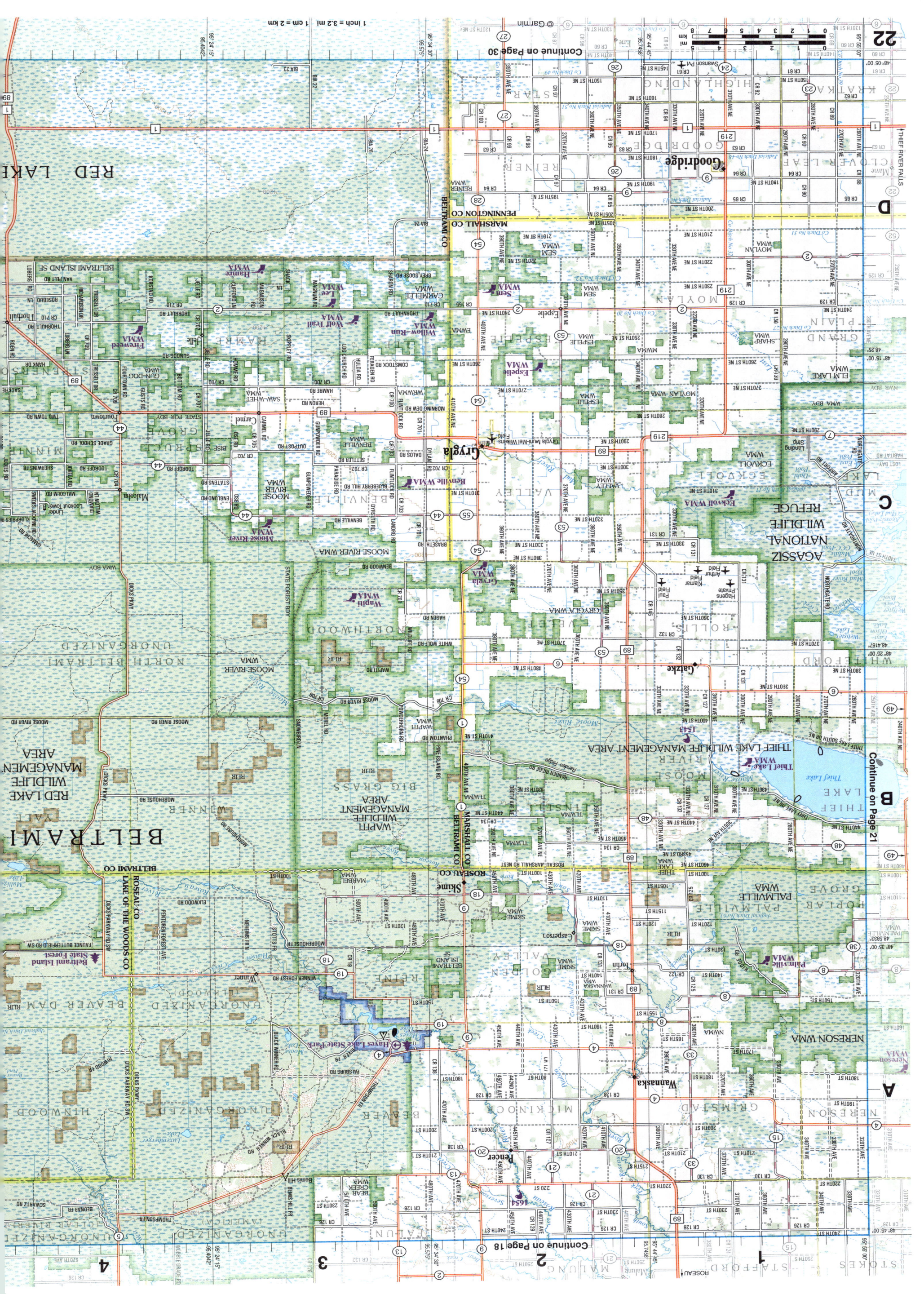

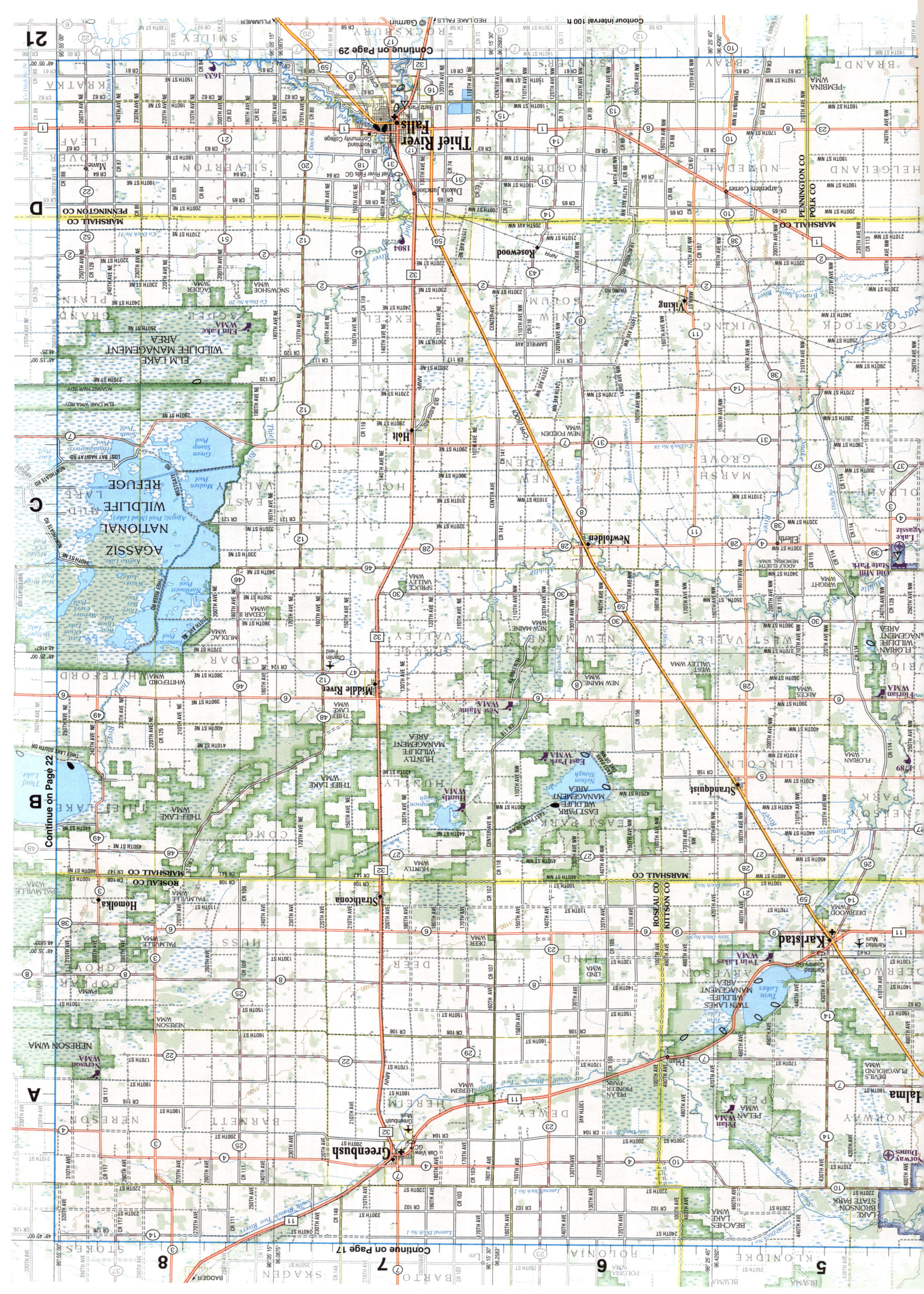

ONTARIO
MANITOBA
MINNESOTA

Auineau Penninsula

Harrison Creek

Falcon Island

A

Penasse
Penasse I
Fort St Charles
Historic Site
Magnusons
Island
Lambert I

Winigo
Island

Windfall
Island

Angle Inlet
Northwest Angle

DAWSON RD NW

Brush
Island
Moose
Bay
Birch I

Honeymoon
Island

Soldiers
Point
Birch Island

Northwest Angle
State Forest

Flag
Island RLR

Oak Island

Channel

NORTHWEST ANGLE
STATE FOREST

Oak
Island
RLR

Oases
Point

Sturgeon

Sevenmile
Swamp

Younges

NORTHWEST ANGLE
RED LAKE
INDIAN RESERVATION
STATE FOREST

Sugar
Point

Fourblock Island

Techout Island

Crowduck Island

Caribou
Bay

49

Little Oak Island

Kirk Island

Shady Island

Norman Island

CANADA
UNITED STATES

Big Island

B

525

A N G L E

Driftwood
Point

Hay Island

Babe Island

Garden Island
State Recreation Area

Stony
Creek

Rooty
Point

Garden Island

Bridges Island

Sand
Point
Bay

Sandy Beach

Big Traverse Bay

Buffalo Bay

Stony
Point

Knight Island

Basil Channel

Bigsby Island

UNITED STATES
CANADA

MINNESOTA
ONTARIO

L A K E   O F   T H E   W O O D S

49.0833°

C

1435

Gull Rock

Long
Point

Long Point

Larry
Bernhoft
WMA

Lake of the Woods Co

Twin Rocks

Lude

Rocky
Point

ROCKY
POINT
WMA

68TH NW

Birch Beach

Currys Island

Oak
Point

Muskeg Bay

Arnessen

17
9

64TH ST NW

LAKEWOOD

60TH ST NW

SOUTH SHORE
WMA

2

LOTWSF

LOTWSF

60TH ST NW

Pine Island

Fourmile
Bay

LOTWSE

9

58TH ST NW

Lake
of the
Woods SF

56TH ST NW

52ND ST NW

Zippel Bay

Wheelers
Point

ZIPPEL
BAY
STATE
PARK

PROSPER

48TH ST NW

Prosper
WMA

CR53

ZIPPEL
WMA

Birch
Lady's-slipper
Ridge

Morris Point

FOUR MILE
BAY WMA

D

17

11

11

Lake
of the
Woods
SF

Angler's

Zippel Bay
State Park

20

8

33

SOUTH SHORE
WMA

12

44TH ST NW

2

40TH ST NW

34

LOTWSE

Hackett

32

RLR

WHEELER

Oak Harbor
Golf & Tennis Club

600

Swift

LAONA

34

CHILDREN

WILDERNESS AVE

ZIPPEL

12

28TH ST NW

172

31

4433

11

8

32ND ST NW

12

LOTWSE

30

RAINY
RIVER

42

Erickson

42

17

Roosevelt

24TH ST NW

CR 58

CR 58

GRACETON
WMA

GRACETON
WMA

UNORGANIZED
OAKS

13

Blueberry
Hill

MCDOUGALD

Graceton
WMA

39

BELTRAMI ISLAND
STATE FOREST

MYHRE

Williams

14

13

12TH ST NW

WABANICA

CR 73

6

11

Continue on Page 23

Contour interval 100 ft

© Garmin

BAUDETTE

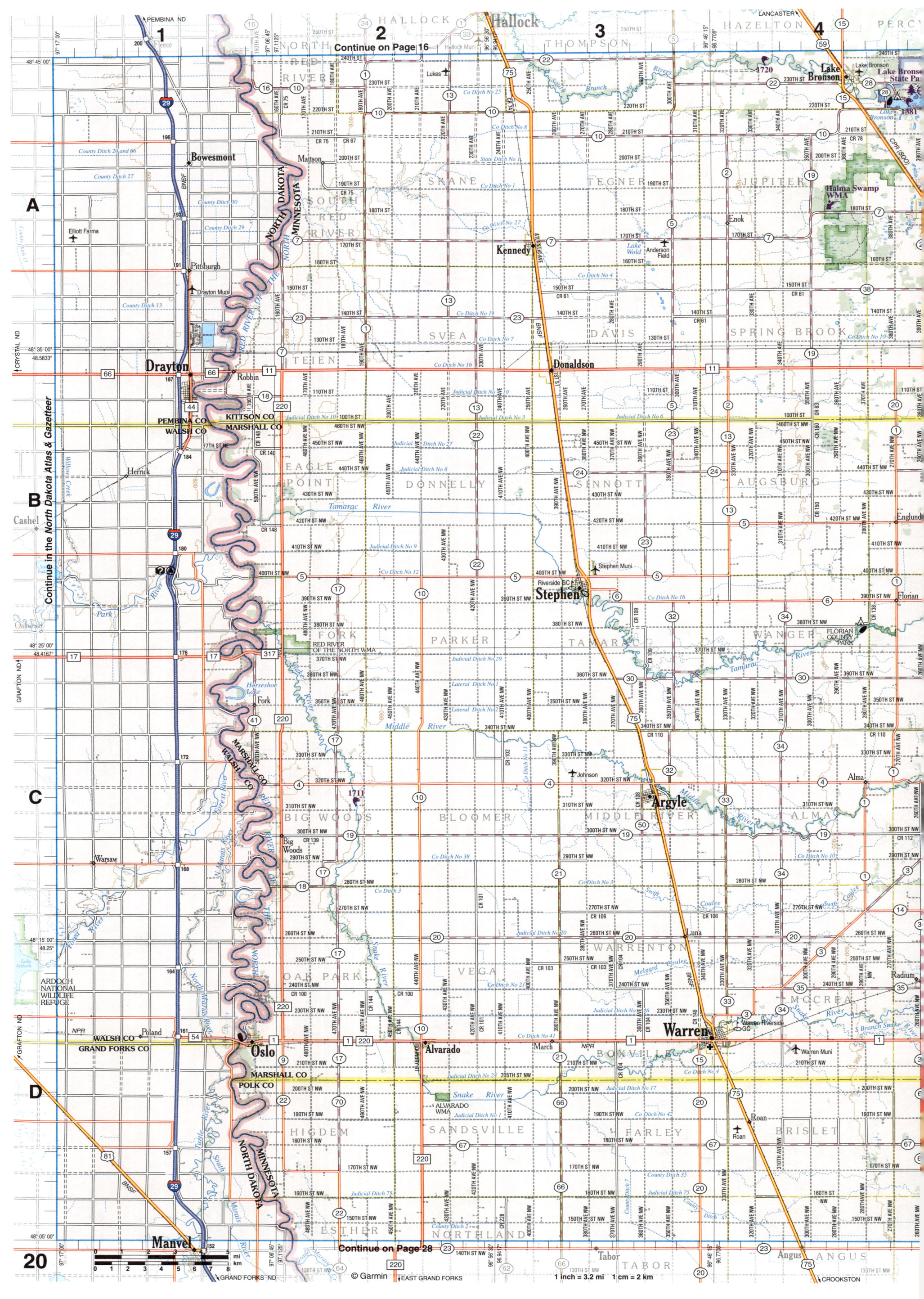

Fishing

Number, Name	Page & Grid	Walleye	Rainbow Trout	Brown Trout	Brook Trout	Lake Trout	Salmon	Northern Pike	Yellow Perch	Largemouth Bass	Smallmouth Bass	Rock Bass	Muskellunge	Channel Catfish	Bullhead Catfish	Bluegill	Pumpkinseed	Black Crappie	Carp
1003 Baby Lake	44 C2	●						●	●	●	●	●	●			●			
1006 Bad Medicine Lake	42 B3	●						●	●										
1009 Badger Creek	87 C6			●	●														
1012 Ball Club Lake	44 A4	●						●	●						●			●	
1015 Balsam Lake	33 D2	●						●	●	●		●				●		●	
1018 Barrett Lake	60 B1	●						●	●			●			●	●	●	●	●
1021 Bass Lake	45 A6	●						●							●				
1024 Bass Lake	83 B7							●	●	●		●			●	●	●	●	
1027 Basswood Lake	36 B1	●						●	●										
1030 Bay Lake	55 C5							●	●						●		●		
1033 Bear Lake	53 C8	●						●	●			●				●		●	
1036 Beaver Creek	78 D3			●	●														
1039 Big Birch Lake	61 B7	●						●		●	●	●			●	●	●	●	
1042 Big Fork River	32 C4	●						●	●	●	●	●	●	●					
1045 Big Kandiyohi Lake	68 C2	●							●					●	●	●		●	●
1048 Big Lake	27 D8	●							●			●							
1051 Big Lake	31 D8	●						●	●	●		●			●	●	●	●	
1054 Big Lake	61 D8	●							●	●					●	●	●	●	●
1057 Big Marine Lake	71 B6	●						●		●					●	●	●	●	
1060 Big Sandy Lake	45 D8	●						●	●			●			●	●		●	
1063 Big Spunk Lake	62 C3	●						●	●	●		●			●	●	●	●	
1066 Big Stone Lake	58 D4	●							●			●			●			●	●
1069 Birch Lake	44 C1							●	●	●		●			●	●		●	
1072 Black Duck Lake	26 D3	●						●	●		●					●		●	
1075 Blackduck Lake	31 C8	●							●			●			●	●		●	
1078 Blue Earth River	83 B7	●						●	●					●					
1081 Blueberry Lake	43 D5							●	●						●			●	●
1084 Blueberry Lake	43 D5	●						●	●	●					●	●	●	●	
1087 Boulder Lake	47 C6	●						●	●									●	
1090 Bowstring Lake	32 D4	●							●						●			●	
1093 Boy Lake	44 B3	●						●	●	●		●			●		●		
1096 Brule Lake	37 B7	●						●											
1099 Buck Lake	33 D8	●						●	●	●						●	●	●	
1102 Buffalo Lake	42 C1	●						●	●		●	●			●	●	●		
1105 Buffalo Lake	69 B8	●						●	●					●	●	●	●		●
1108 Buffalo River	41 D6	●						●	●					●					
1111 Burlington Bay; Lake Superior	48 D1		●			●	●												
1114 Burntside Lake	35 A8	●				●		●			●	●							
1117 Cameron Lake	29 C8														●				
1120 Camp Creek	86 C3			●	●														
1123 Cannon River	77 B6	●		●				●	●	●	●	●		●					
1126 Caribou Lake	37 B8	●						●	●									●	
1129 Carrie Lake	68 C3	●						●	●	●					●	●		●	●
1132 Cascade River	37 C8		●	●	●		●												
1135 Cass Lake	32 D1	●						●	●			●							
1138 Cedar Lake	76 C3	●						●							●	●		●	●
1141 Cedar River	85 D6							●	●	●		●		●					
1144 Chippewa River	60 D2	●						●	●										
1147 Clearwater Lake	37 B1					●			●								●		
1150 Clearwater Lake	31 C5	●						●	●			●			●	●			
1153 Clearwater Lake	69 A7	●						●		●		●			●	●	●		●
1156 Clearwater River	30 A1	●	●	●				●	●										
1159 Clitherall Lake	52 C2	●						●	●	●	●	●				●	●	●	
1162 Cokato Lake	69 B7	●							●		●					●		●	●
1165 Coon Lake	33 B7							●	●							●	●	●	
1168 Cotton Lake	42 D2	●						●	●	●		●			●	●	●	●	
1171 Cottonwood River	71 C4	●						●	●		●	●		●					
1174 Crane Lake	27 C5	●						●	●		●								
1177 Crescent Lake	37 C7	●									●		●						
1180 Crooked Creek	87 C7		●	●															
1183 Crooked Lake	33 D8							●	●							●		●	
1186 Cross Lake Reservoi-	54 A3	●						●	●	●		●			●	●	●	●	
1189 Crow River	70 B1	●						●	●		●	●		●					
1192 Cut Foot Sioux Lake	72 D3	●						●	●	●		●			●		●		
1195 Dead Lake	52 B1	●						●		●					●	●	●	●	
1198 Deer Lake	23 B7	●						●	●	●		●				●	●		
1201 Deer Lake	45 A6	●							●	●	●	●				●	●	●	
1204 Des Moines River	81 A6	●						●						●					
1207 Detroit Lake	42 D1	●						●	●	●					●	●	●	●	
1210 Devil Track Lake	38 C1	●						●	●		●								
1213 Diamond Lake	68 B3	●						●	●						●	●		●	●
1216 Eagle Lake	68 B2	●						●	●						●	●			
1219 East Battle Lake	52 C3	●						●	●	●						●	●	●	
1222 East Beaver Bay; Lake Superior	48 B4		●			●	●												
1225 Echo Lake	27 D5	●						●										●	
1228 Edward Lake	52 B3							●		●					●	●	●	●	
1231 Elbow Lake	34 A4	●							●							●			
1234 Elbow Lake	38 E1	●						●	●										
1237 Elbow Lake	42 B3	●						●	●	●		●			●	●	●		
1240 Farm Island Lake	55 B5	●						●		●		●			●	●	●	●	●
1243 Fish Hook Lake	43 C6	●						●	●	●		●			●	●	●		
1246 Fish Trap Lake	53 D8	●						●	●	●		●				●	●	●	
1249 Flour Lake	38 B1	●							●		●								
1252 Flute Reed River	38 C3		●		●														
1255 Forest Lake	71 A6	●						●	●							●	●	●	
1258 Forestville Creek	86 C2			●															
1261 Four Mile Lake	37 D5	●							●									●	
1264 French Lake	69 B7	●						●	●						●	●		●	●
1267 French Lake	76 C3	●						●	●	●			●			●		●	●
1270 Garfield Lake	43 B7	●						●	●	●		●				●	●		
1273 Garvin Brook	87 A5			●	●														
1276 Gooseberry River	48 A2		●	●	●														
1279 Grace Lake	43 A7	●						●	●			●			●	●	●		
1282 Grand Marais; Lake Superior	38 D2		●			●	●												
1285 Granite Point; Lake Superior	48 D1			●	●	●	●												
1288 Green Lake	68 A2	●						●		●	●	●			●			●	
1291 Green Lake	63 D7	●						●	●						●	●		●	
1294 Green Lake	71 A6	●						●	●	●					●	●	●	●	
1297 Greenwood Lake	38 B2					●					●								
1300 Greenwood Lake	48 A2	●						●	●										
1303 Grindstone Lake	36 D2		●			●					●	●							
1306 Gull Lake	54 B2	●				●		●	●			●			●	●		●	
1309 Gunflint Lake	37 A7										●								
1312 Hanging Horn Lake	56 B3							●								●		●	
1315 Hay Creek	77 B8			●															
1318 Height Of Land Lake	42 D2	●						●	●	●					●	●	●		
1321 Hill Lake	45 C6	●						●	●	●		●				●		●	
1324 Horseshoe Bay; Lake Superior	38 C4		●	●	●		●												
1327 Horseshoe Lake	62 D1	●									●			●		●		●	
1333 Howard Lake	69 C7	●						●	●	●					●	●	●	●	
1336 Ice Cracking Lake	42 C3	●						●		●		●			●	●	●	●	
1339 Island Lake	42 C3	●							●	●	●	●			●	●	●	●	
1342 Jessie Lake	33 D5	●						●	●			●						●	
1345 Kabekona Lake	43 B7	●							●	●	●	●			●	●	●		
1348 Kabetogama Lake	26 B1	●						●	●		●	●						●	
1351 Kettle River	64 B3	●						●	●	●	●	●	●						
1354 Kitchi Lake	32 B1	●						●	●	●		●							
1357 Knife Lake	63 A8	●						●	●							●		●	
1360 Knife River	48 D1		●	●	●														
1363 Lac la Croix	27 C7	●				●		●											
1366 Lac qui Parle Lake	66 B4	●						●	●			●		●	●			●	●
1369 Lac qui Parle River	66 D3	●						●						●					
1372 Lake Alexander	53 D8	●							●	●	●	●				●	●	●	
1375 Lake Belle Taine	43 C6	●						●		●	●				●	●	●	●	
1378 Lake Bemidji	31 D7	●							●										
1381 Lake Bronson	20 A4	●						●	●	●		●			●		●		
1384 Lake Carlos	60 A4	●						●		●		●			●	●	●	●	●
1387 Lake George	43 B6	●						●		●					●	●	●		
1390 Lake Hattie	44 D1	●						●	●	●		●			●	●	●	●	
1393 Lake Ida	60 A3	●						●		●	●	●			●	●	●	●	
1396 Lake Independence	30 C2	●						●	●				●			●	●	●	
1399 Lake Itasca	43 B5	●						●	●							●			
1402 Lake Jennie	69 C6	●						●	●						●	●	●	●	●
1405 Lake Koronis	68 A4	●						●	●	●	●	●			●	●			
1408 Lake Le Homme Dieu	60 A4	●						●		●		●			●	●	●	●	●
1411 Lake Lida	51 A8	●						●	●	●	●	●				●	●	●	
1414 Lake Lizzie	51 A8	●						●	●	●	●	●				●	●		
1417 Lake Mary	60 B3								●	●					●	●		●	●
1420 Lake Melissa	52 A1	●						●	●	●		●			●	●	●		
1423 Lake Miltona	60 A4	●							●	●	●	●	●		●	●	●	●	
1426 Lake Minnetonka	70 C2	●						●	●							●		●	●
1429 Lake Minnewaska	60 C3	●						●	●	●					●	●	●	●	●
1432 Lake Minnewawa	55 A8	●						●	●	●					●	●	●	●	
1435 Lake of the Woods	19 C6	●						●	●										
1438 Lake Osakis	61 B5	●						●	●	●	●				●	●		●	●
1441 Lake Pepin	78 B2	●										●		●				●	
1444 Lake Plantagenet	43 A6	●						●	●										
1447 Lake Traverse	58 C4	●						●	●			●		●	●				

Recreation Areas

Name, Location	Page & Grid	Administration	Acreage	Camping	Hiking	Horseback Riding	Biking	Boating	Fishing	Swimming	Cross-Country Skiing	Snowmobiling	Historic Site
Afton State Park, Afton	71 D7	MDNR	1,695	●	●		●	●	●		●		
Badoura State Forest, Badoura	43 D8	MDNR	4,520	●	●								
Banning State Park, Sandstone	56 D2	MDNR	6,201	●	●		●	●	●		●	●	
Battleground State Forest, Federal Dam	44 B2	MDNR	17,969	●	●		●		●	●			
Bear Head Lake State Park, Soudan	35 B7	MDNR	4,523	●	●			●	●	●		●	
Bear Island State Forest, Winton	36 C1	MDNR	157,814		●		●	●	●		●		
Beaver Creek Valley State Park, Caledonia	87 C6	MDNR	1,187	●	●				●				
Beltrami Island State Forest, Winner	22 A4	MDNR	703,366	●	●	●						●	
Big Bog State Recreation Area, Waskish	24 D1	MDNR	9,400	●	●			●	●	●		●	
Big Fork State Forest, Pomroy	32 B4	MDNR	127,929	●	●		●	●	●	●	●		
Big Stone Lake State Park, Beardsley	58 D4	MDNR	986	●	●			●	●	●			
Birch Lakes State Forest, Ward Springs	61 B7	MDNR	710	●	●		●	●	●	●		●	
Blackduck State Forest, Blackduck	32 C1	MDNR	125,529		●				●		●	●	
Blue Mounds State Park, Luverne	80 C3	MDNR	1,826	●	●			●	●	●		●	
Boundary Waters Canoe Area Wilderness, Forest Center	36 B4	USFS	1,000,000	●				●	●		●		
Bowstring State Forest, Deer River	33 D5	MDNR	526,569	●	●		●	●	●	●	●	●	
Buena Vista State Forest, Turtle River	31 C7	MDNR	122,333	●				●			●	●	
Buffalo River State Park, Muskoda	41 D5	MDNR	1,322	●	●				●	●	●		
Burntside State Forest, Ely	35 B8	MDNR	74,815		●			●	●				
Camden State Park, Lynd	72 C4	MDNR	2,245	●	●		●		●		●	●	
Carley State Park, Viola	78 D2	MDNR	209	●	●				●				
Cascade River State Park, Grand Marais	37 D8	MDNR	2,865	●	●				●		●	●	
Charles A. Lindbergh State Park, Little Falls	62 A1	MDNR	436	●	●			●	●		●		●
Chengwatana State Forest, Pine City	64 B3	MDNR	29,039	●	●	●	●	●	●		●	●	
Chippewa National Forest, Marcell	33 C6	USFS	660,000	●	●	●	●	●	●		●	●	
Cloquet Valley State Forest, Whiteface	47 B6	MDNR	327,098	●	●			●	●			●	
Crow Wing State Forest, Crosby	54 B3	MDNR	33,713	●	●			●	●	●			
Crow Wing State Park, Brainerd	54 C2	MDNR	2,871	●	●			●	●		●	●	●
Cuyuna Country State Recreation Area, Crosby	54 B4	MDNR	1,824	●	●		●	●	●				
DAR State Forest, Askov	56 D3	MDNR	643	●									
Emily State Forest, Emily	54 A4	MDNR	639	●	●								
Father Hennepin State Park, Isle	55 D7	MDNR	320	●	●			●	●	●	●		
Finland State Forest, Whyte	48 A2	MDNR	311,970	●	●			●	●		●	●	
Flandrau State Park, New Ulm	75 C5	MDNR	1,006	●	●			●	●	●	●	●	
Fond Du Lac State Forest, Cromwell	56 A3	MDNR	64,505	●	●		●	●			●	●	
Foothills State Forest, Poplar	53 A8	MDNR	46,896	●	●		●	●		●	●	●	
Forestville/Mystery Cave State Park, Preston	86 C2	MDNR	3,170	●	●	●			●		●	●	
Fort Ridgely State Park, Fairfax	74 B3	MDNR	1,040	●	●	●	●				●	●	●
Fort Snelling State Park, St. Paul	70 D4	MDNR	2,931		●		●	●	●	●	●		●
Franz Jevne State Park, Birchdale	24 A3	MDNR	118	●	●				●		●		
Frontenac State Park, Old Frontenac	78 B2	MDNR	2,803	●	●		●				●	●	
Garden Island State Recreation Area, Oak Island	19 B7	MDNR	734					●	●	●		●	
General C. C. Andrews State Forest, Moose Lake	56 C3	MDNR	7,770	●	●	●	●	●	●		●		
George H. Crosby Manitou State Park, Schroeder	49 A5	MDNR	6,682	●	●			●	●				
George Washington State Forest, Togo	33 A7	MDNR	320,534	●	●	●	●	●	●	●	●	●	
Glacial Lakes State Park, Starbuck	60 D3	MDNR	2,423	●	●	●	●		●		●	●	
Glendalough State Park, Battle Lake	52 C2	MDNR	1,931	●	●		●	●	●	●	●		
Golden Anniversary State Forest, Grand Rapids	45 B7	MDNR	7,287	●			●	●	●	●	●		
Gooseberry Falls State Park, Two Harbors	48 C3	MDNR	1,687	●	●		●				●	●	●
Grand Portage State Forest, Hovland	38 B3	MDNR	100,172	●	●			●	●		●	●	
Grand Portage State Park, Grand Portage	39 B6	MDNR	278		●								
Great River Bluffs State Park, Dakota	87 A7	MDNR	3,067	●	●						●		
Hayes Lake State Park, Winner	22 A3	MDNR	2,958	●	●	●	●	●	●	●	●	●	
Hill River State Forest, Grand Rapids	45 C6	MDNR	24,854	●	●			●	●	●		●	
Huntersville State Forest, Hubbard	53 A7	MDNR	33,963	●	●	●		●		●	●		
Insula Lake State Forest, Forest Center	36 C4	MDNR	609	●	●				●				
Interstate State Park, Taylors Falls	71 A8	MDNR	298	●	●			●	●				
Itasca State Park, lake Itasca	43 B5	MDNR	32,690	●	●		●	●	●	●	●	●	●
Jay Cooke State Park, Brownell	57 A5	MDNR	8,781	●	●	●	●	●			●	●	
John A. Latsch State Park, Czechville	78 D4	MDNR	1,871	●	●								
Judge C.R. Magney State Park, Hovland	38 C3	MDNR	4,643	●	●				●				
Kabetogama State Forest, Cusson	26 D2	MDNR	619,287	●	●		●	●	●		●	●	
Kilen Woods State Park, Lakefield	82 C1	MDNR	548	●	●			●			●	●	
Koochiching State Forest, Ashlake	26 D1	MDNR	567,985	●	●			●	●		●	●	
Lac qui Parle State Park, Milan	67 C5	MDNR	911	●	●	●		●	●	●	●		
Lake Bemidji State Park, Lavinia	31 D7	MDNR	1,726	●	●		●	●	●	●	●	●	
Lake Bronson State Park, Lake Bronson	20 A4	MDNR	3,598	●	●		●		●	●	●	●	●
Lake Carlos State Park, Carlos	60 A4	MDNR	1,236	●	●	●		●	●	●	●	●	
Lake Isabella State Forest, Forest Center	36 C4	MDNR	638	●	●			●					
Lake Jeanette State Forest, Soudan	27 D6	MDNR	11,521	●				●	●				
Lake Louise State Park, LeRoy	85 D8	MDNR	1,147	●	●	●	●	●		●	●	●	
Lake Maria State Park, Monticello	69 A8	MDNR	1,614	●	●	●			●		●		
Lake of the Woods State Forest, Carp	23 B8	MDNR	142,331	●				●	●			●	
Lake Shetek State Park, Currie	73 D6	MDNR	1,108	●	●		●		●	●	●	●	●
Land O'Lakes State Forest, Remer	44 C4	MDNR	51,498	●	●	●	●	●	●	●	●		
Lost River State Forest, Roseau	18 C2	MDNR	54,915	●	●							●	
Lyons State Forest, Staples	53 B7	MDNR	14,789	●	●			●					
Maplewood State Park, Pelican Rapids	51 B8	MDNR	9,264	●	●	●		●	●	●	●	●	
McCarthy Beach State Park, Side Lake	34 C1	MDNR	2,359	●	●	●	●		●	●	●	●	
Mille Lacs Kathio State Park, Vineland	54 D5	MDNR	10,554	●	●	●				●	●	●	●
Minneopa State Park, Mankato	75 D7	MDNR	2,691	●	●				●		●		
Minnesota Valley State Recreation Area, Jordan	76 A1	MDNR	5,501	●	●	●	●				●	●	
Mississppi Headwaters State Forest, Becida	31 D6	MDNR	45,290	●	●		●	●	●	●		●	
Monson Lake State Park, Sunburg	67 A8	MDNR	187	●	●				●				
Moose Lake State Park, Moose Lake	56 B3	MDNR	1,199	●	●				●	●	●	●	
Myre–Big Island State Park, Albert Lea	84 C4	MDNR	2,028	●	●		●	●	●		●	●	
Nemadji State Forest, Moose Lake	57 C5	MDNR	90,270	●	●	●	●	●	●	●	●		
Nerstrand–Big Woods State Park, Angle Inlet	77 C5	MDNR	2,882	●	●						●	●	
Northwest Angle State Forest, Lutsen	19 A6	MDNR	144,412	●	●			●	●			●	
Pat Bayle State Forest, Grand Marais	37 C8	MDNR	180,403	●	●		●	●	●	●		●	
Paul Bunyan State Forest, Park Rapids	43 C7	MDNR	150,113	●	●		●				●	●	
Pillsbury State Forest, Pillager	54 B1	MDNR	25,612	●	●	●	●	●	●	●	●		
Pine Island State Forest, Margie	24 D2	MDNR	900,133		●			●	●		●	●	
Red Lake State Forest, Shotley	31 A8	MDNR	84,105	●	●				●				
Red River State Recreation Area, Grand Forks	28 A2	MDNR	1,230	●	●		●	●	●	●			
Remer State Forest, Remer	45 D5	MDNR	12,850	●	●								
Rice Lake State Park, Owatonna	77 D5	MDNR	1,071	●	●			●			●	●	
Richard J. Dorer Memorial Hardwood State Forest, Chatfield	86 B4	MDNR	1,016,204	●	●	●	●	●	●		●		
Rum River State Forest, Miloca	63 B6	MDNR	40,605	●	●			●				●	
Sakatah Lake State Park, Waterville	76 D3	MDNR	842	●	●		●		●		●	●	
Sand Dunes State Forest, Big Lake	63 D5	MDNR	11,040	●	●	●	●	●	●	●	●	●	
Savanna Portage State Park, Balsam	46 D1	MDNR	15,818	●	●		●		●	●	●	●	●
Savanna State Forest, Sheshabee	45 D8	MDNR	238,954	●	●			●	●	●	●	●	
Scenic State Park, Bigfork	33 C6	MDNR	3,360	●	●		●		●	●	●	●	
Schoolcraft State Park, Remer	45 B5	MDNR	295	●	●			●	●	●			
Sibley State Park, New London	68 A2	MDNR	2,509	●	●	●	●	●	●		●	●	
Smokey Bear State Forest, Little Fork	23 B6	MDNR	12,276	●	●								
Smoky Hills State Forest, Osage	42 C4	MDNR	25,278	●					●			●	
Snake River State Forest, Isle	55 D8	MDNR	9,635	●	●							●	
Solana State Forest, McGrath	55 C8	MDNR	68,141	●				●				●	
Split Rock Creek State Park, Jasper	80 B2	MDNR	1,303	●	●				●	●			
Split Rock Lighthouse State Park, Silver Bay	48 C3	MDNR	2,192	●			●				●		●
St. Croix State Forest, Danbury	65 A5	MDNR	42,152	●	●	●	●	●		●	●	●	
St. Croix State Park, Pine City	64 A4	MDNR	33,895	●	●	●	●	●	●		●	●	
Sturgeon River State Forest, Cooke	34 B2	MDNR	146,691	●	●		●	●	●				
Superior National Forest, Ely	35 B8	USFS	3,000,000	●	●	●	●	●	●		●	●	
Temperance River State Park, Schroeder	49 A6	MDNR	5,070	●	●				●		●	●	
Tettegouche State Park, Silver Bay	48 B4	MDNR	9,349	●	●		●				●	●	
Two Inlets State Forest, Two Inlets	42 C4	MDNR	28,051	●	●			●	●	●		●	
Upper Sioux Agency State Park, Wood Lake	73 A7	MDNR	1,281	●	●	●					●	●	●
Voyageurs National Park, Kabetogama	26 B1	NPS	217,000	●	●			●	●	●	●	●	
Waukenabo State Forest, Palisade	45 D7	MDNR	15,461	●	●								
Wealthwood State Forest, Wealthwood	55 C6	MDNR	15,042	●				●				●	
Welsh Lake State Forest, Cass Lake	43 A8	MDNR	19,797	●	●	●	●		●			●	
White Earth State Forest, Bagley	42 A4	MDNR	155,390	●	●		●	●	●			●	
Whiteface River State Forest, Meadowlands	46 C4	MDNR	4,429	●	●								
Whitewater State Park, St. Charles	86 A3	MDNR	2,745	●	●				●	●	●		
Wild River State Park, Almelund	64 D4	MDNR	6,767	●	●	●	●	●			●		
William O'Brien State Park, Mario St. Croix	71 B7	MDNR	1,620	●	●		●	●	●	●	●		
Zippel Bay State Park, Williams	19 D7	MDNR	2,906	●					●	●	●		

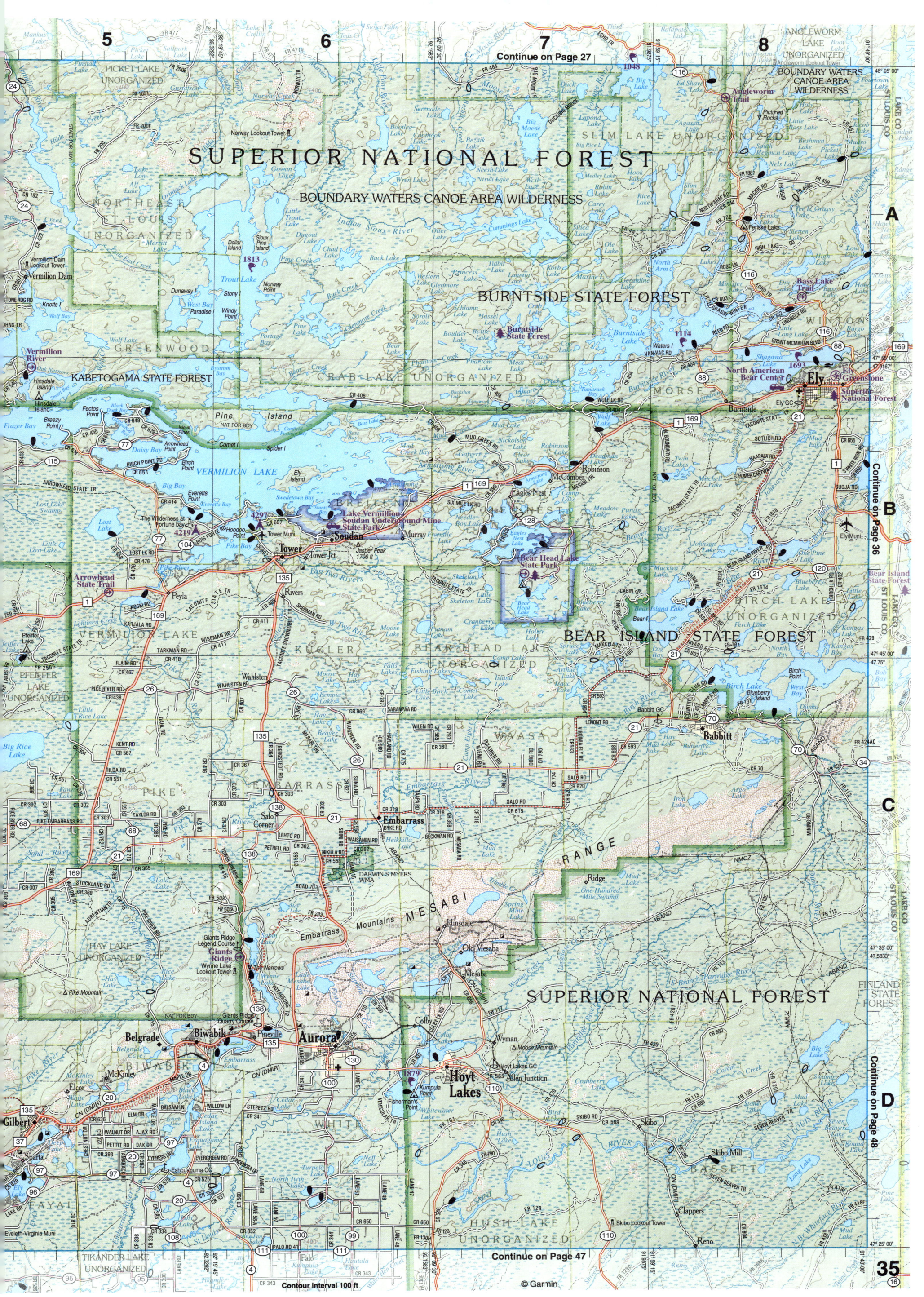

SUPERIOR NATIONAL FOREST

BOUNDARY WATERS CANOE AREA WILDERNESS

BURNTSIDE STATE FOREST

KABETOGAMA STATE FOREST

CRAB LAKE UNORGANIZED

BEAR ISLAND STATE FOREST

MESABI RANGE

SUPERIOR NATIONAL FOREST

Continue on Page 36

Continue on Page 48

Contour interval 100 ft

© Garmin

35

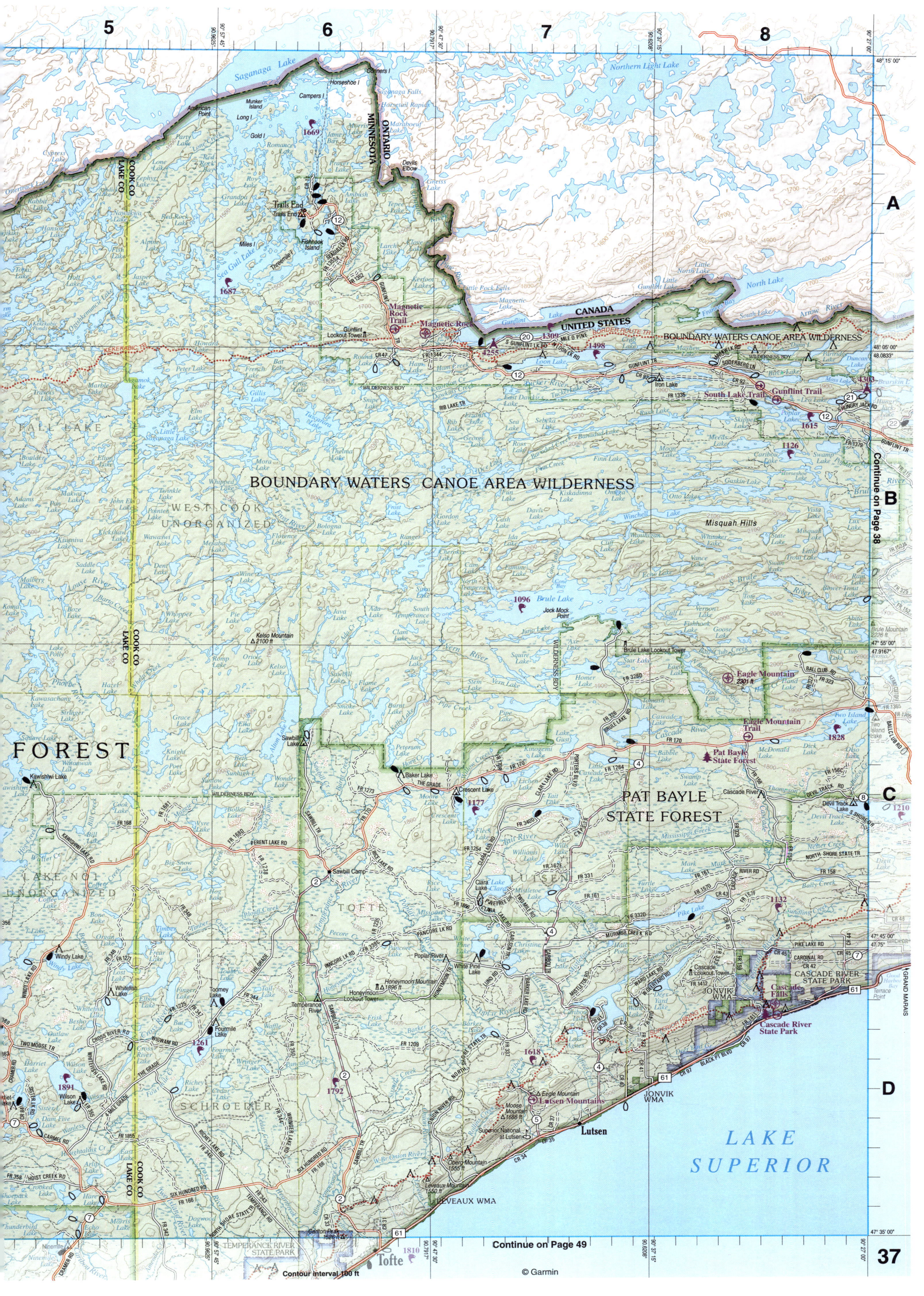

Continue on Page 38

Continue on Page 49

© Garmin

37

LAKE

Continue in the
Wisconsin Atlas & Gazetteer

© Garmin

1 inch = 3.2 mi   1 cm = 2 km

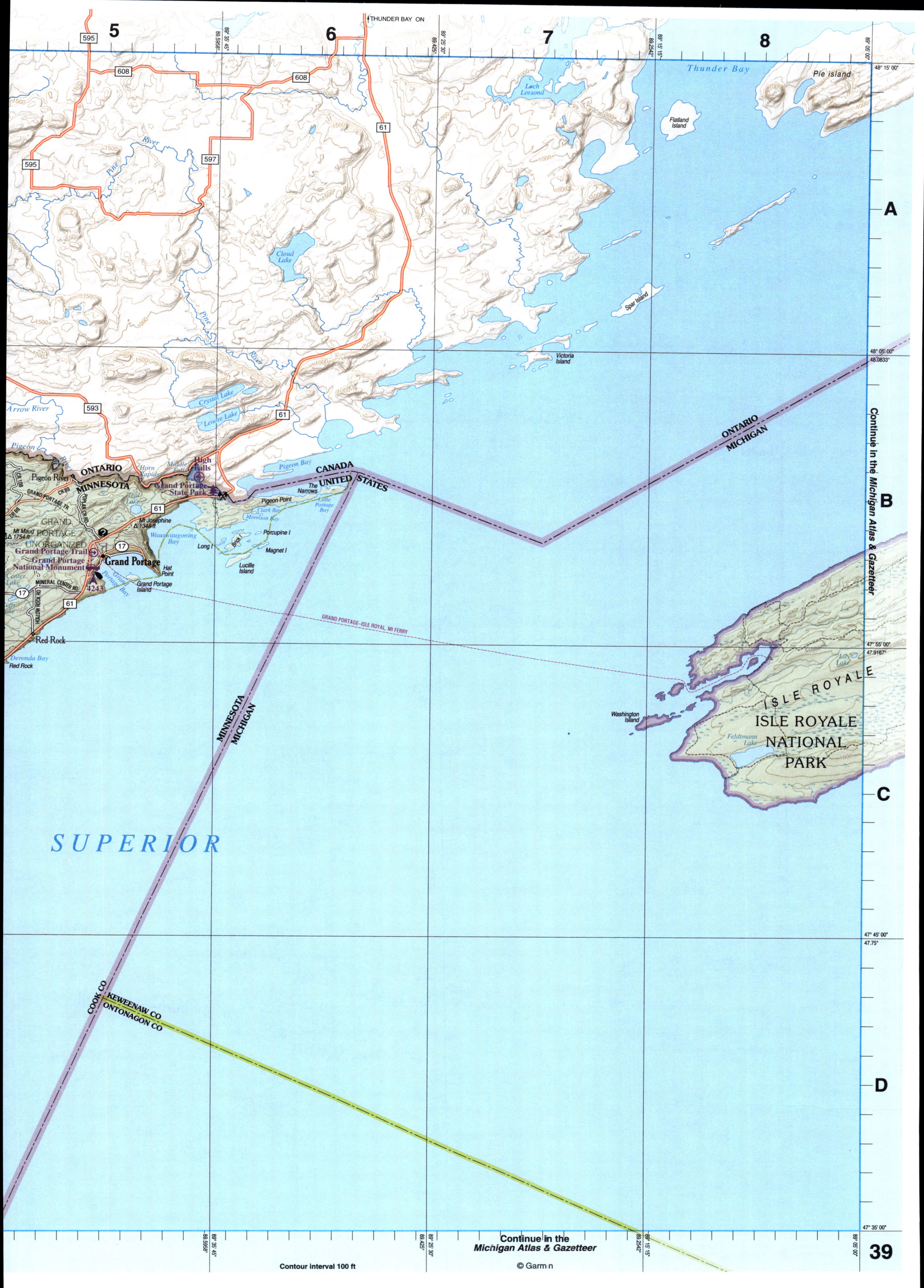

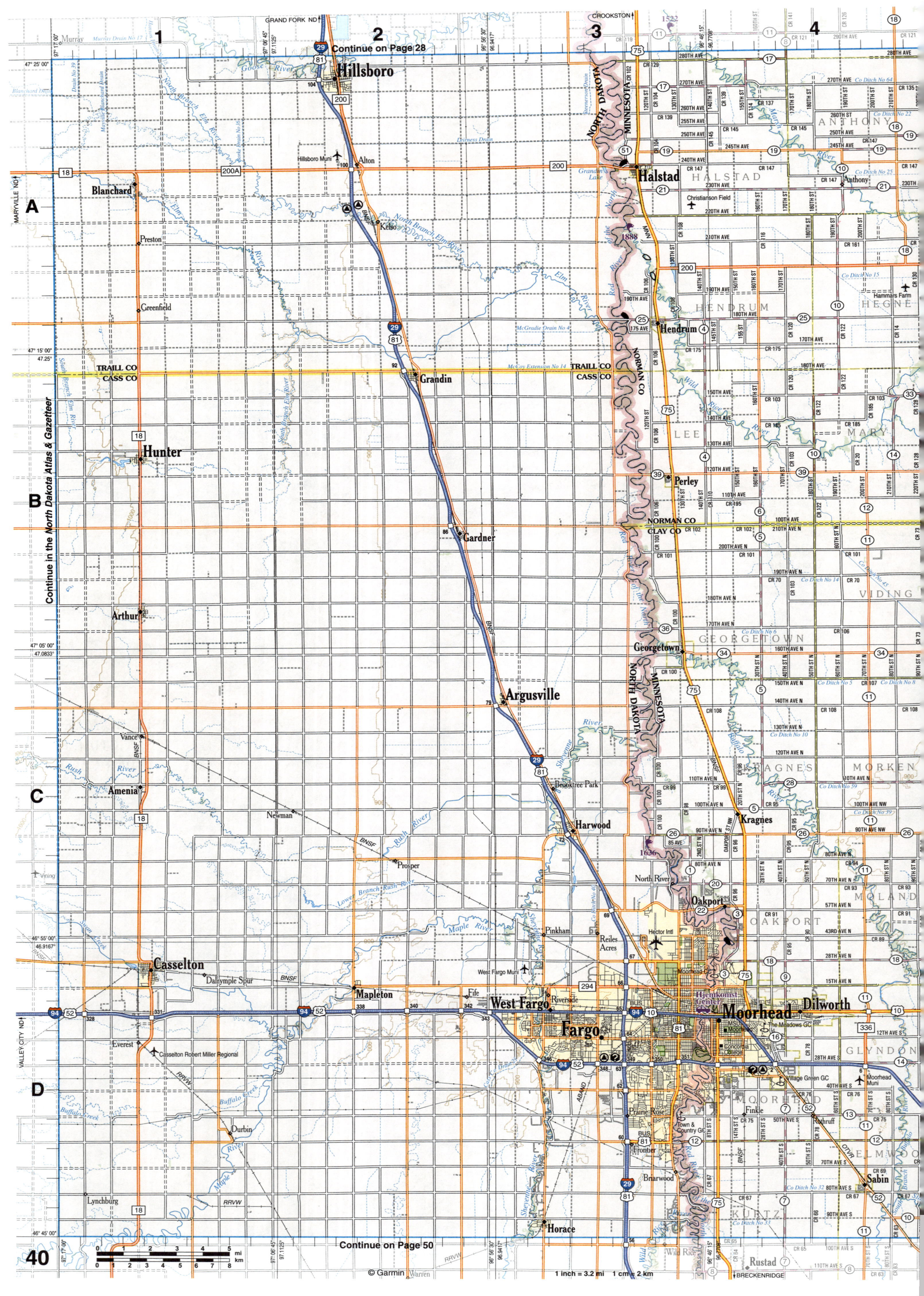

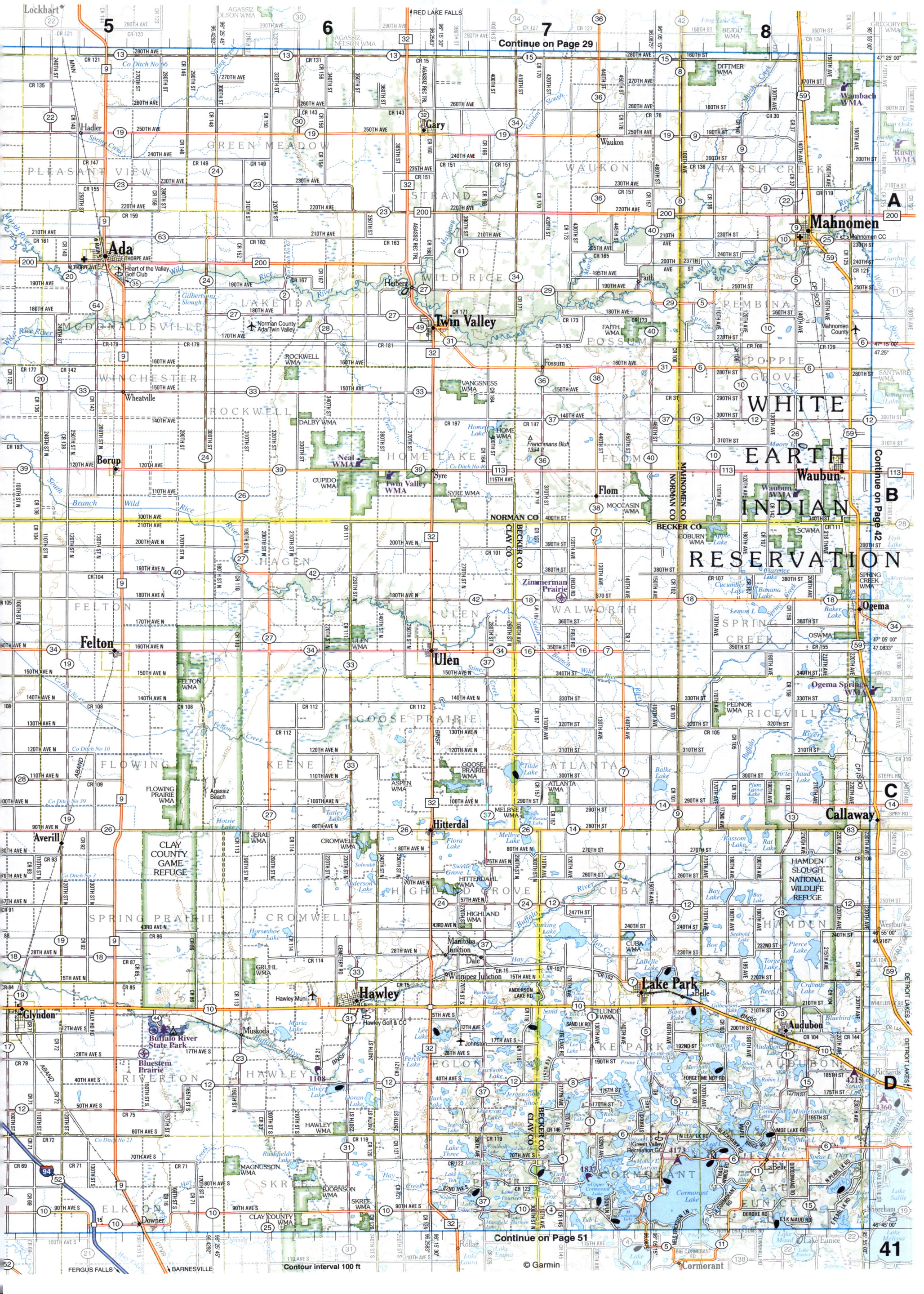

Continue on Page 29

Continue on Page 42

Continue on Page 51

Contour interval 100 ft

© Garmin

41

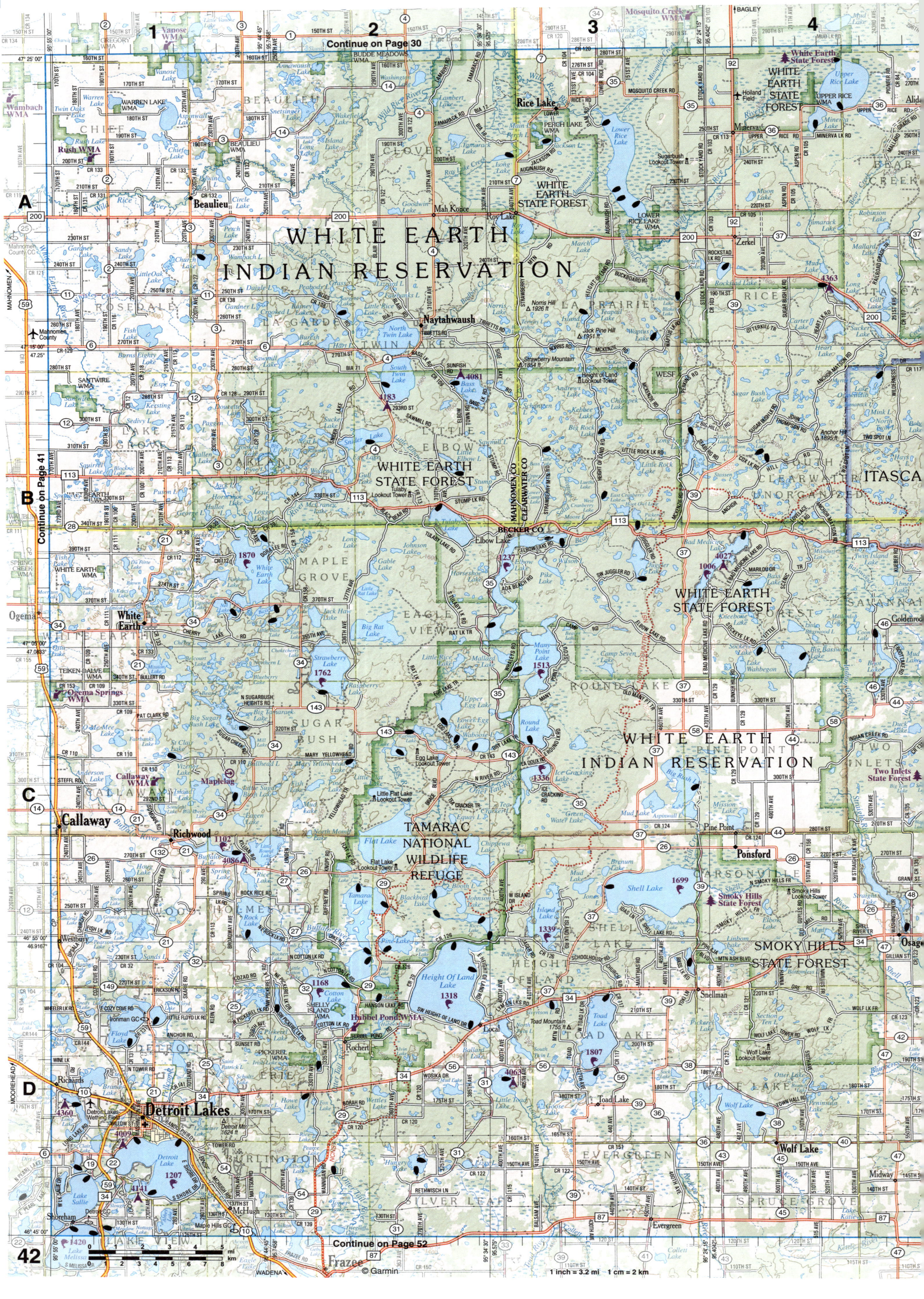

Continue on Page 30

Continue on Page 41

WHITE EARTH
INDIAN RESERVATION

WHITE EARTH
STATE FOREST

WHITE EARTH
STATE FOREST

WHITE EARTH
INDIAN RESERVATION

TAMARAC
NATIONAL
WILDLIFE
REFUGE

SMOKY HILLS
STATE FOREST

Detroit Lakes

Continue on Page 52

42

1 inch = 3.2 mi   1 cm = 2 km

© Garmin

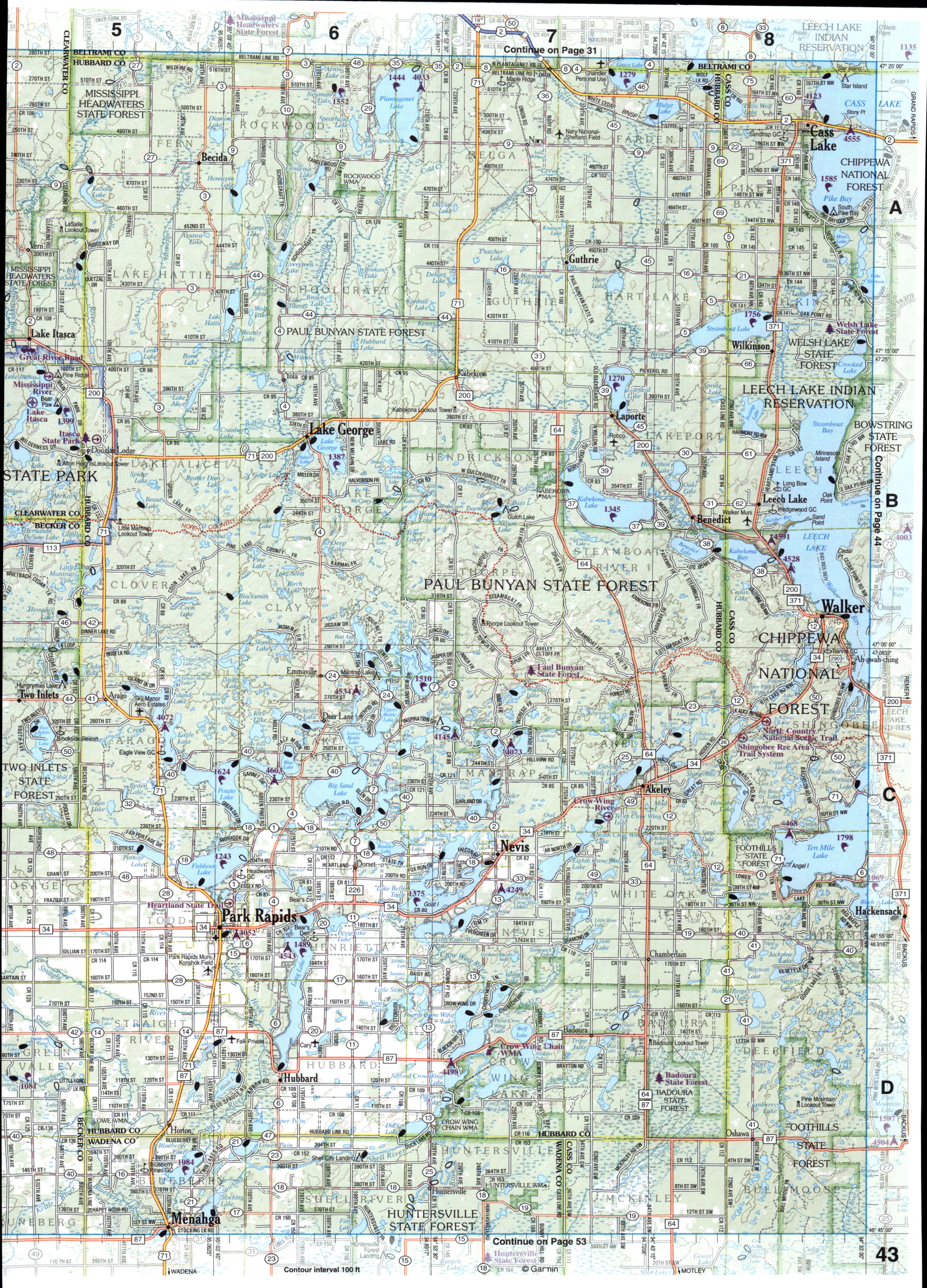

Continue on Page 31
Continue on Page 44
Continue on Page 53

43

Continue on Page 32

Continue on Page 43

Continue on Page 54

44

1 inch = 3.2 mi   1 cm = 2 km

© Garmin

Continue on Page 33

Continue on Page 46

Continue on Page 55

Contour interval 100 ft

© Garmin

45

Continue on Page 35

SUPERIOR NATIONAL FOREST

CLOQUET VALLEY STATE FOREST

Continue on Page 48

LAKE SUPERIOR

Duluth

Continue on Page 57

Contour interval 100 ft

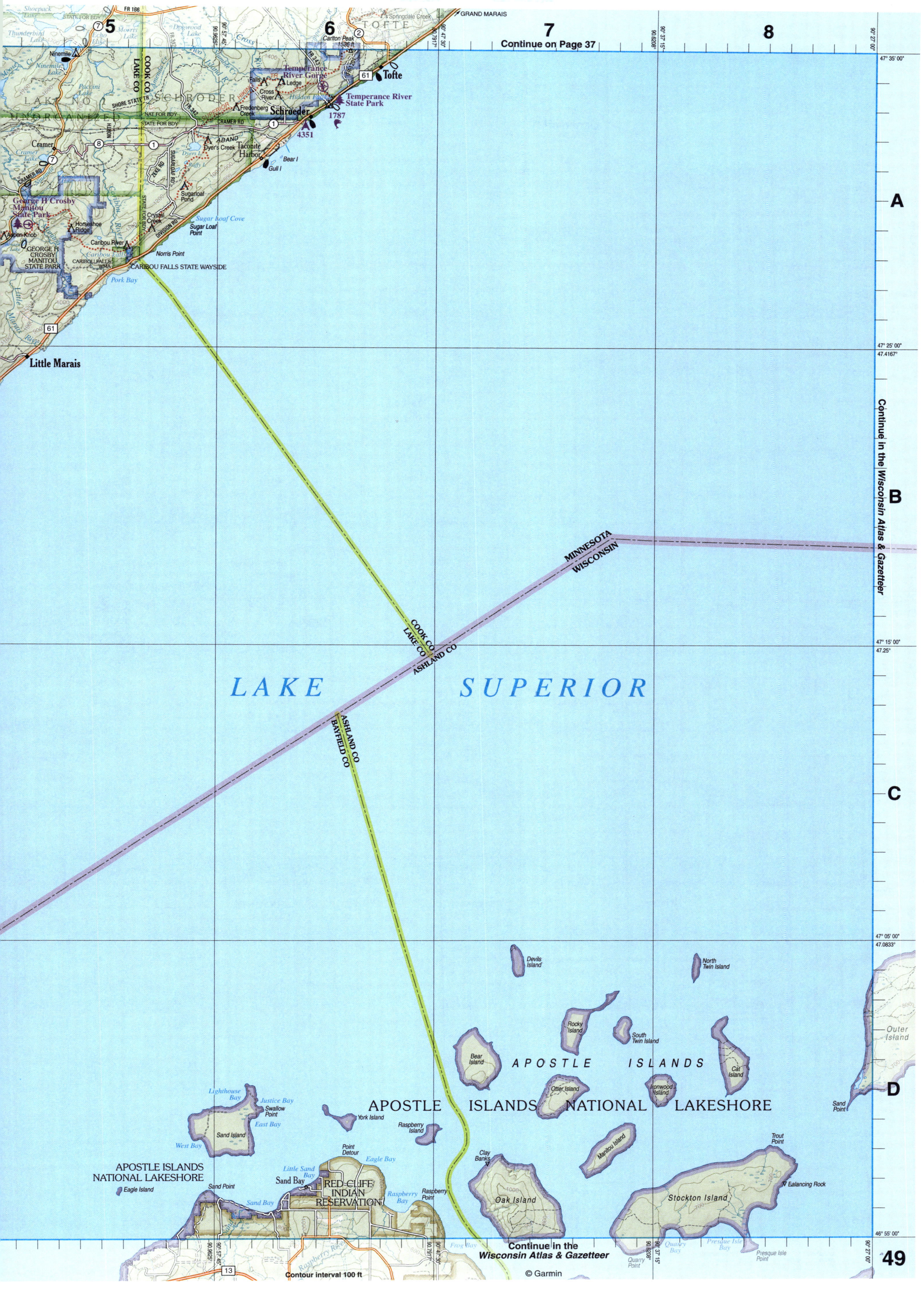

Continue on Page 37

Continue in the Wisconsin Atlas & Gazetteer

A

B

C

D

47° 35' 00"

47° 25' 00"
47.4167°

47° 15' 00"
47.25°

47° 05' 00"
47.0833°

46° 55' 00"

GRAND MARAIS

TOFTE

Temperance
River Gorge
Ledge

Tofte

Temperance River
State Park

Cross
River

Hidden Falls

Schroeder

1787

4351

ABAND
Dyer's Creek
Taconite
Harbor

Bear I

Gull I

Sugarloaf
Pond

Sugar Loaf Cove

Sugar Loaf
Point

Crystal
Creek

Norris Point

CARIBOU FALLS STATE WAYSIDE

Caribou River

Caribou Falls WMA

Pork Bay

Little Marais

George H Crosby
Manitou State Park

Horseshoe
Ridge

Aspen Knob

GEORGE H
CROSBY
MANITOU
STATE PARK

Ninemile
Lake

Shoepack
Lake

Thunderbird
Lake

Morris
Lake

Dogwood
Lake

Cross
Lake

Springdale Creek

Cramer

Cramer
Lake

COOK CO
LAKE CO

SCHRODER

FR 166

LAKE NO
UNORGANIZED

COOK CO
LAKE CO

ASHLAND CO

ASHLAND CO
BAYFIELD CO

MINNESOTA
WISCONSIN

LAKE SUPERIOR

Devils
Island

North
Twin Island

Rocky
Island

Rocky
Island

South
Twin Island

Cat
Island

APOSTLE ISLANDS

Bear
Island

Otter Island

Ironwood
Island

Sand
Point

Outer
Island

APOSTLE ISLANDS NATIONAL LAKESHORE

Lighthouse
Bay

Justice Bay

Swallow
Point

East Bay

Sand Island

West Bay

York Island

Raspberry
Island

Manitou Island

Trout
Point

Point
Detour

Little Sand
Bay

Eagle Bay

Sand Bay

Clay
Banks

Balancing Rock

Stockton Island

APOSTLE ISLANDS
NATIONAL LAKESHORE

Eagle Island

Sand Point

Sand Bay

RED CLIFF
INDIAN
RESERVATION

Raspberry
Bay

Raspberry
Point

Oak Island

Quarry
Point

Quarry
Bay

Presque Isle
Bay

Presque Isle
Point

90° 45' 00"
90° 37' 30"
90° 30' 00"
90° 37' 15"
90° 30'

90° 27' 00"

Continue in the
Wisconsin Atlas & Gazetteer

Contour interval 100 ft

© Garmin

49

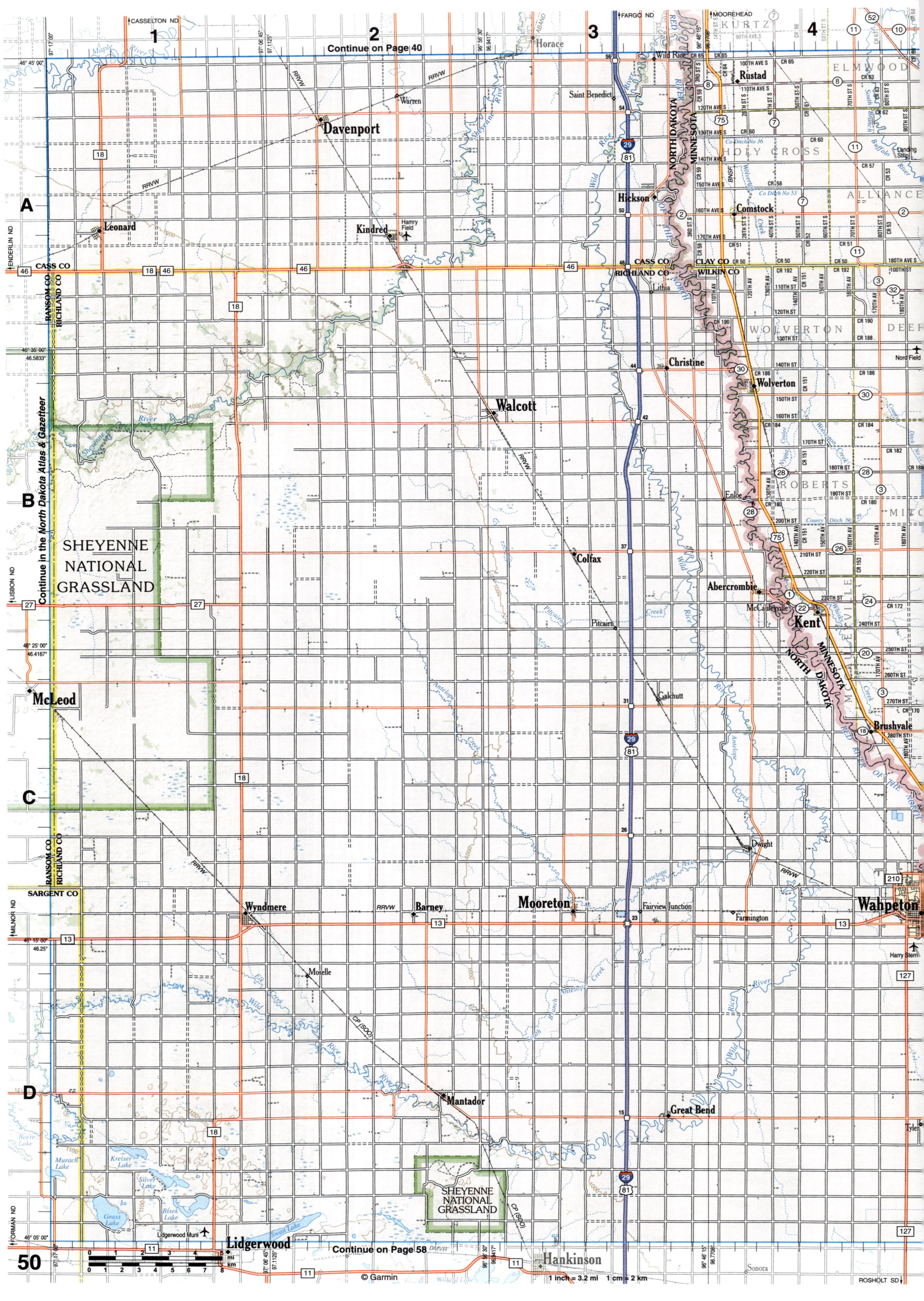

CASSELTON ND

Continue on Page 40

MOOREHEAD
KURTZ

Horace

Warren

FARGO ND

Wild Rice

Rustad

Saint Benedict

ELMWOOD

Davenport

HOLY CROSS

Hickson

Comstock

A

CASS CO

Leonard

Kindred

Hamry Field

ALLIANCE

CASS CO

CLAY CO

18 46

46

CASS CO

RICHLAND CO

WILKIN CO

18

WOLVERTON

DEER

Litha

Christine

B

SHEYENNE
NATIONAL
GRASSLAND

Walcott

Wolverton

North Field

ROBERTS

Enloe

27

27

Colfax

Abercrombie

Kent

C

McCauleyville

RANSOM CO
RICHLAND CO

McLeod

Galchutt

MINNESOTA

NORTH DAKOTA

Brushvale

18

Dwight

SARGENT CO

Wyndmere

Barney

Mooreton

Fairview Junction

Wahpeton

13

13

Farmington

13

Moselle

Harry Stern

127

D

Mantador

Great Bend

Tyle

15

18

SHEYENNE
NATIONAL
GRASSLAND

Kreiser
Lake

Muracil
Lake

Silver
Lake

Bisek
Lake

Grass
Lake

Ludgerwood Muni

50

Lidgerwood

Continue on Page 58

Hankinson

Sonora

© Garmin

1 inch = 3.2 mi 1 cm = 2 km

ROSHOLT SD

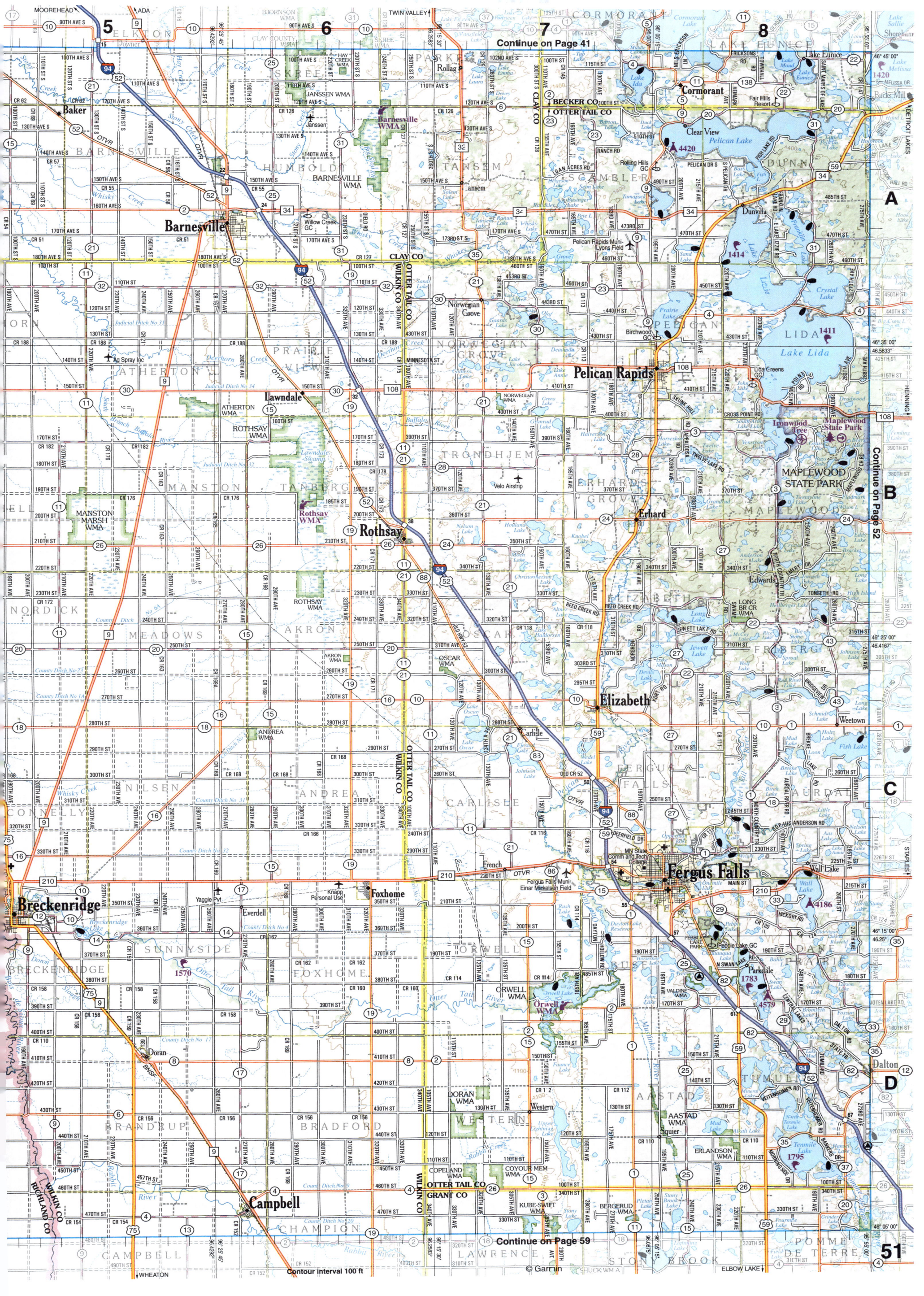

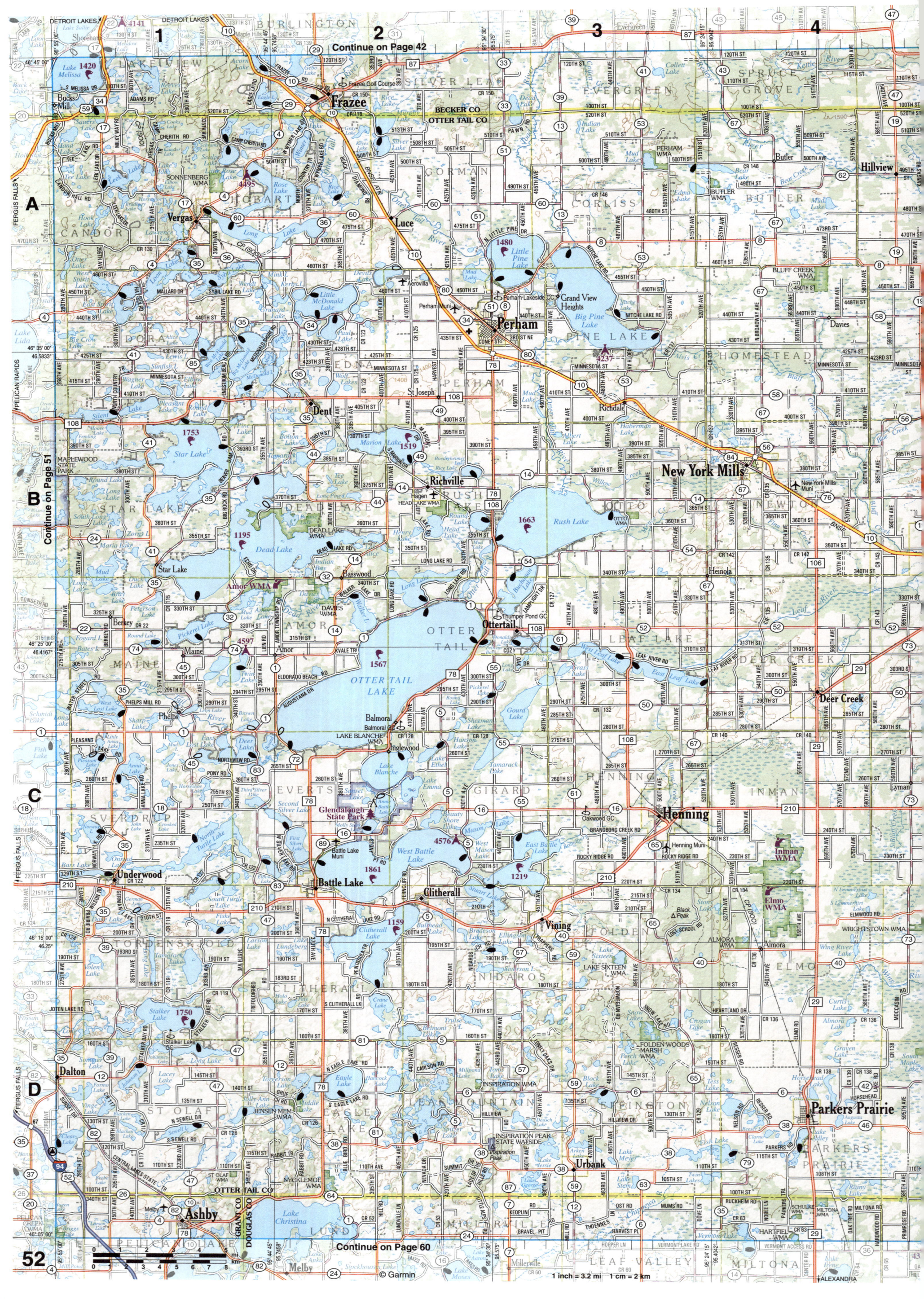

Continue on Page 51

1 inch = 3.2 mi   1 cm = 2 km

© Garmin

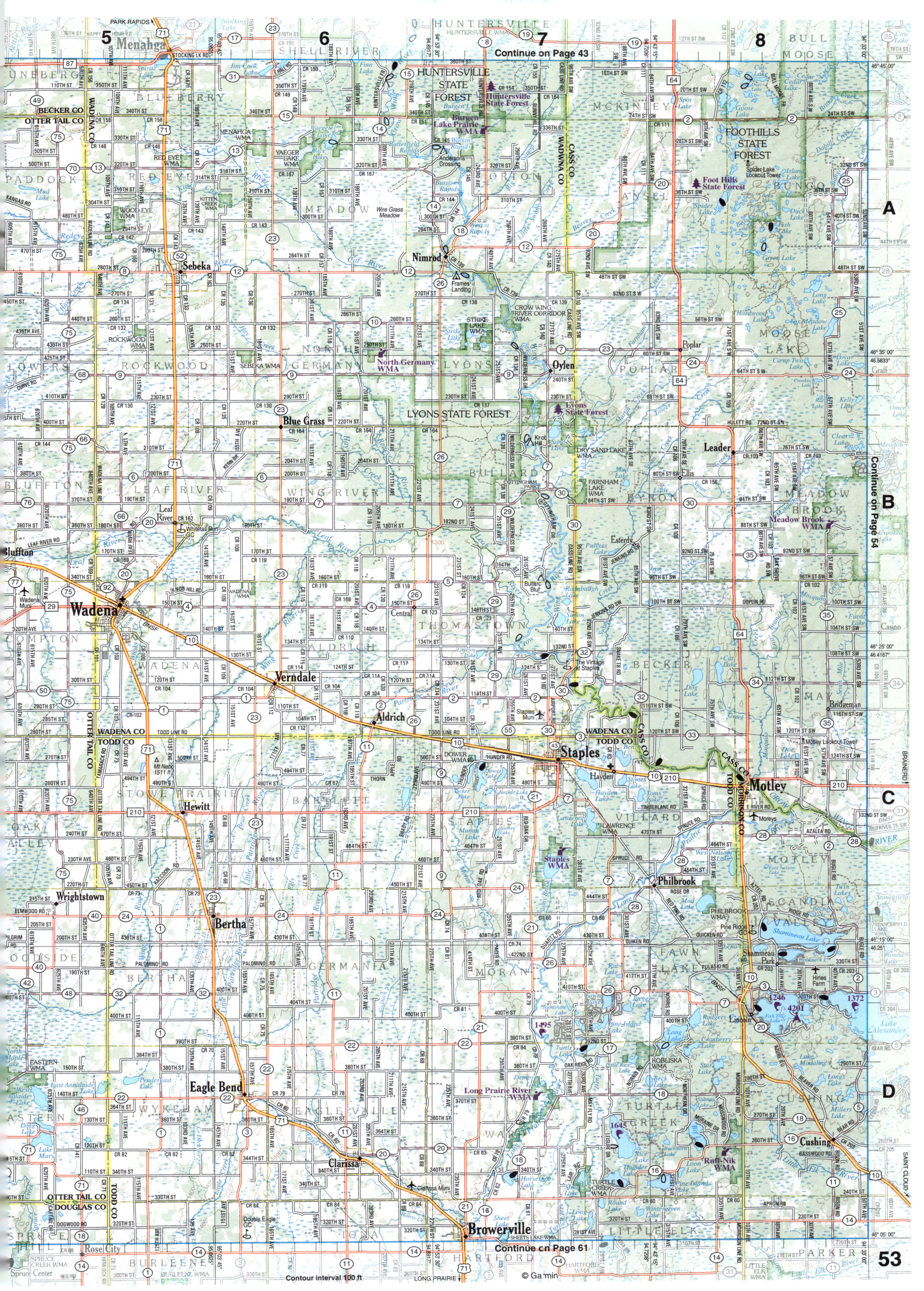

Continue on Page 43

Continue on Page 54

Continue on Page 61

Contour interval 100 ft

© Garmin

53

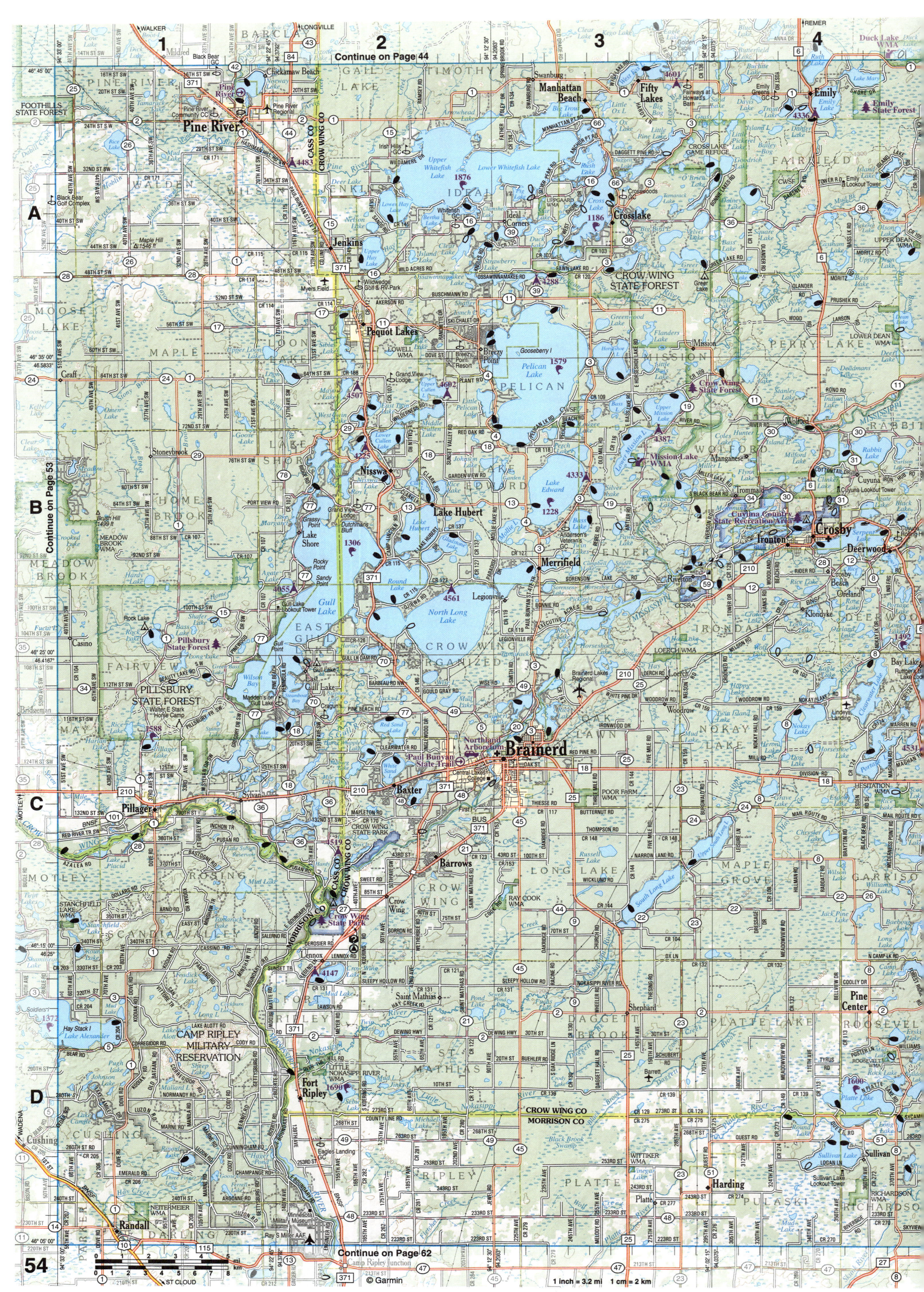

Continue on Page 44

Continue on Page 53

Continue on Page 62

54

1 inch = 3.2 mi   1 cm = 2 km

© Garmin

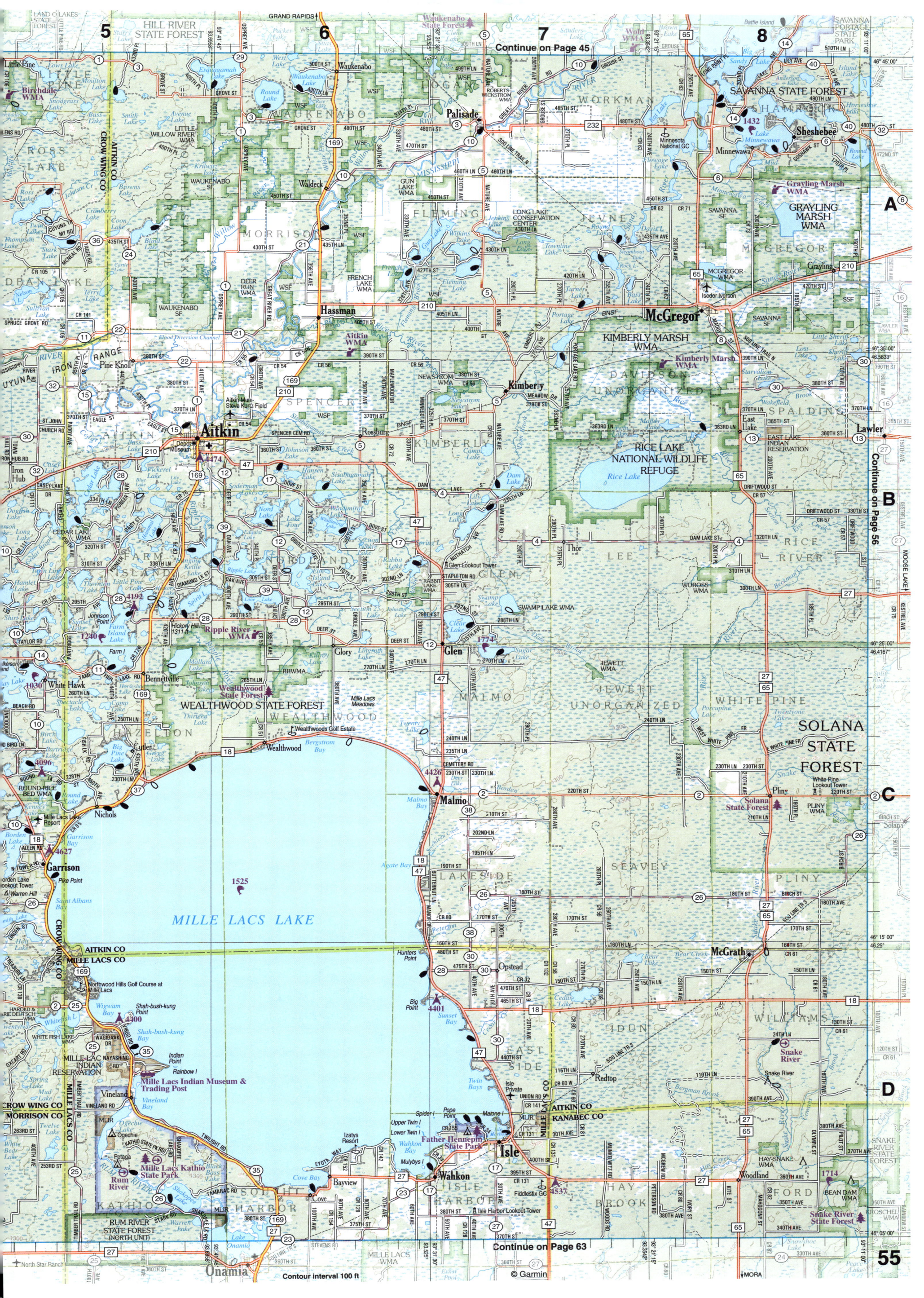

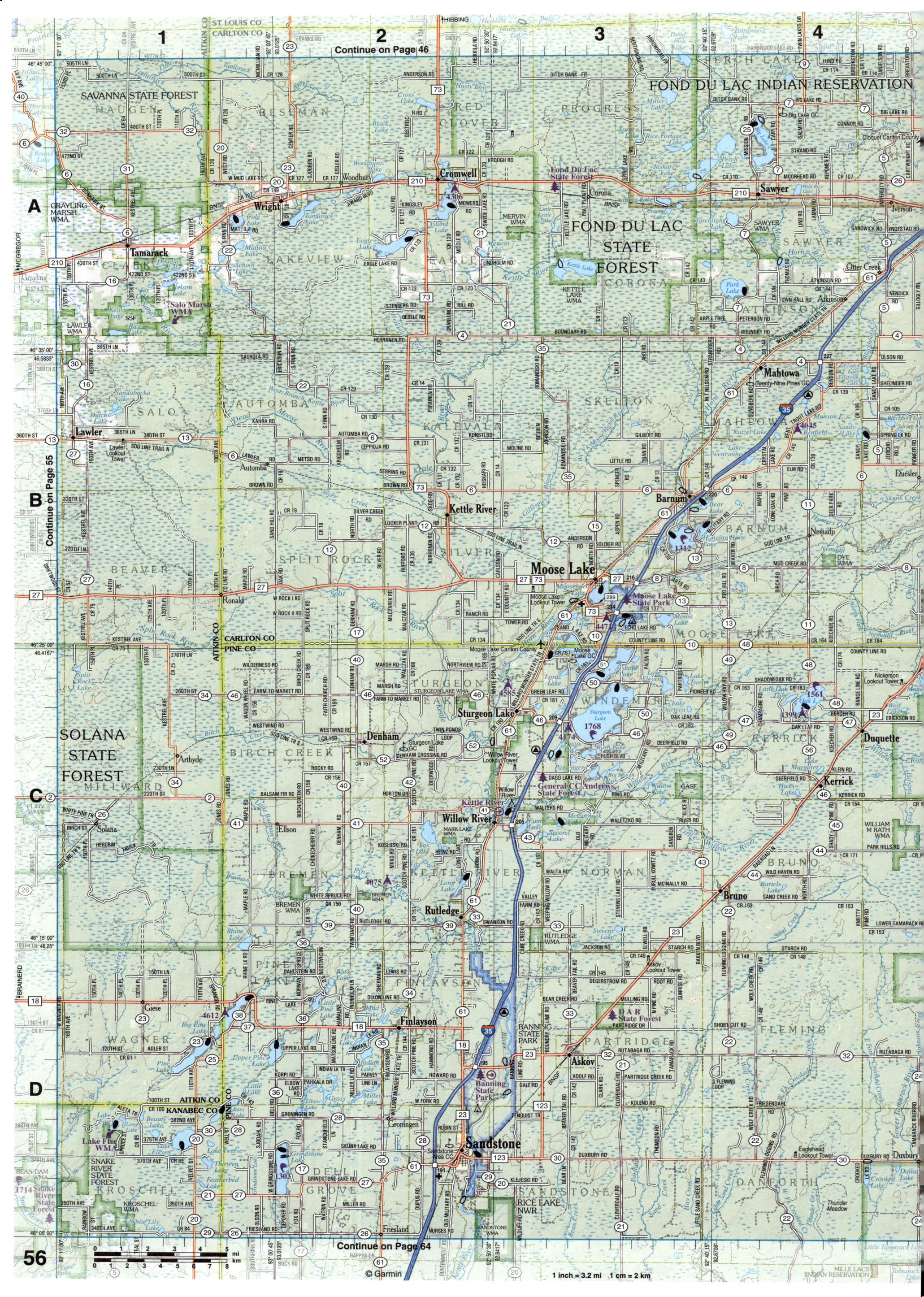

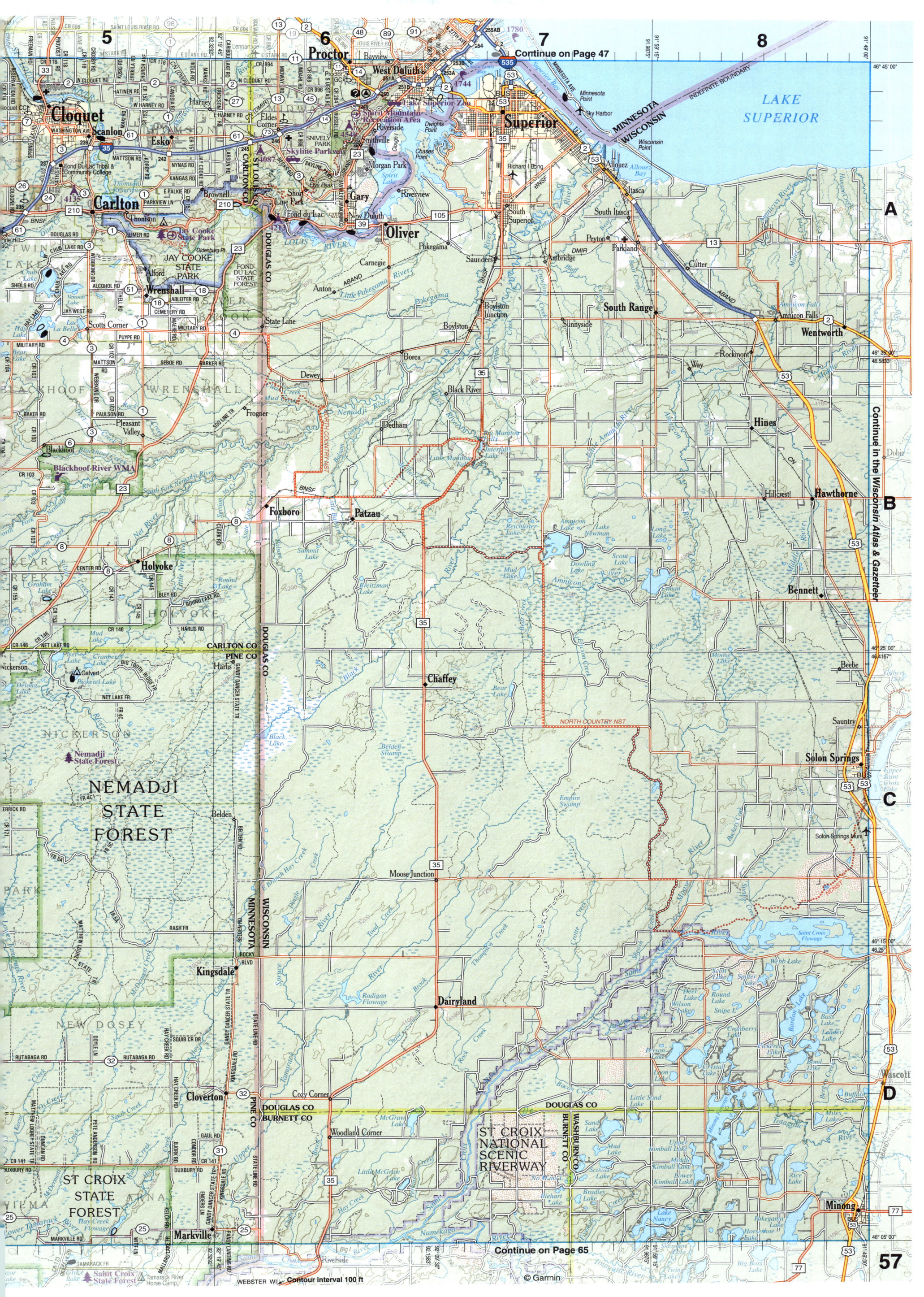

Continue on Page 47

LAKE SUPERIOR

5 Proctor **6** **7** **8**

Cloquet

Scanlon

Esko

Carlton

Thomson

Wrenshall

Scotts Corner

Pleasant Valley

Blackhoof

Blackhoof River WMA

JAY COOKE STATE PARK

FOND DU LAC STATE FOREST

West Duluth

Spirit Mountain Recreation Area

Riverside

Smithville

Morgan Park

Gary

New Duluth

Fond du Lac

Short Line Park

Skyline Parkway

Superior

Minnesota Point

Sky Harbor

Allouez

Itasca

South Itasca

Richard I Bong

South Superior

Carnegie

Anton

Little Pokegama

Saunders

Boylston Junction

Boylston

Borea

Dewey

Frogner

Dedham

Black River

Manitou Falls

Little Manitou Falls

Interfalls Lake

Foxboro

Patzau

Holyoke

Chaffey

South Range

Sunnyside

Way

Rockmont

Amnicon Falls

Wentworth

Hines

Hillcrest

Hawthorne

Bennett

Beebe

Sauntry

Solon Springs

Solon Springs Muni

NEMADJI STATE FOREST

Belden

Kingsdale

Dairyland

Moose Junction

Cloverton

Cozy Corner

DOUGLAS CO BURNETT CO

Woodland Corner

McGraw

ST CROIX NATIONAL SCENIC RIVERWAY

ST CROIX STATE FOREST

Markville

Minong

Wascott

CARLTON CO / PINE CO

DOUGLAS CO

MINNESOTA / WISCONSIN

NORTH COUNTRY NST

NEW DOSEY

Nemadji State Forest

NICKERSON

Rutabaga Rd

MINNESOTA / WISCONSIN

Continue on Page 65

WEBSTER WI Contour interval 100 ft

© Garmin

Continue in the Wisconsin Atlas & Gazetteer

A

B

C

D

57

Continue on Page 50

LAKE TRAVERSE INDIAN RESERVATION

Continue in the North Dakota Atlas & Gazetteer

Continue in the South Dakota Atlas & Gazetteer

58

Continue in the South Dakota Atlas & Gazetteer

© Garmin

1 inch = 3.2 mi   1 cm = 2 km

Continue on Page 51

Continue on Page 60

Continue on Page 66

Contour interval 100 ft

© Garmin

59

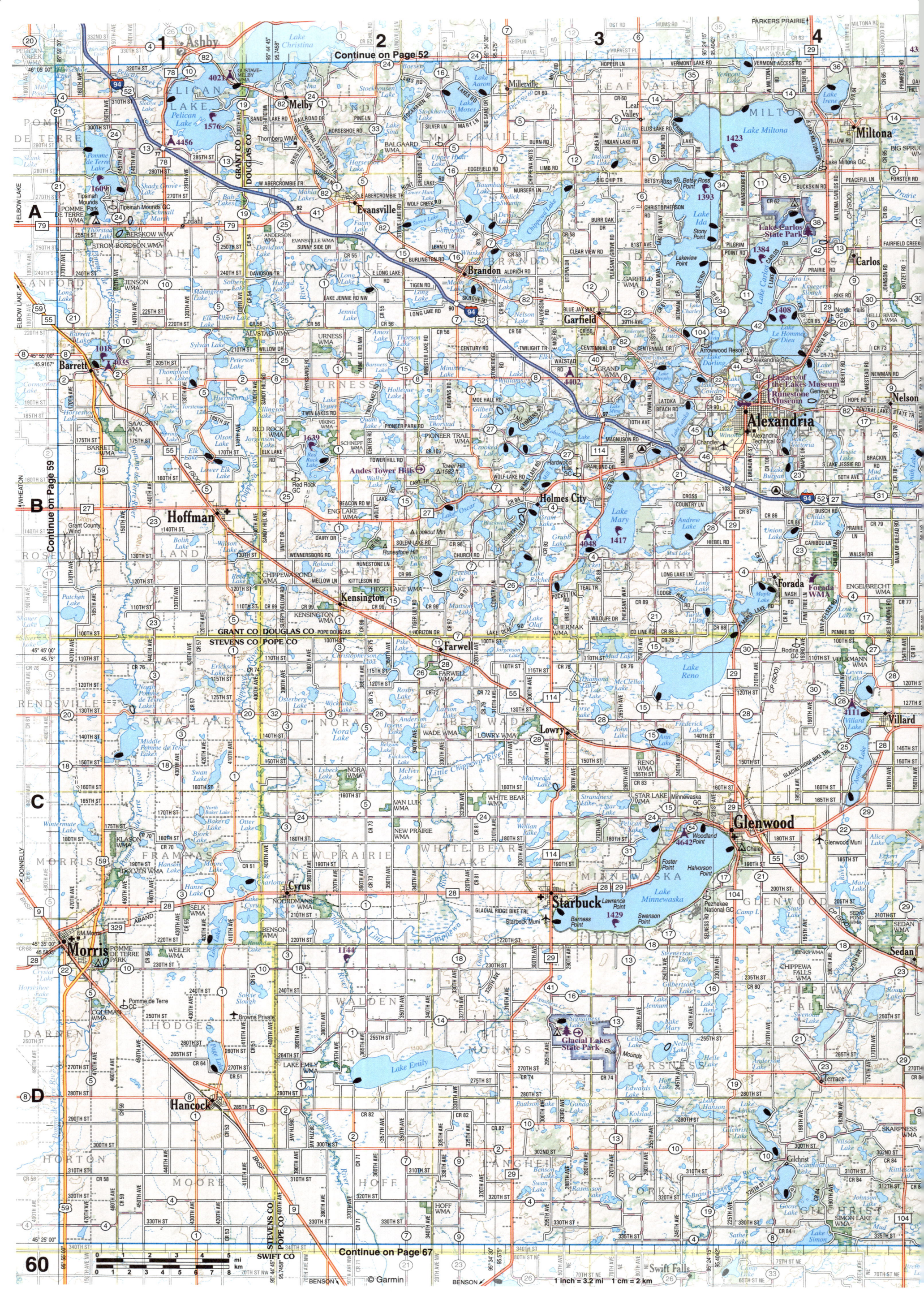

Continue on Page 52

Continue on Page 59

Continue on Page 67

© Garmin

1 inch = 3.2 mi   1 cm = 2 km

Continue on Page 62

Contour interval 100 ft

© Garmin

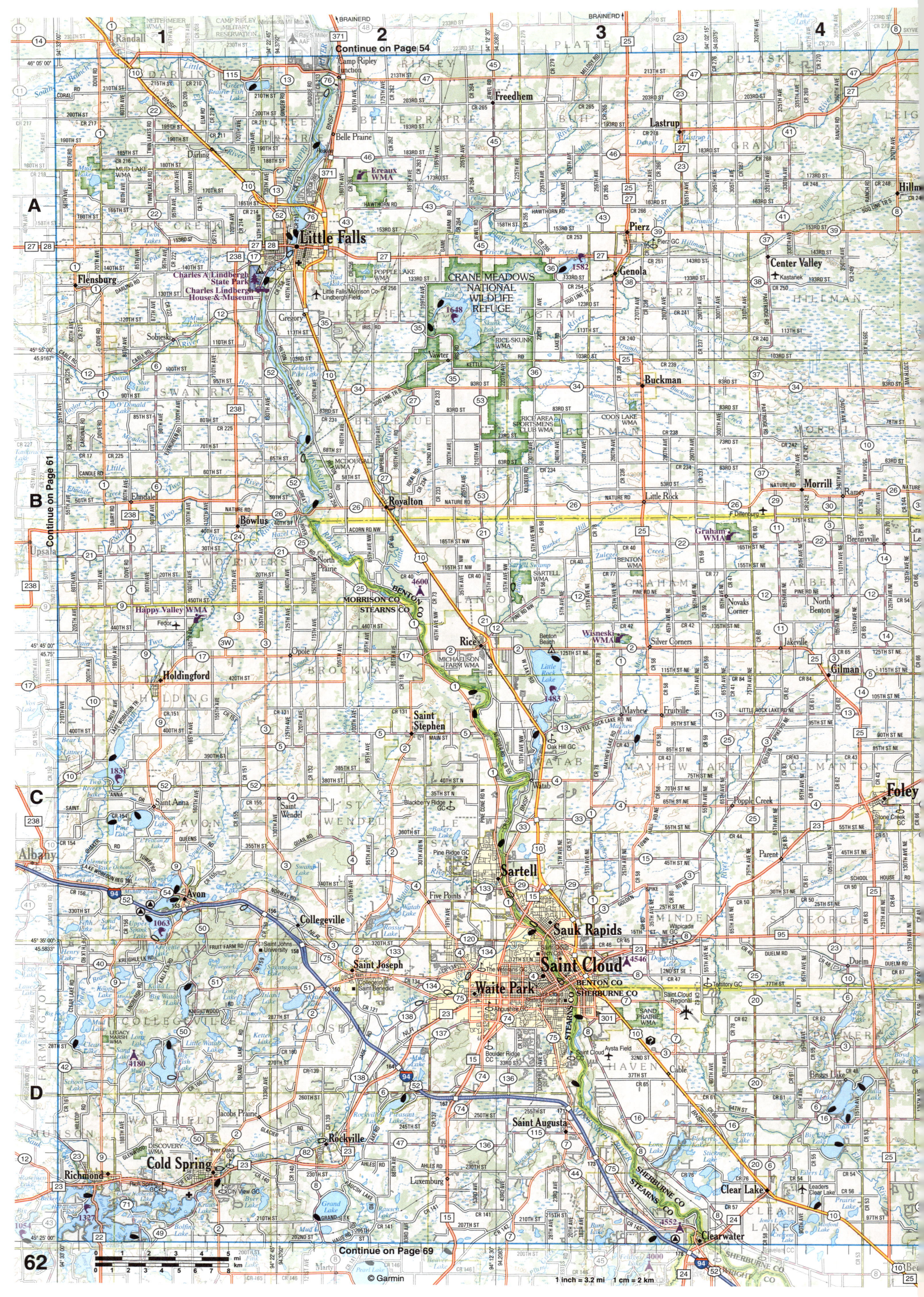

Continue on Page 54

Continue on Page 61

Continue on Page 69

62

1 inch = 3.2 mi   1 cm = 2 km

© Garmin

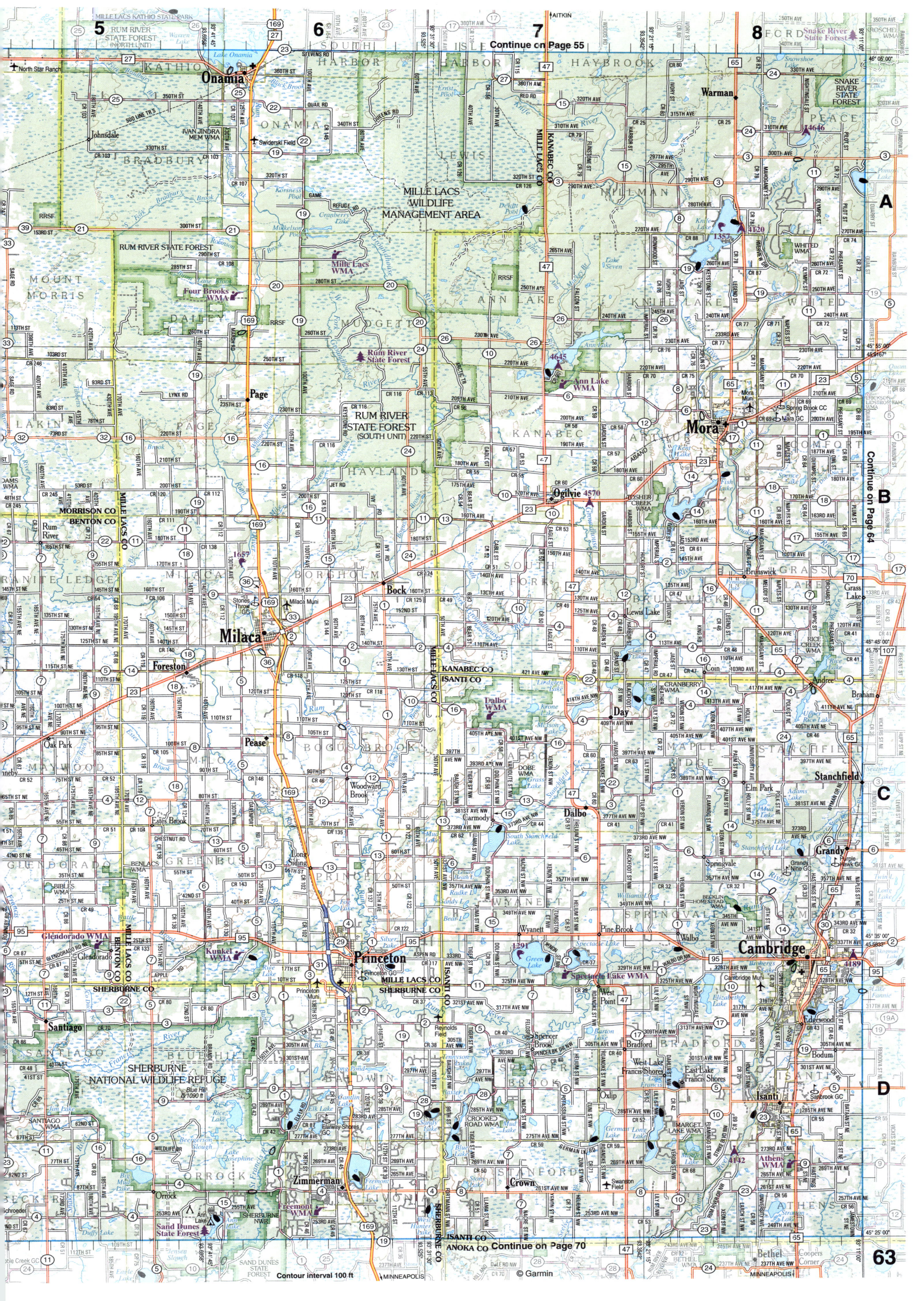

Continue on Page 64

Continue on Page 70

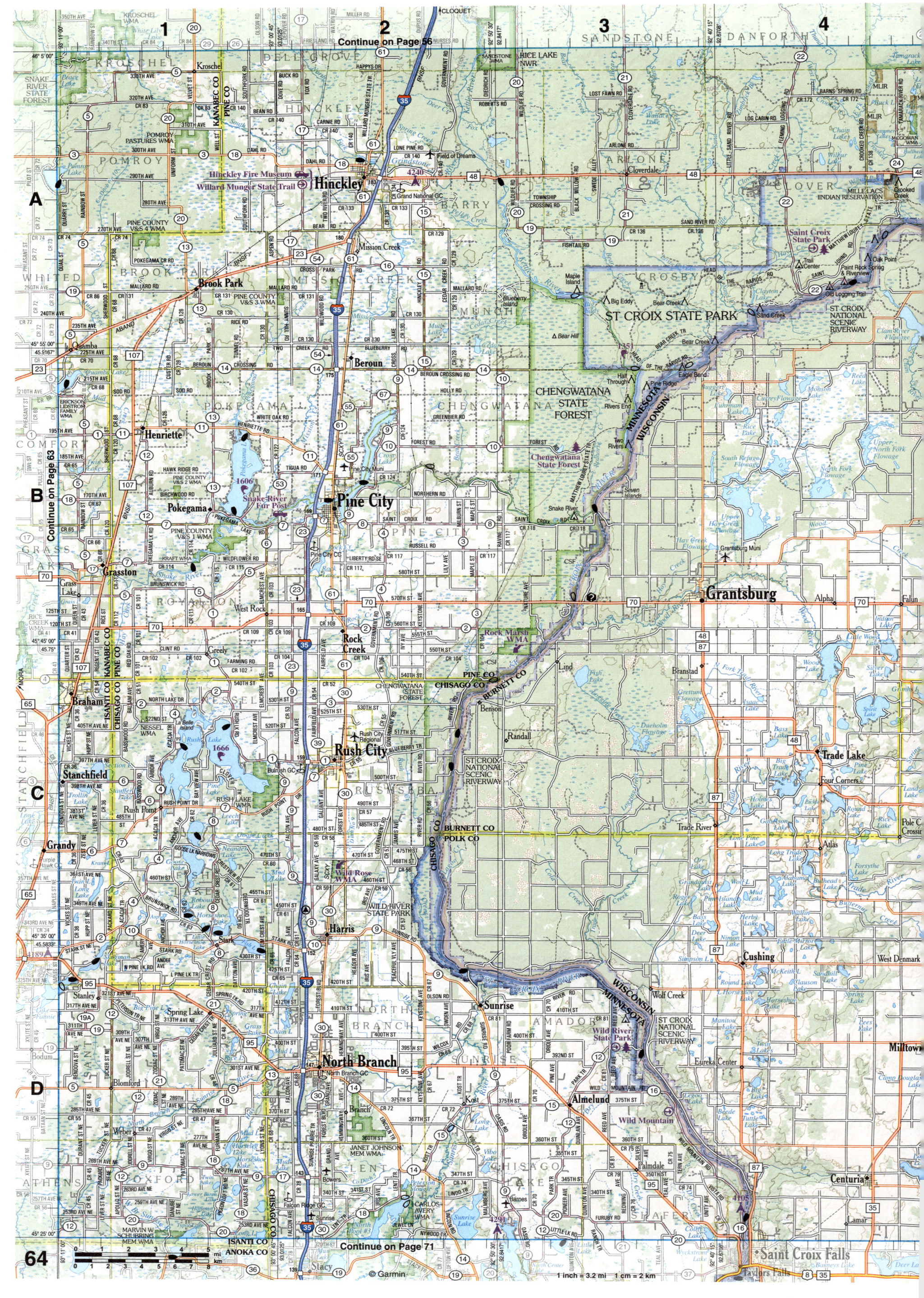

Continue on Page 56

A

Continue on Page 63

B

C

D

Continue on Page 71

1 inch = 3.2 mi   1 cm = 2 km

© Garmin

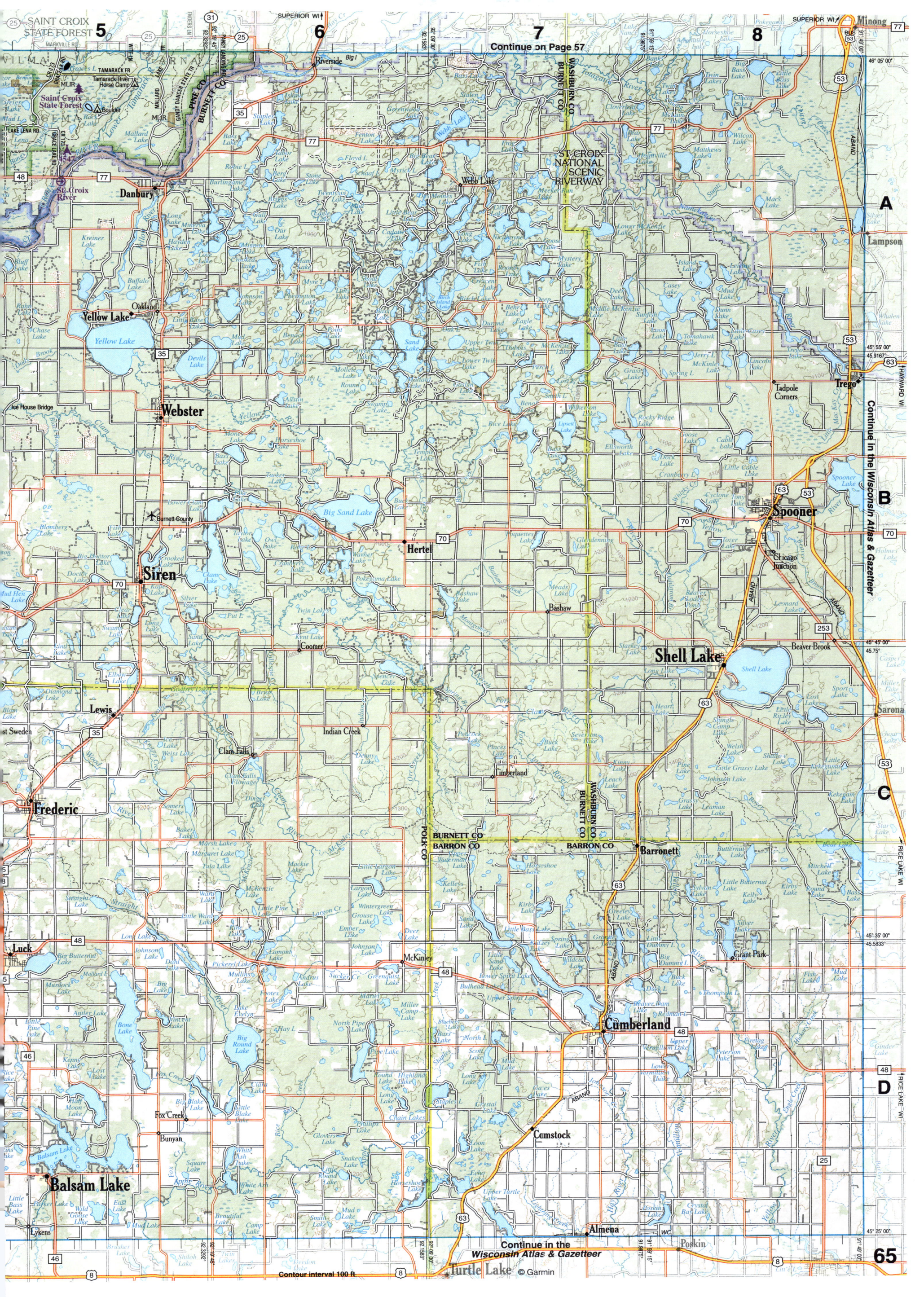

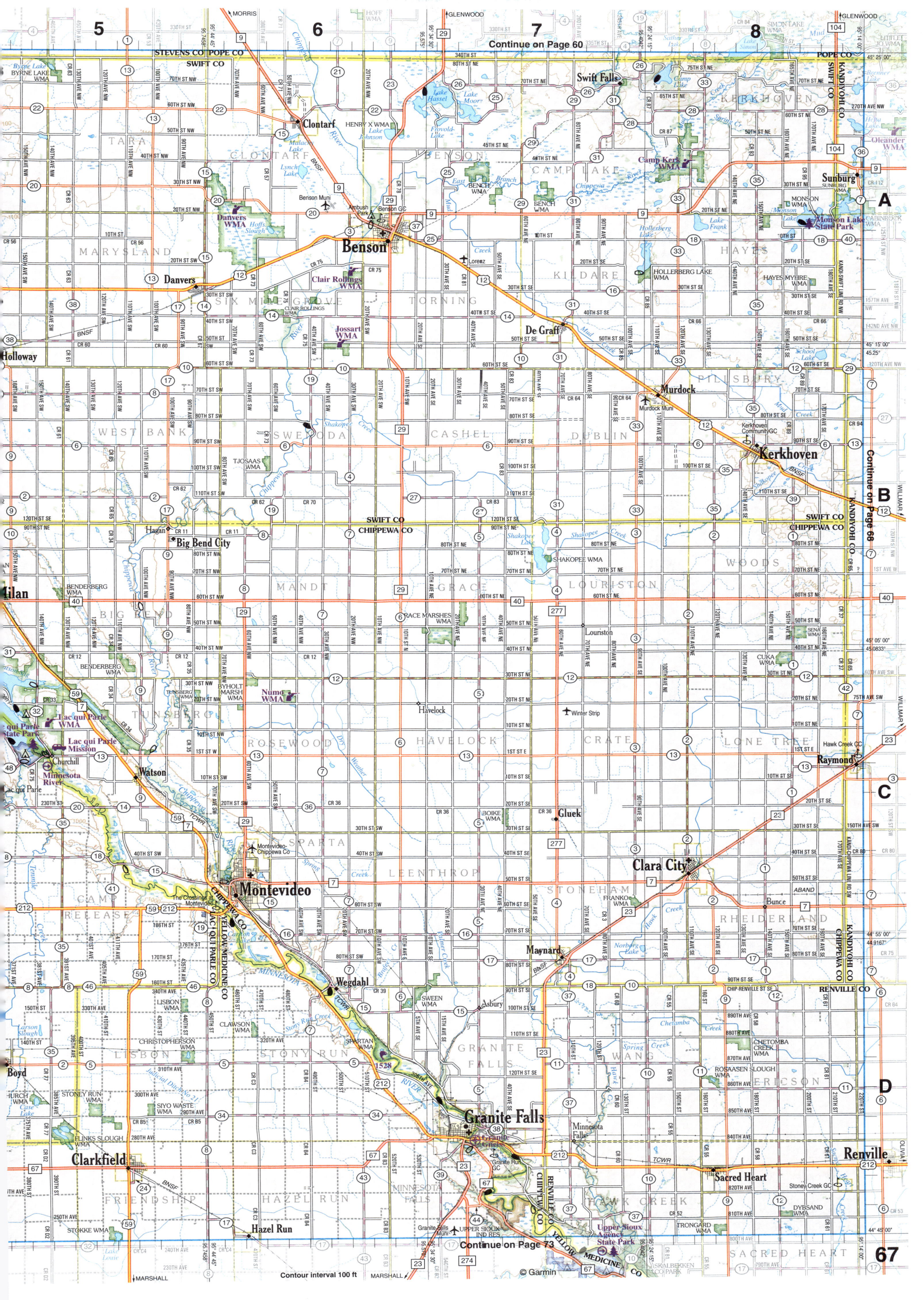

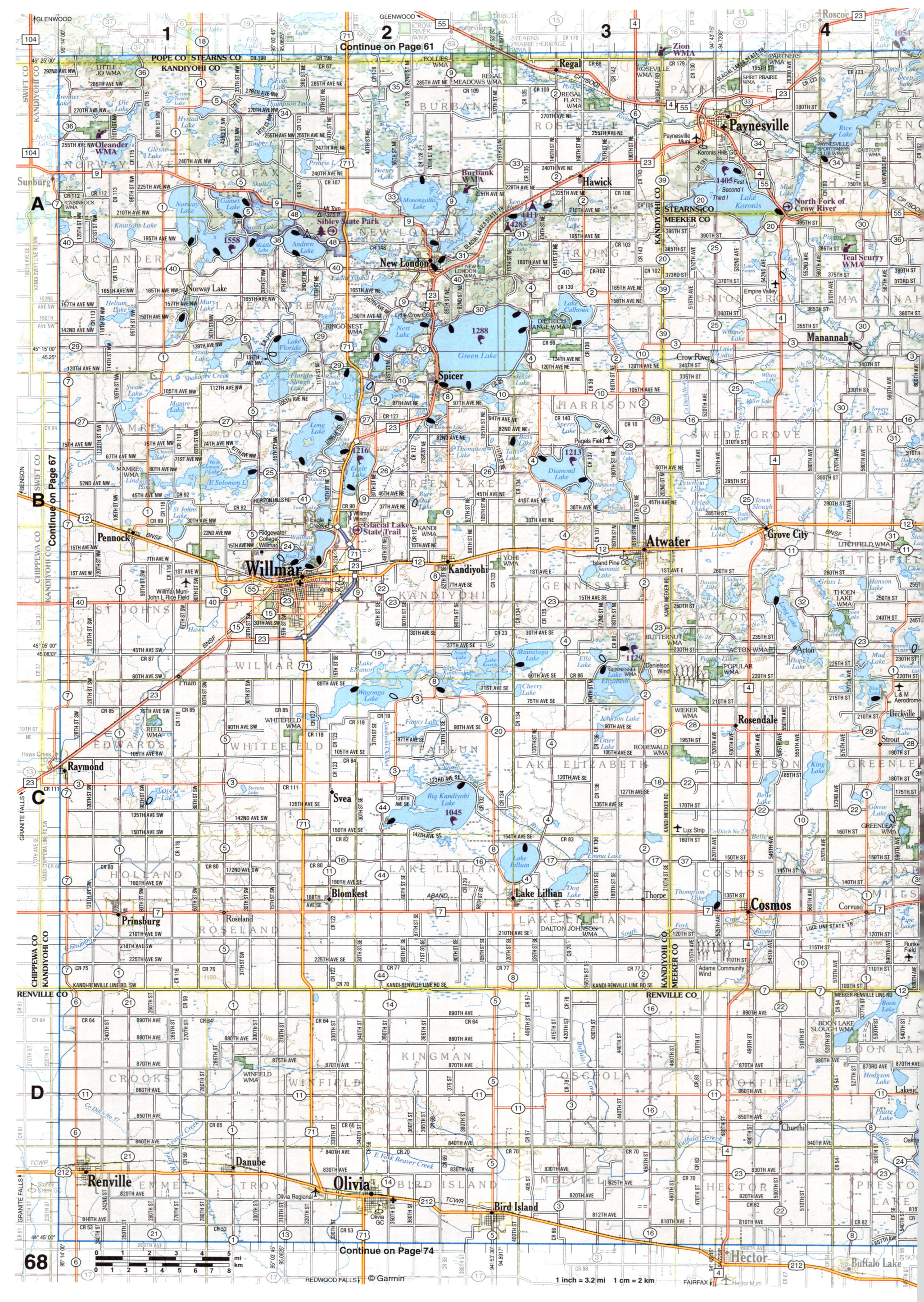

Continue on Page 61

Continue on Page 67

Continue on Page 74

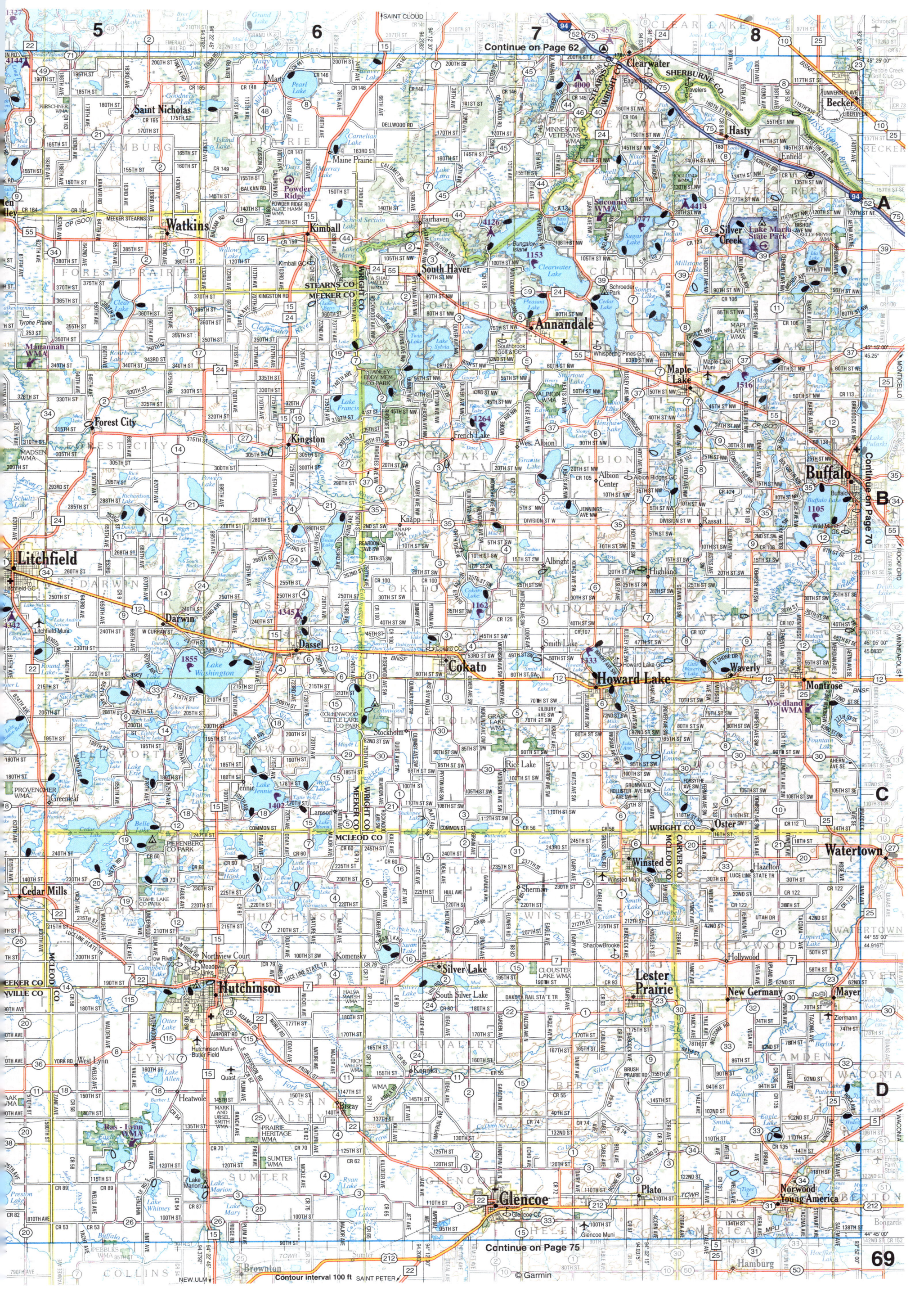

Continue on Page 70

Contour interval 100 ft

© Garmin

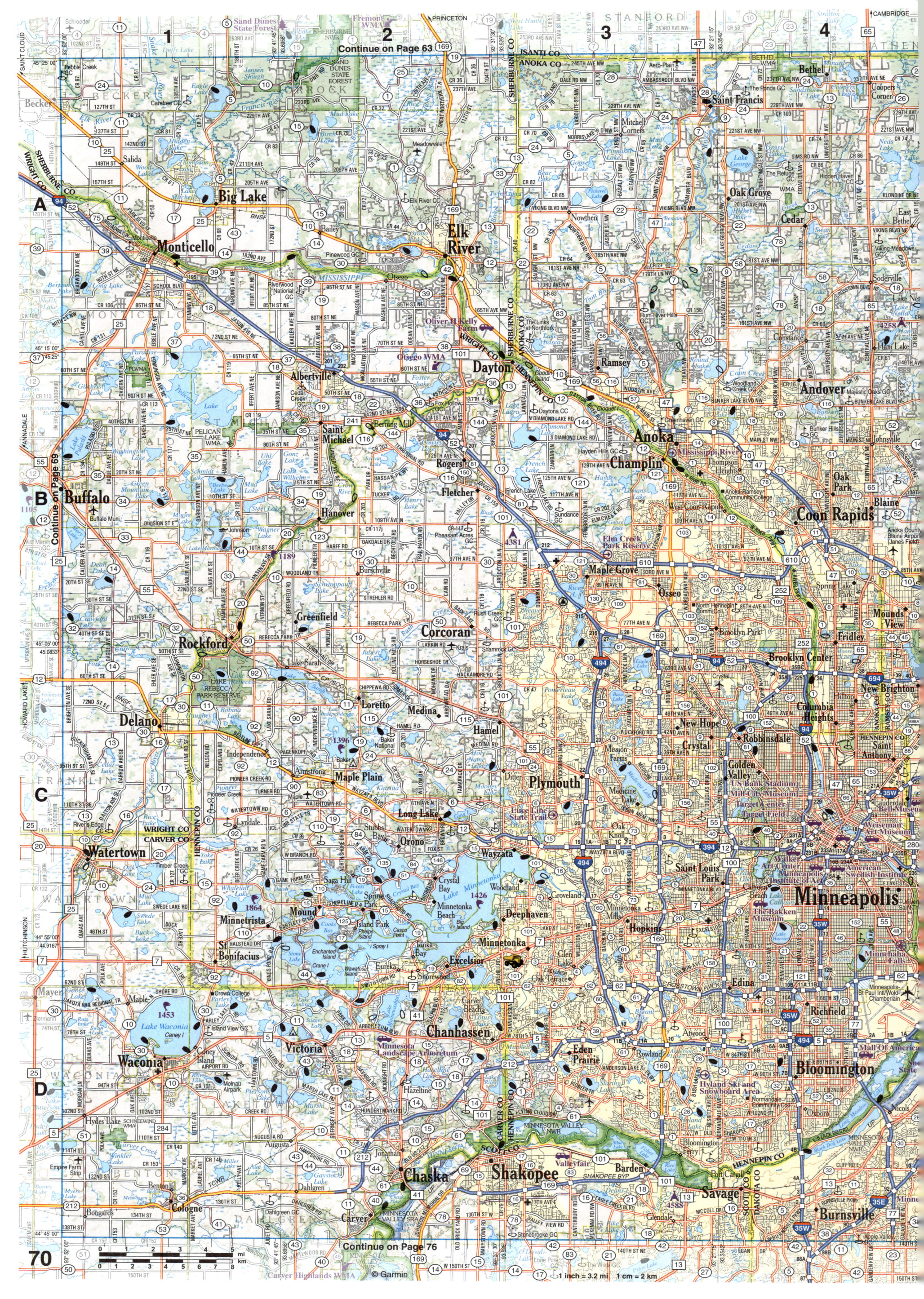

Continue on Page 63

Continue on Page 69

Continue on Page 76

© Garmin

1 inch = 3.2 mi.   1 cm = 2 km

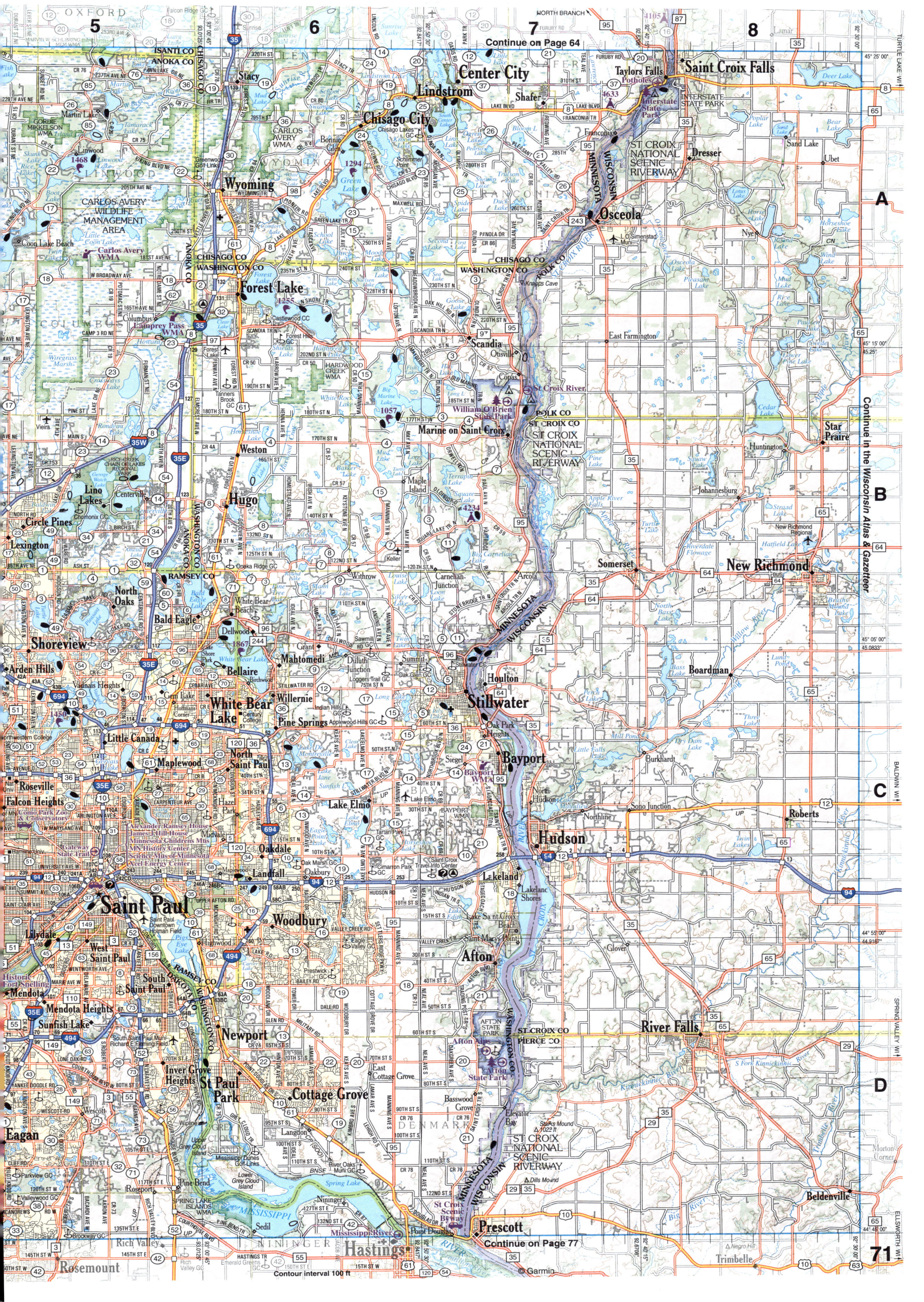

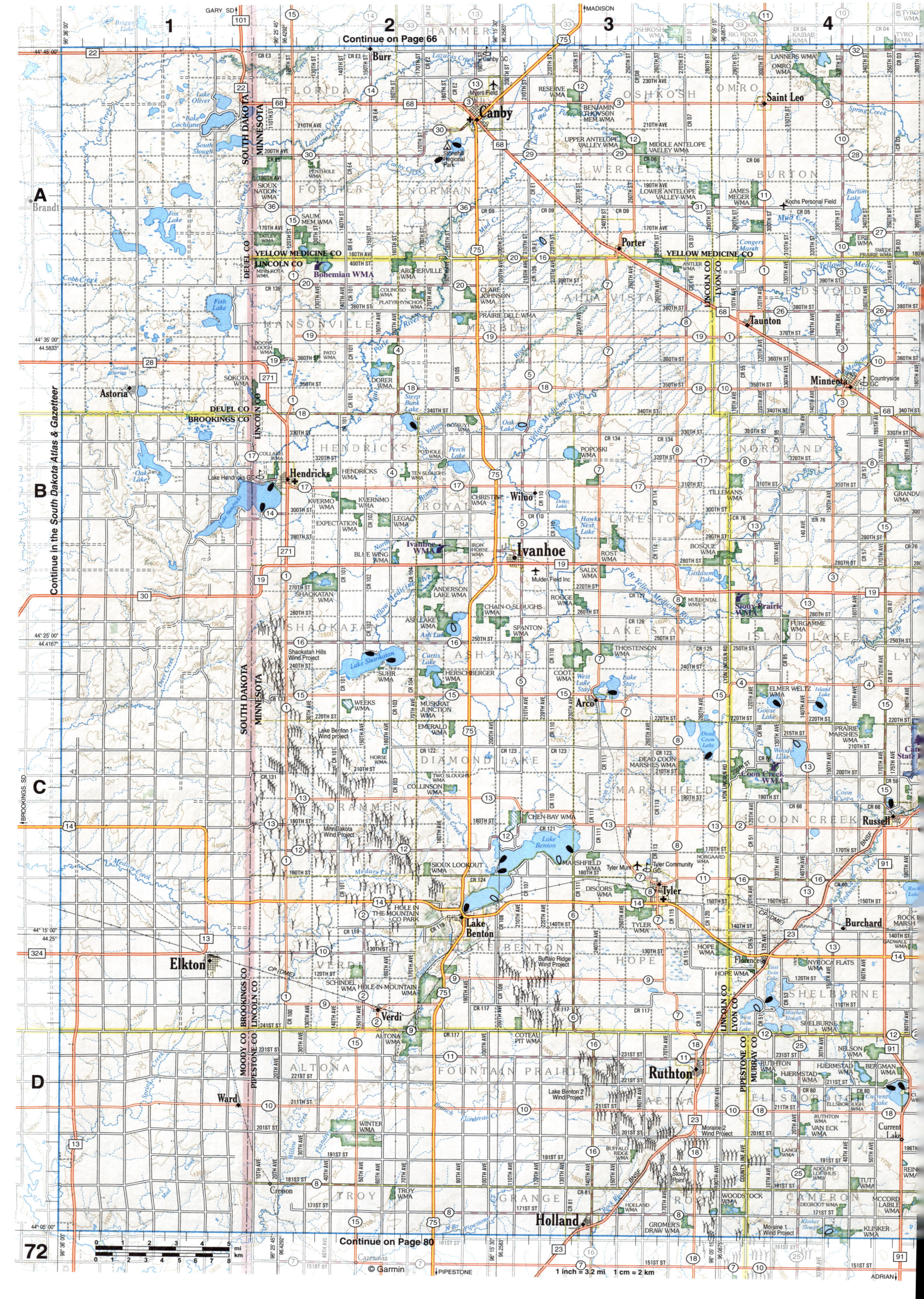

Continue on Page 66

Continue on Page 80

© Garmin

1 inch = 3.2 mi   1 cm = 2 km

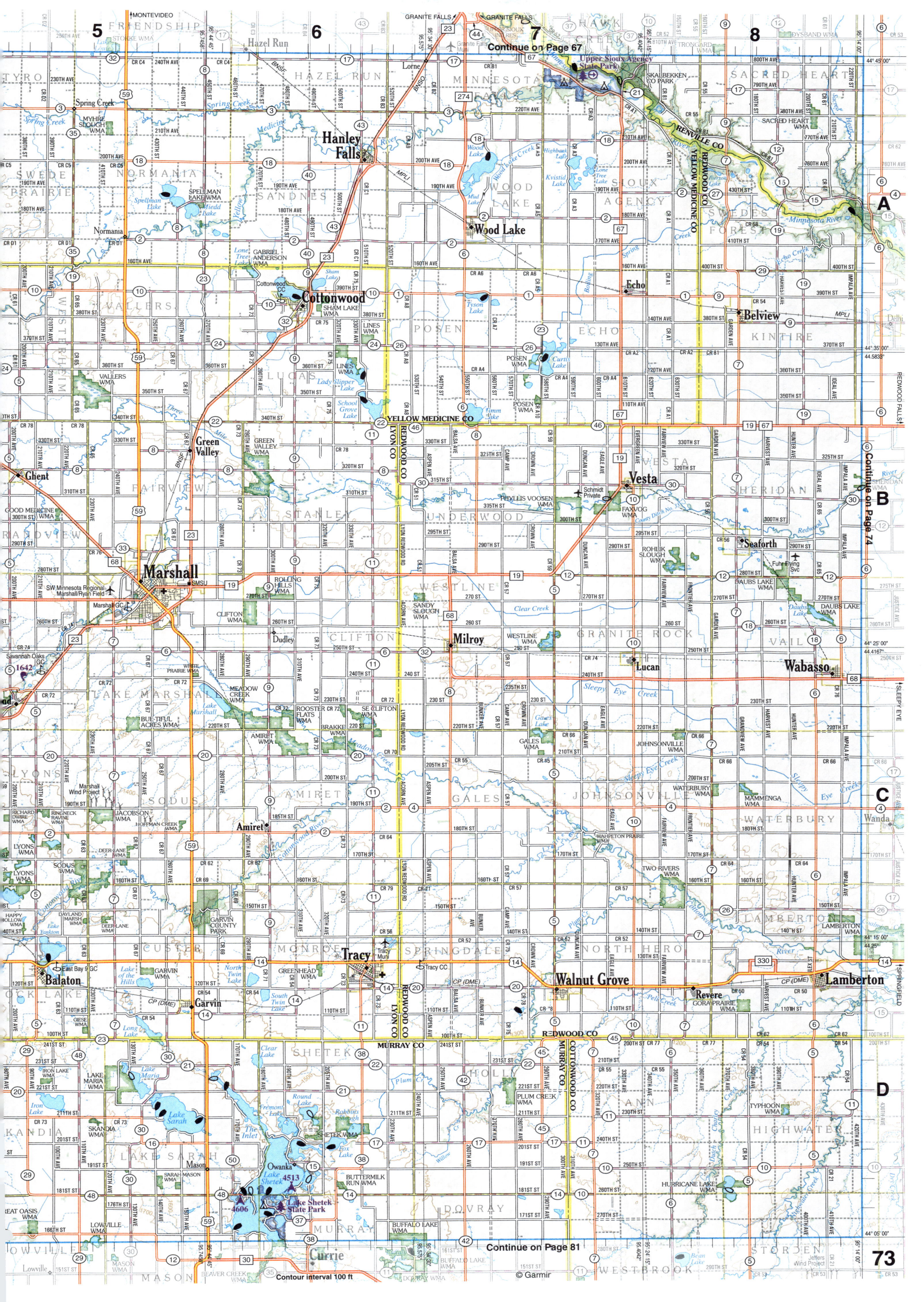

Continue on Page 67

Continue on Page 74

Continue on Page 81

Contour interval 100 ft

© Garmin

73

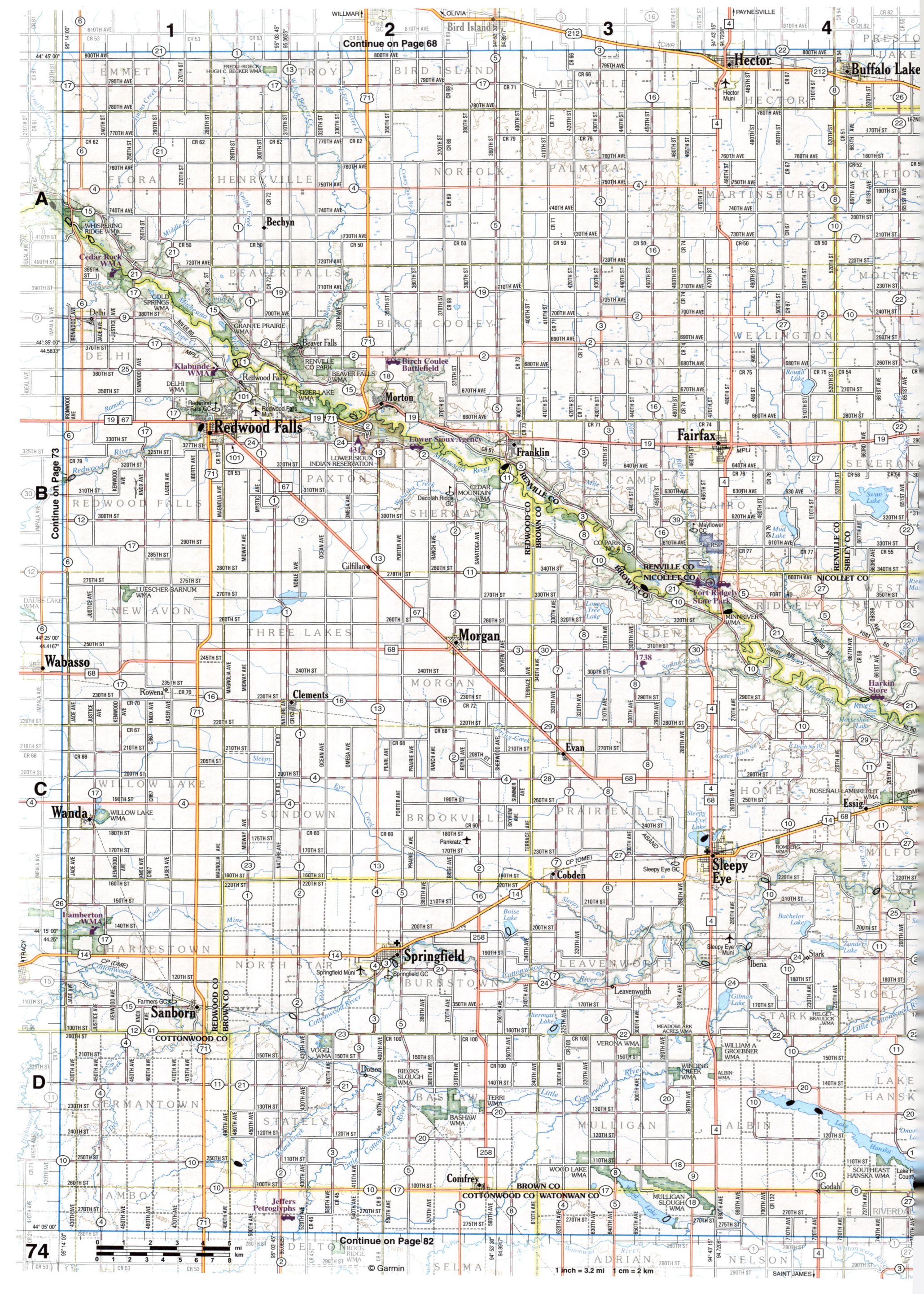

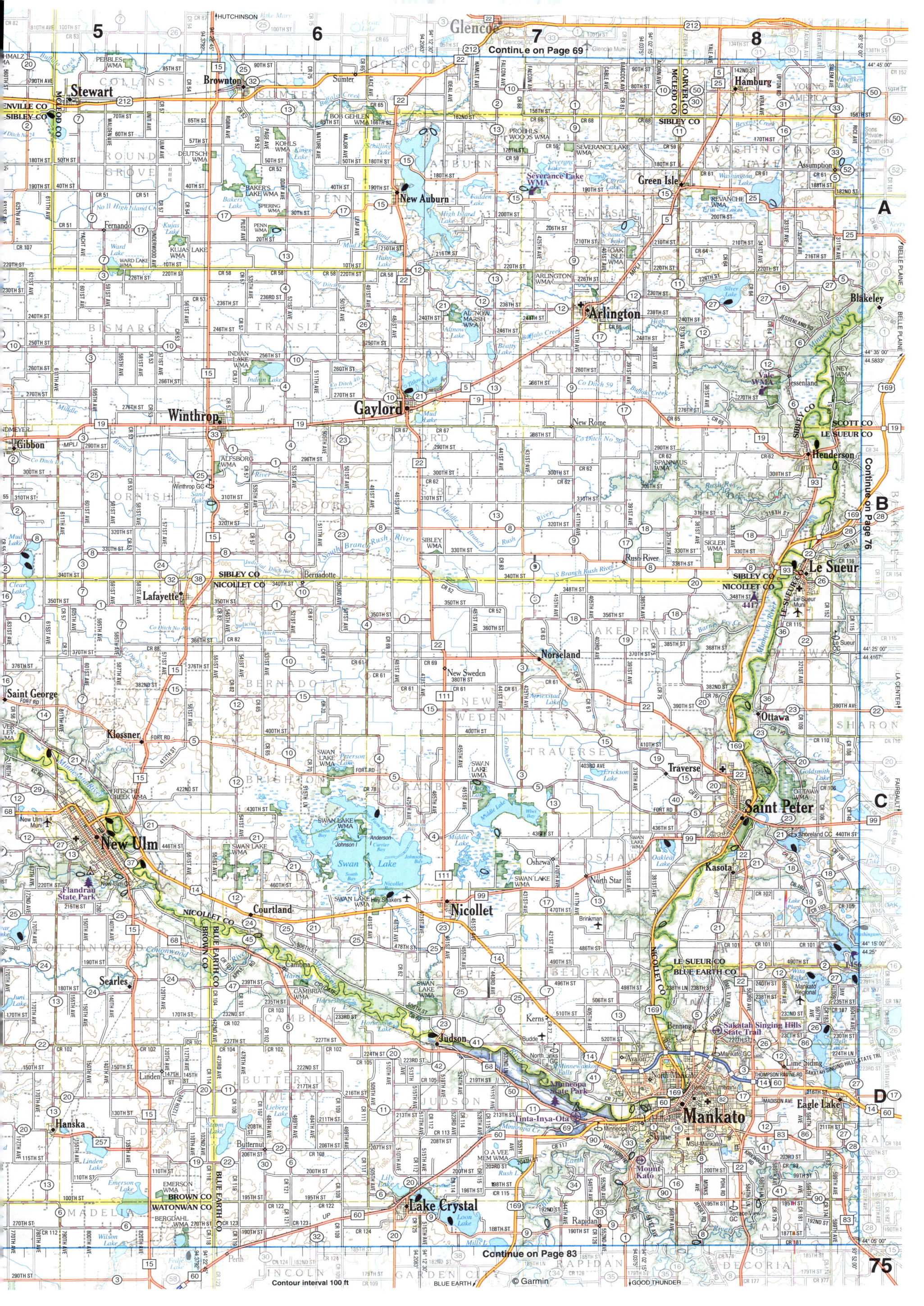

Continue on Page 69

Continue on Page 76

Continue on Page 83

Contour interval 100 ft   © Garmin

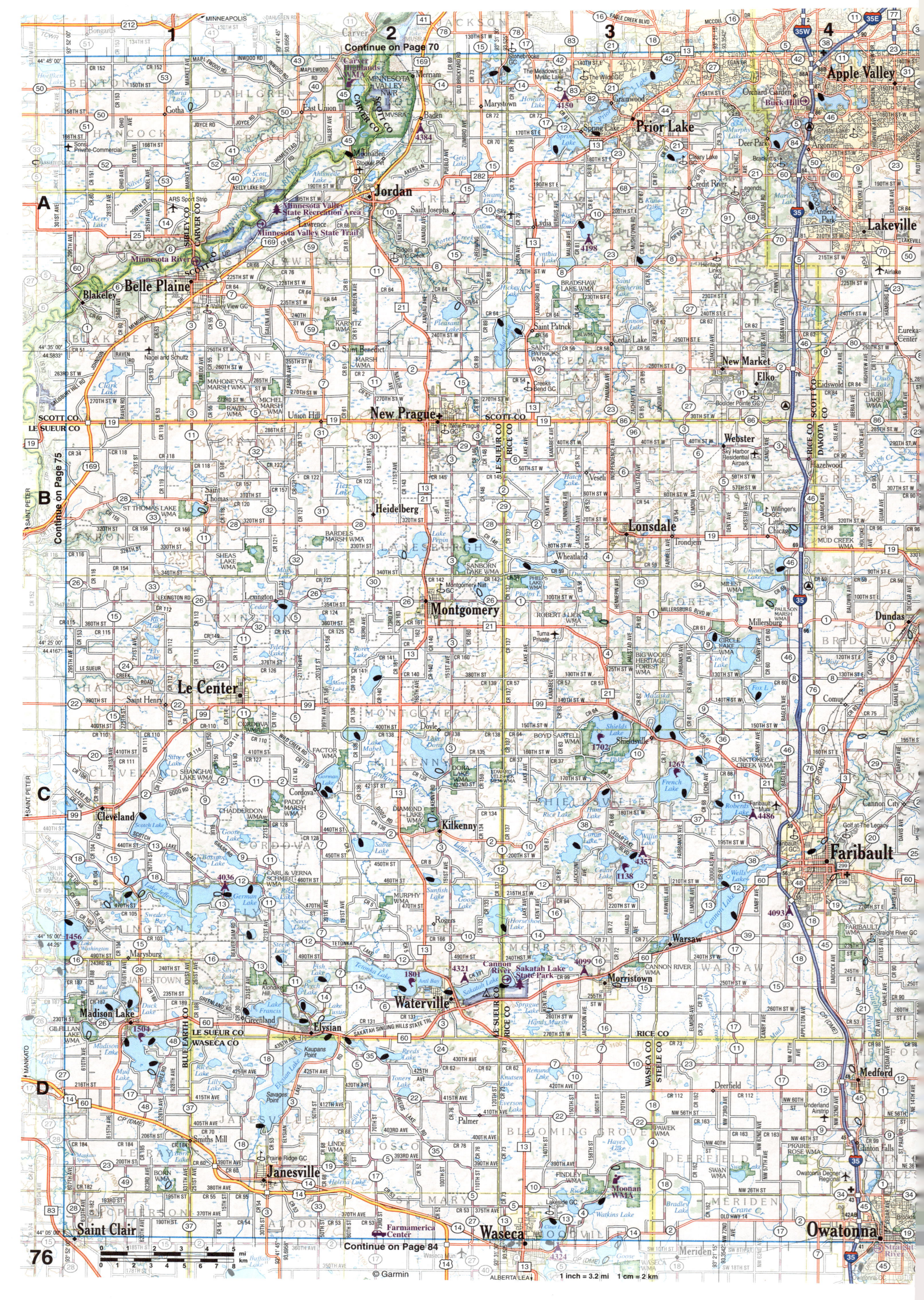

Continue on Page 70

Continue on Page 75

A

B

C

D

Apple Valley

Lakeville

Prior Lake

Jordan

Belle Plaine

Blakeley

New Market

Elko

New Prague

Webster

Lonsdale

Dundas

Heidelberg

Montgomery

Le Center

Faribault

Cleveland

Kilkenny

Cannon City

Cordova

Warsaw

Waterville

Morristown

Madison Lake

Elysian

Medford

Janesville

Saint Clair

Waseca

Owatonna

Continue on Page 84

mi
km
0 1 2 3 4 5 6

© Garmin

1 inch = 3.2 mi   1 cm = 2 km

Continue on Page 78

Contour interval 100 ft

© Garmin

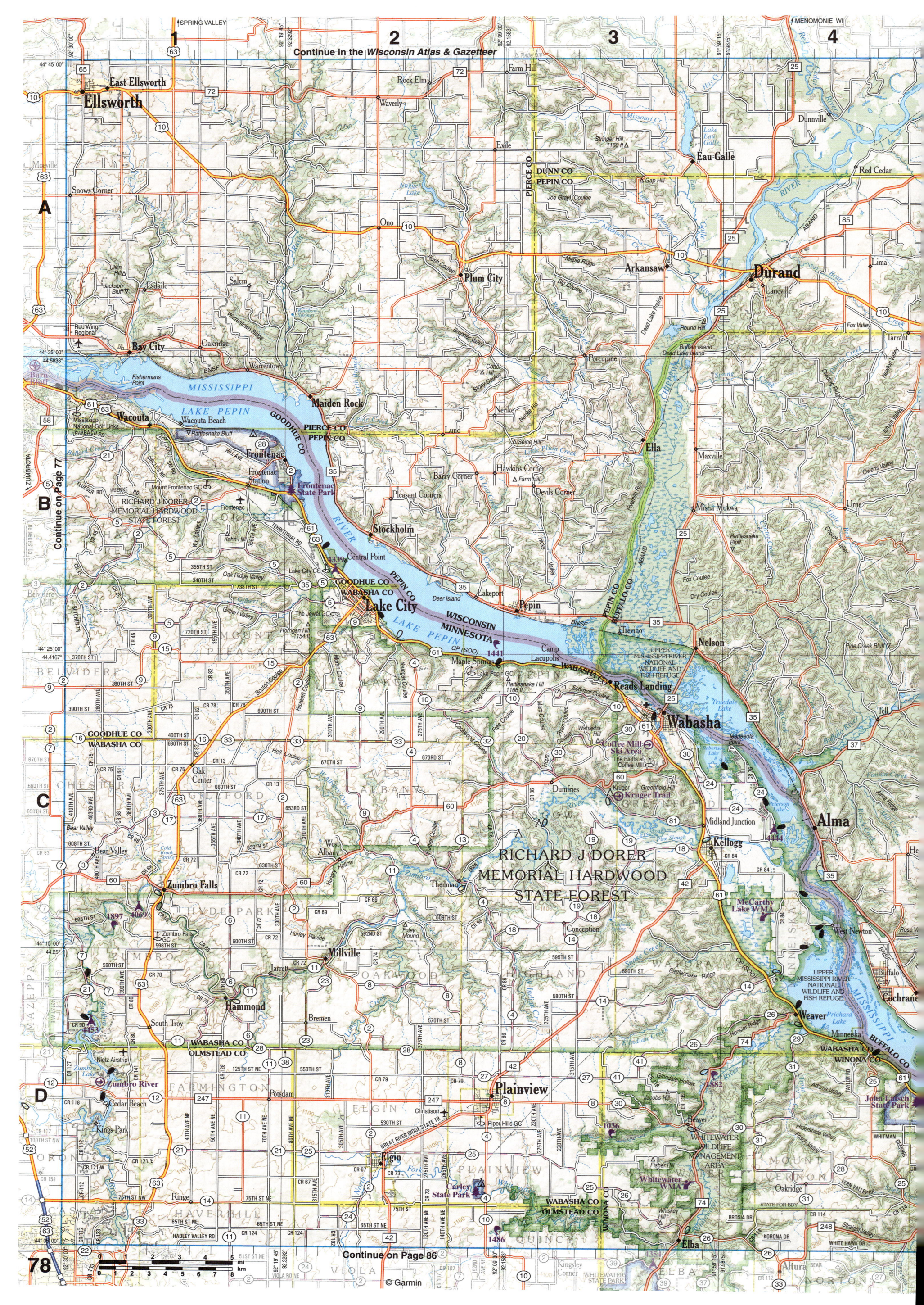

Continue on Page 77

Continue on Page 86

© Garmin

5   6   7   8

Meridean
Caryville
Rock Falls
Candy Corners
Mount Hope Corners
Brackett
Cleghorn
Nix Corner
Foster
Hale Corner
Augusta
Rodell
Moldenhauer Hill

DUNN CO
PEPIN CO
EAU CLAIRE CO
PEPIN CO

A

EAU CLAIRE CO
BUFFALO CO
TREMPEALEAU CO
BUFFALO CO

Steinke Valley
Mondovi
Eleva
Strum
Osseo

EAU CLAIRE CO
TREMPEALEAU CO
JACKSON CO
TREMPEALEAU CO

Chimney Rock
Tom Mountain
Gilmanton
Modena
Lookout
Chimney Rock
Pleasantville
Hale
York

Eagle Peak

B

Praag
Russell
Elk Creek
Coral City
Pigeon Falls

Montana
Independence
Whitehall
Taylor

Waumandee
Larkin Valley
Gransberg Hill
Blair
Blair

C

Cream
Glencoe
North Creek
Weaver Hill
Welch Coulee
Square Bluff

Arcadia
Chapultepec
Upper French Creek
Iduna
Hess
Franklin
Beachs Corners

Wagners Coulee

D

WISCONSIN
MINNESOTA
Fountain City
Tamarack
Frenchville
Ettrick

UPPER MISSISSIPPI RIVER NATIONAL WILDLIFE AND FISH REFUGE

TREMPEALEAU CO
BUFFALO CO

Pine Creek
Dodge
Johnson Peak
Platt Valley

ngstone
Minnesota City

Peacock Hill
North Bend

Galesville

Contour interval 100 ft

© Garmin

Butman Corners

79

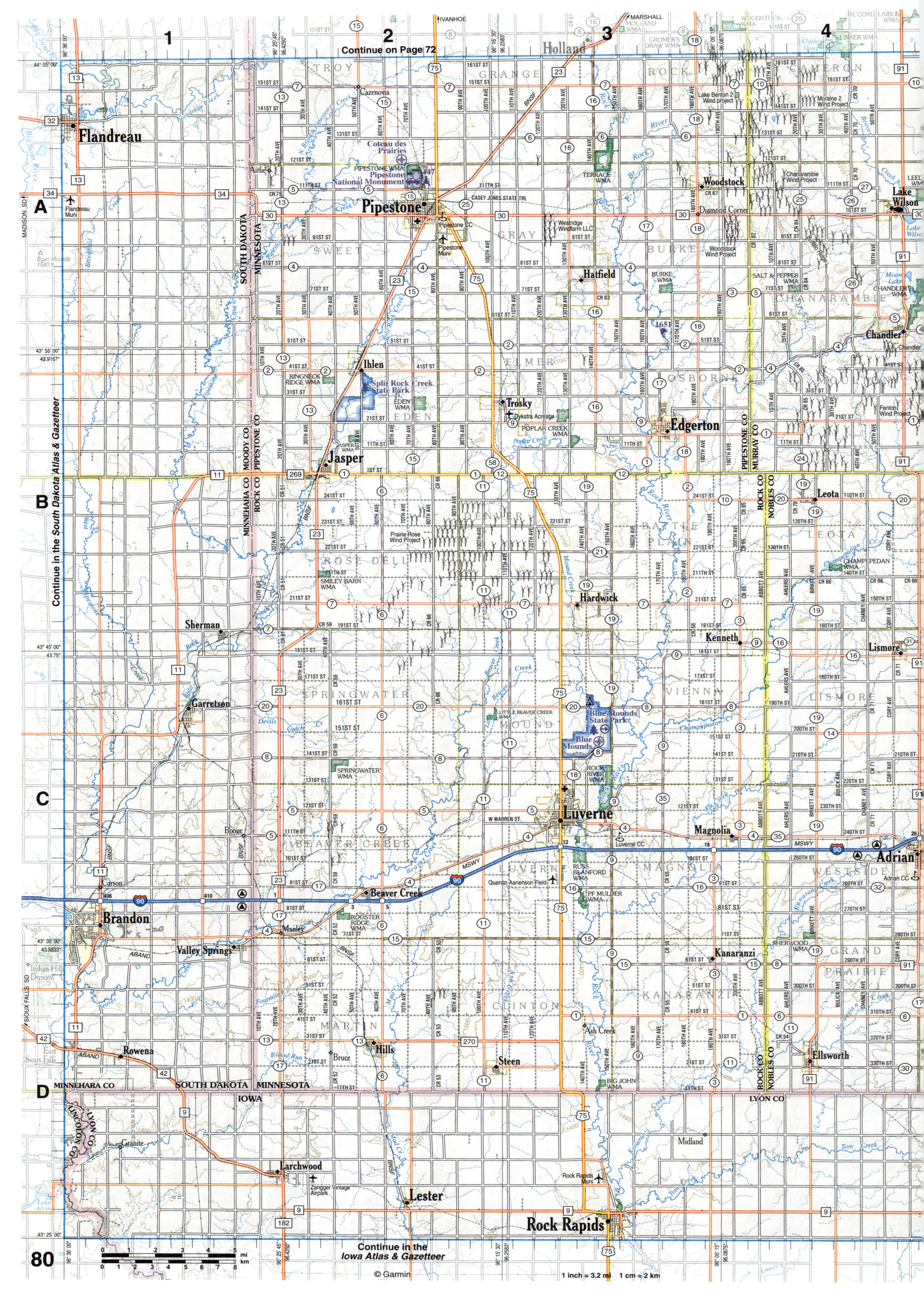

Continue on Page 72

1 **2** **3** **4**

A

B

C

D

Flandreau

Pipestone

Hatfield

Woodstock

Lake Wilson

Chandler

Ihlen

Trosky

Edgerton

Jasper

Leota

Sherman

Hardwick

Kenneth

Lismore

Garretson

Luverne

Magnolia

Adrian

Brandon

Beaver Creek

Valley Springs

Kanaranzi

Rowena

Hills

Steen

Ellsworth

Larchwood

Lester

Rock Rapids

Continue in the Iowa Atlas & Gazetteer

© Garmin

1 inch = 3.2 mi   1 cm = 2 km

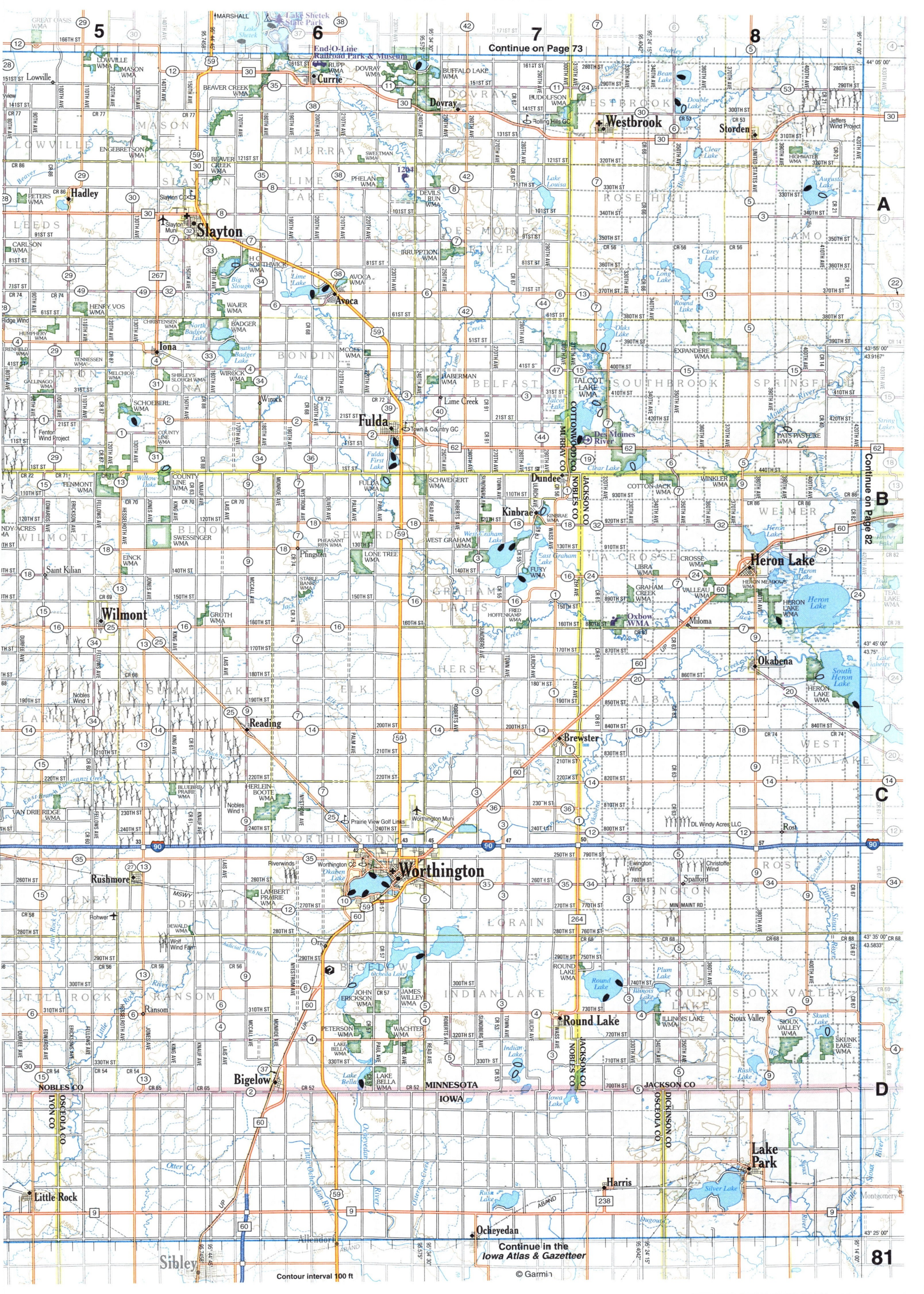

Continue on Page 73

Continue on Page 82

Great Oasis WMA
Lake Shetek State Park
End-O-Line Railroad Park & Museum
Marshall

Lowville
Lowville WMA
Mason WMA
Currie
Beaver Creek WMA
Dovray Buffalo Lake WMA
Rudolfson WMA
Westbrook
Storden
Jeffers Wind Project
Rolling Hills GC
MASON
MURRAY
Sweetman WMA
Phelan WMA
Devils Run WMA
WESTBROOK
Clear Lake
Augusta Lake
Hadley
SLAYTON
LIME LAKE
Slayton Co
DES MOINES RIVER
ROSE HILL
STORDEN
Highwater WMA
A
Peters WMA
Carey Lake
Long Lake
Slayton Muni
Northwick
Big Slough
Lime Lake
Avoca WMA
Avoca
IRRUPTION WMA
Round Lake
LEEDS
CARLSON WMA
Henry Vos WMA
Humphrey WMA
Christensen WMA
Wajer WMA
Badger WMA
North Badger Lake
South Badger Lake
McCoe WMA
HABERMAN WMA
BELFAST
Talcot Lake WMA
SOUTHBROOK
SPRINGFIELD
Oaks Lake
EXPANDERE WMA
PATS PASTURE
Freenfield WMA
Iona
Melchior WMA
Tennessen WMA
Gallinago WMA
IONA
Shirley's Slough WMA
Wirock WMA
Wirock
BONDIN
Lime Creek
Des Moines River
Talcot Lake
Clear Lake
WEIMER
Fenton Wind Project
Schoeberl WMA
Fulda
Town & Country GC
Fulda First Lake
County Line WMA
MURRAY CO
COTTONWOOD CO
NOBLES CO
JACKSON CO
FENMONT WMA
Wilton WMA
Fulda WMA
SCHWEIGERT WMA
Dundee
COTTON-JACK WMA
WINKLER WMA
Heron Lake
B
BLOOM
Swessinger WMA
EINCK WMA
Kinbrae
West Graham WMA
West Graham Lake
East Graham Lake
LA CROSSE
CROSSE WMA
LIBRA WMA
Heron Lake
HERON MEADOWS
Saint Kilian
Phingsten
LONE TREE WMA
PHEASANT RUN WMA
GRAHAM LAKES
FURY WMA
GRAHAM CREEK WMA
VALLEAU WMA
Oxbow WMA
Miloma
HERON LAKE WMA
Wilmont
WILMONT
GROTH WMA
STABLE BANKS WMA
FRED HOFFENKAMP WMA
HERSEY
ELK
ALBA
Okabena
South Heron Lake
HERON LAKE WMA
SUMMIT LAKE
LARKIN
Reading
WEST HERON LAKE
VAN DRIE RIDGE WMA
Nobles Wind 1
HERLEIN-BOOTH WMA
BLUEBIRD PRAIRIE WMA
Nobles Wind 1
Brewster
DL Windy Acres LLC
Ross
C
Prairie View Golf Links
Worthington Muni
WORTHINGTON
Ewington Wind
Christoffer Wind
Spafford
EWINGTON
Rushmore
Riverwinds
Worthington
Okabena Lake
LAMBERT PRAIRIE WMA
OLNEY
DEWALD
MSWY
Rohwer
DEWALD WMA
Wolf Wind Farm
LORAIN
LITTLE ROCK
RANSOM
Ransom
BIGELOW
Ocheda Lake
INDIAN LAKE
Round Lake
Plum Lake
ROUND LAKE WMA
Illinois Lake
ROUND SIOUX VALLEY
SIOUX VALLEY WMA
JOHN ERICKSON WMA
JAMES WILLEY WMA
WACHTER WMA
PETERSON WMA
LAKE BELLA WMA
Round Lake
Indian Lake
Illinois Lake
Sioux Valley
Skunk Lake
SKUNK LAKE WMA
Bigelow
Lake Bella
Lake Bella WMA
NOBLES CO
OSCEOLA CO
JACKSON CO
DICKINSON CO
Rush Lake
D
NOBLES CO
MINNESOTA
IOWA
LYON CO
OSCEOLA CO
Lake Park
Little Rock
Harris
Silver Lake
Ocheyedan

Continue in the Iowa Atlas & Gazetteer

Sibley

Contour interval 100 ft

© Garmin

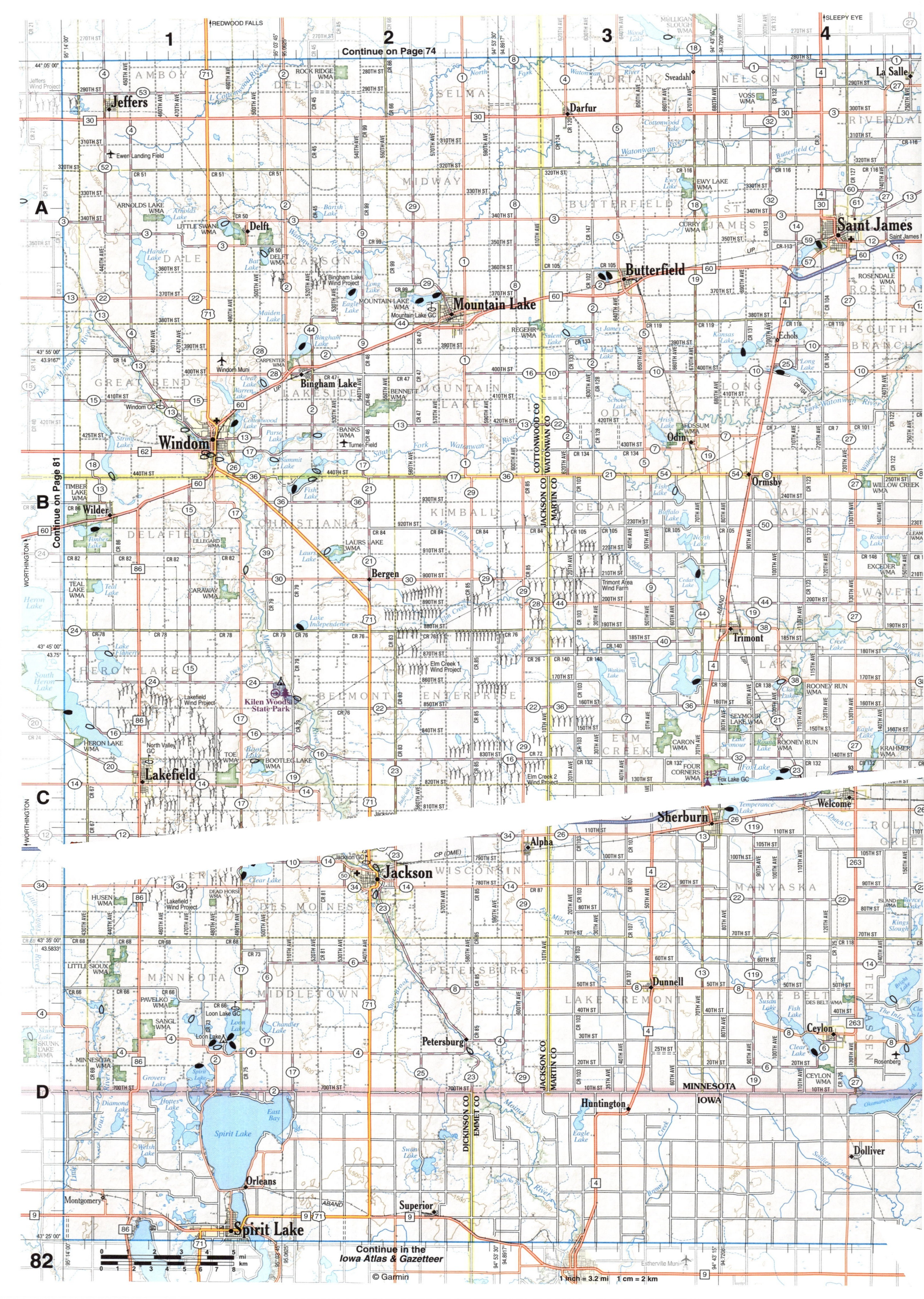

Continue on Page 74

Continue on Page 81

1   2   3   4

A

B

C

D

82

Continue in the
Iowa Atlas & Gazetteer

© Garmin

1 inch = 3.2 mi   1 cm = 2 km

Continue on Page 76

Continue on Page 83

Continue in the
Iowa Atlas & Gazetteer

© Garmin

1 inch = 3.2 mi   1 cm = 2 km

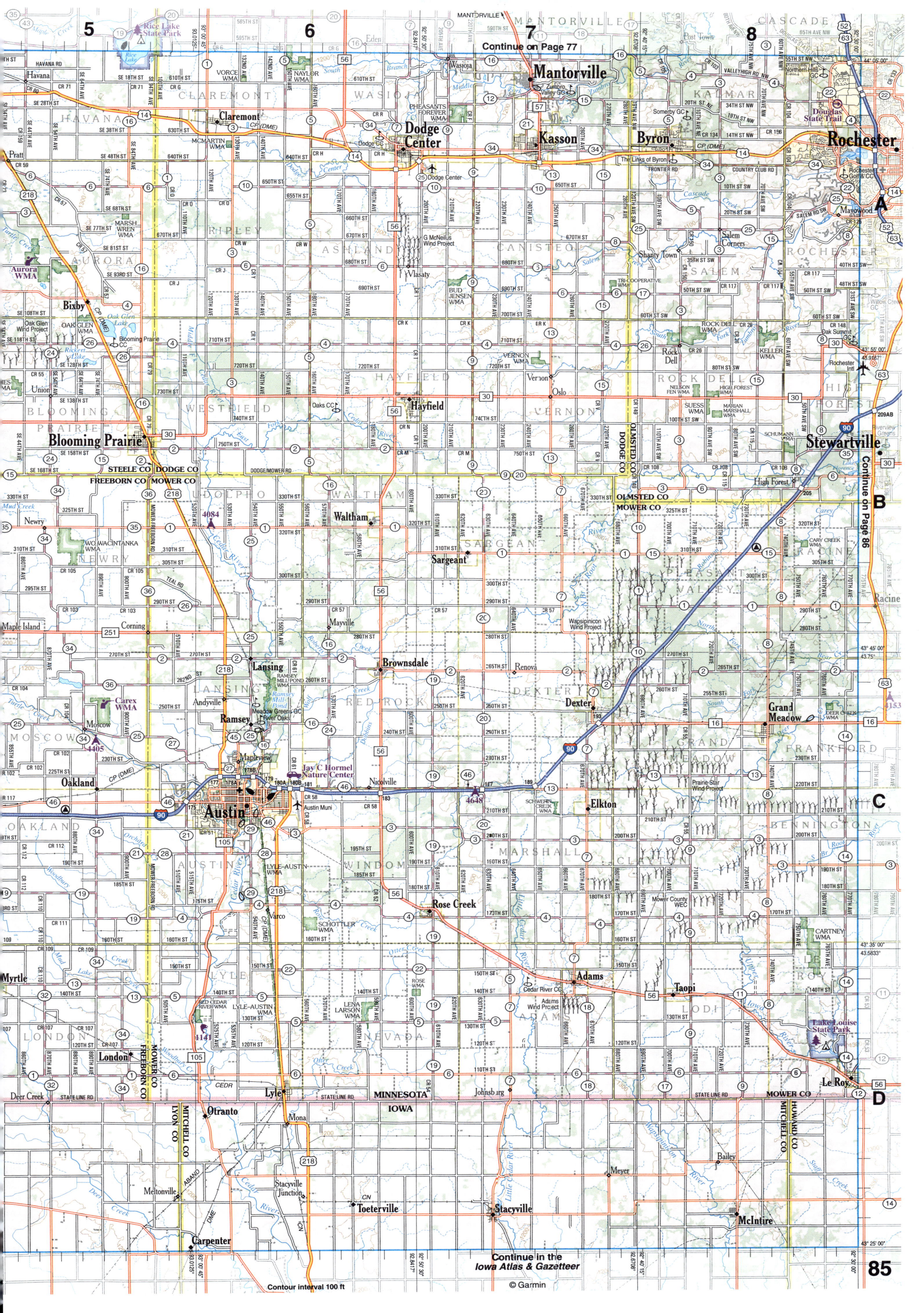

Continue on Page 77

Continue in the
Iowa Atlas & Gazetteer

Contour interval 100 ft

© Garmin

Continue on Page 78

Continue on Page 85

1   **2**   **3**   **4**

A

B

C

D

Rochester

Stewartville

Chatfield

Fountain

Lanesboro

Whalan

Preston

Spring Valley

Wykoff

Racine

Ostrander

Etna

Mystery
Cave

Greenleafton

Harmony

Canton

York

Granger

Chester

Lime Springs

Viola

Eyota

Dover

Saint Charles

Utica

Lewiston

Troy

Simpson

Marion

Predmore

Pleasant Grove

Cummingsville

Saratoga

Clyde

Fremont

Altura

RICHARD J DORER
MEMORIAL HARDWOOD
STATE FOREST

Whitewater
State Park

Chimney
Rock

RICHARD J DORER
MEMORIAL HARDWOOD
STATE FOREST

RICHARD J DORER
MEMORIAL HARDWOOD
STATE FOREST

RICHARD J DORE

STAT

Forestville/Mystery Cave
State Park

Forestville

Carimona

Big Spring

Cherry Grove

Bristol

Lenora

Henrytown

Ainherst

Niagara
Cave

Prosper

Douglas

Burr Oak

Kendallville

Bonair

Florenceville

MINNESOTA

IOWA

MOWER CO

FILLMORE CO

OLMSTED CO

WINONA CO

FILLMORE CO

HOWARD CO

WINNESHIEK CO

Continue in the
Iowa Atlas & Gazetteer

0 1 2 3 4 5 mi
0 1 2 3 4 5 6 7 8 km

© Garmin

1 inch = 3.2 mi   1 cm = 2 km

NEW HAMPTON IA   DECORAH IA

Continue on Page 79

Continue in the Wisconsin Atlas & Gazetteer

Name, Location	Page & Grid	Acreage	Deer	Bear	Rabbit	Turkey	Sharptail Grouse	Ruffed Grouse	Pheasant	Dove	Waterfowl
Agassiz-Olson WMA, Flaming	29 D6	1,532	●						●		
Aitkin WMA, Hassman	55 A6	3,138	●	●	●		●	●			
Amor WMA, Amor	52 B1	720	●	●	●	●			●		
Anchor Lake WMA, Melrude	47 A5	180	●	●	●			●			
Ann Lake WMA, Ogilvie	63 B7	1,702	●	●	●	●		●	●		●
Athens WMA, Isanti	63 D8	192	●	●	●	●			●		
Aurora WMA, Bixby	85 A5	639	●		●	●			●	●	●
Barnesville WMA, Rollag	51 A6	1,630	●						●		
Bayport WMA, Bayport	71 C7	452	●		●	●			●		
Beaches Lake WMA, Lancaster	16 D4	17,652	●		●		●		●		●
Bejou WMA, Bejou	29 D8	1,937	●		●				●		
Benville WMA, Grygla	22 C3	1,194	●		●		●		●		
Birchdale WMA, Little Pine	55 A5	1,426	●	●	●				●		
Blackhoof River WMA, Blackhoof	57 B5	3,798	●	●	●			●			
Bohemian WMA, Burr	72 A2	665	●		●				●	●	●
Brandsvold WMA, Fosston	30 C1	144	●		●				●		
Burbank WMA, New London	68 A2	447	●		●	●			●		●
Burgen Lake Prairie WMA, Nimrod	53 A7	2,281	●	●	●				●		
Burnham WMA, Melvin	29 C6	990	●		●				●		●
Caerulean WMA, Bellingham	66 B2	187	●		●				●		
Callaway WMA, Galloway	42 C1	317	●		●			●			
Camp Kerk WMA, Swift Falls	67 A8	1,023	●		●				●		
Canosia WMA, Four Corners	47 D6	2,489	●		●			●			
Carex WMA, Moscow	85 C5	332	●		●	●			●	●	●
Caribou WMA, Caribou	17 C5	13,659	●	●	●		●		●		
Carlos Avery WMA, Linwood	71 A5	23,747	●	●	●	●		●	●		●
Carp Swamp WMA, Baudette	23 A8	14,014	●	●	●			●			●
Carver Highlands WMA, Carver	76 A2	302			●	●			●		
Cedar Rock WMA, Delhi	74 A1	640	●		●	●			●		
Chicog WMA, Melvin	29 C6	2,434	●		●				●		●
Clair Rollings WMA, Benson	67 A2	401	●		●				●		
Coon Creek WMA, Russell	72 C4	1,049	●		●				●	●	●
Crane WMA, Roland	30 B2	985	●	●	●	●			●		
Crow Wing Chain WMA, Badoura	43 D7	3,267	●	●	●	●		●			●
Dalbo WMA, Carmody	63 C7	2,802	●		●	●			●		
Danvers WMA, Danvers	67 A6	2,950	●		●				●	●	●
Duck Lake WMA, Emily	54 A4	1,041	●	●	●	●			●		
Dugdale WMA, Tilden Junction	29 C6	960	●	●	●	●			●		
East Park WMA, Newfolden	21 B6	10,427	●	●	●		●	●	●		
Eckvoll WMA, Gatzke	22 C1	6,499	●	●	●			●			
Eldorado WMA, Herman	59 C7	300	●		●				●	●	●
Elm Lake WMA, Holt	21 D8	15,560	●		●		●		●		
Elmo WMA, Almora	52 C4	1,508	●		●				●		●
Ereaux WMA, Belle Prairie	62 A2	527	●		●	●		●	●	●	
Erskine WMA, Erskine	29 C8	1,221	●		●		●		●		●
Espelie WMA, Espelie	22 C2	3,644	●	●	●		●	●			
Fireweed WMA, Fourtown	22 D4	2,266	●	●	●			●			
Florian WMA, Florian	21 B5	1,529	●	●	●				●		●
Florida Creek WMA, Haydenville	66 D2	849	●		●				●		●
Forada WMA, Forada	60 B4	829	●		●	●			●		
Four Brooks WMA, Page	63 A6	3,670	●	●	●			●			
Freemont WMA, Lake Fremont	63 D6	165	●		●	●			●		●
Glendorado WMA, Glendorado	63 D5	213	●		●	●			●		
Godfrey WMA, Melvin	29 C6	145	●	●	●				●		
Gold Portage WMA, Island View	26 B1	902									●
Gordon W. Yeager WMA, Rochester	86 A1	241	●		●	●			●		
Gores Pool #3 WMA, Etter	77 A7	6,449	●		●	●			●		●
Graceton WMA, Graceton	19 D7	10,709	●	●	●		●	●			●
Graham WMA, Morrill	62 B4	369	●		●	●		●			
Grayling Marsh WMA, Minnewawa	55 A8	9,634	●	●	●			●			●
Great Scott WMA, Scott	34 D3	284	●		●			●			
Grey Eagle WMA, Ward Springs	61 B7	1,400	●		●	●	●		●	●	●
Grygla WMA, Grygla	22 C2	3,366	●	●	●			●			
Halma Swamp WMA, Halma	20 A4	840	●	●	●		●		●		
Hamre WMA, Jelle	22 D3	4,530	●	●	●			●			
Happy Valley WMA, Holdingford	62 B1	206	●		●	●			●		
Haydenville WMA, Haydenville	66 C2	464	●		●				●		●
Higinbotham WMA, Saint Hilaire	29 A6	984	●		●				●		
Hubbel Pond WMA, Detroit Lakes	42 D2	3,342	●	●	●			●	●		●
Huntly WMA, Strathcona	21 B7	6,506	●	●	●		●		●		
Inman WMA, Almora	52 C4	1,324	●		●				●		●
Ivanhoe WMA, Ivanhoe	72 B2	382	●		●				●	●	●
Jossart WMA, Benson	67 A2	160	●		●				●		
Kibler WMA, Bellingham	66 B2	654	●		●				●		●
Kimberly Marsh WMA, McGregor	55 B8	10,596	●	●	●			●			●
Klabunde WMA, Redwood Falls	74 B1	202	●		●				●		
Kunkel WMA, Brickton	63 D6	2,635	●	●	●	●			●		●
Lac qui Parle WMA, Churchill	67 C5	33,490	●		●	●			●	●	●
Lake Five WMA, Sandstone	56 D1	276	●		●			●			
Lamberton WMA, Sanborn	74 C1	642	●		●				●		

Name, Location	Page & Grid	Acreage	Deer	Bear	Rabbit	Turkey	Sharptail Grouse	Ruffed Grouse	Pheasant	Dove	Waterfowl
Lamprey Pass WMA, Forest Lake	71 A5	1,332	●	●	●				●	●	●
Lee WMA, Jelle	22 D3	2,244	●	●	●			●	●	●	
Liberty WMA, Melvin	29 D6	1,360	●		●				●		
Little Elk WMA, Browerville	61 A8	1,480	●		●			●	●		●
Long Prairie River WMA, Browerville	53 D7	965	●		●			●			
Lost Marsh WMA, Pemberton	84 A1	329	●		●				●		●
Manannah WMA, Forest City	69 B5	320	●		●	●			●	●	●
Maple Meadows WMA, Maple Bay	29 C7	1,360	●		●				●		●
McCarthy Lake WMA, West Newton	78 C4	2,886	●		●	●		●			●
Meadow Brook WMA, Casino	53 B8	5,772	●		●			●			●
Mentor Prairie WMA, Mentor	29 C7	2,144	●		●				●		●
Mille Lacs WMA, Page	63 A6	38,729	●	●	●			●			●
Mission Lake WMA, Crosby	54 B3	118	●		●			●			
Moonan WMA, Meriden	76 D3	955	●		●	●			●	●	●
Moose River WMA, Carmel	22 C3	21,275	●	●	●			●			●
Moose-Willow WMA, Hill City	45 C6	16,946	●	●	●			●			●
Morph Meadows WMA, Pennington	32 D2	4,894	●	●	●			●			●
Mosquito Creek WMA, Minerva	30 D3	747	●		●				●		
Mound Prairie WMA, Mound Prairie	87 B7	378	●		●	●		●		●	
Mud Goose WMA, Elevenmile Corner	44 B4	17,055	●	●	●			●			●
Mulejohn WMA, Weme	30 C2	122	●		●				●		
Neal WMA, Syre	41 B6	1,673	●		●		●		●		
Nereson WMA, Wannaska	21 A8	9,583	●	●	●		●	●	●		
New Maine WMA, Middle River	21 B6	2,667	●	●	●		●		●		
North Germany WMA, Nimrod	53 A6	278	●	●	●			●			
Numo WMA, Watson	67 C6	140	●		●				●	●	●
Ogema Springs WMA, Ogema	41 C8	508	●		●				●		
Old Red Lake Trail WMA, Leonard	30 C4	1,135	●	●	●			●			
Oleander WMA, Sunburg	68 A1	376	●		●				●		●
Orwell WMA, Western	51 D7	2,129	●		●				●		●
Otsego WMA, Rogers	70 B2	200	●		●	●		●	●		●
Oxbow WMA, Miloma	81 B7	236	●		●				●		●
Palmville WMA, Torfin	22 A1	14,891	●	●	●		●	●	●		
Pelan WMA, Pelan	21 A5	3,610	●	●	●		●		●		
Pembina WMA, Dorothy	29 A5	4,097	●		●		●		●		
Polk WMA, Erskine	29 C8	2,764	●		●				●		●
Prairie Lake Deer Yard WMA, Canisteo	45 A7	600	●	●	●			●			
Ras-Lynn WMA, Hutchinson	69 D1	1,224	●		●				●	●	●
Red Lake WMA, Fuance	23 B5	320,149	●	●	●		●	●	●	●	●
Ripple River WMA, Glory	55 B6	5,274	●	●	●			●			●
Rock Marsh WMA, Benson	64 C3	623	●		●				●		●
Roseau River WMA, Pinecreek	17 C8	74,784	●	●	●		●	●	●		●
Rothsay WMA, Lawndale	51 B6	3,891	●		●		●		●		●
Ruff-Nik WMA, Cushing	53 D8	1,059	●	●	●			●	●		
Rush WMA, Beaulieu	42 A1	715	●	●	●			●		●	
Salo Marsh WMA, Tamarack	56 A1	2,030	●	●	●			●			●
Sax WMA, Sax Station	46 B4	954	●	●	●			●			
Sem WMA, Espelie	22 D2	2,838	●	●	●			●			
Severance Lake WMA, Arlington	75 A7	54	●		●				●	●	●
Sioux Prairie WMA, Arco	72 B4	387	●		●				●	●	●
Skull Lake WMA, Lancaster	16 C4	7,452	●		●		●		●		●
Somerset WMA, Owatonna	84 A4	394	●		●	●			●		●
Spectacle WMA, West Point	63 D7	511	●		●	●			●		●
Staples WMA, Staples	53 C7	1,428	●		●			●	●		
Suconnix WMA, Annandale	69 A7	1,006	●		●	●		●	●		●
Swan River Deer Yard WMA, Swan River	4568	909	●	●	●			●			
Teal Scurry WMA, Manannah	68 A4	158	●		●				●		●
Thief Lake WMA, Gatzke	22 B1	54,957	●	●	●		●	●	●		●
Timber Doodle WMA, Brooks	29 C8	158	●		●			●	●		●
Twin Lakes WMA, Karlstad	21 A5	8,874	●	●	●		●		●		●
Twin Valley WMA, Syre	41 B6	919	●		●		●		●		
Tympanuchus WMA, Benoit	29 C5	848	●		●		●		●		
Vale WMA, Jessenland	75 B8	299	●		●	●			●		●
Vanose WMA, Beaulieu	30 D1	2,498	●	●	●			●			
Vermillion River WMA, Farmington	77 A5	837	●		●	●			●		●
Vermilya WMA, Saratoga	86 A3	198	●		●	●			●		
Vision WMA, Elrosa	61 D6	234	●		●				●		●
Walnut Lake WMA, Bricelyn	84 C1	2,516	●		●				●		●
Wambach WMA, Mahnomen	41 A8	1,280	●		●				●		●
Wapiti WMA, Grygla	22 C3	31,759	●	●	●			●			
Waubun WMA, Waubun	41 B8	1,926	●		●		●		●		
Whitewater WMA, Elba	78 D3	27,305	●		●	●		●			●
Wild Rose WMA, Harris	64 C2	101	●		●	●		●	●		
Willow-Run WMA, Grygla	22 D2	3,564	●	●	●			●			
Wisneski WMA, Silver Corners	62 B3	164	●		●	●			●		
Wold WMA, Libby	45 D7	426	●	●	●			●			
Wolf Trail WMA, Carmel	22 D3	7,793	●	●	●			●			
Woodland WMA, Montrose	69 C8	701	●		●	●			●		
Zim WMA, Sax Station	46 B4	901	●	●	●			●			
Zion WMA, Lake Henry	61 D7	217	●		●				●		●